# Permanently
# New Yorkers

*Final Digs of the Notable and Notorious*

## PATRICIA BROOKS

**INSIDERS' GUIDE®**

GUILFORD, CONNECTICUT

AN IMPRINT OF THE GLOBE PEQUOT PRESS

The contact information and hours of operation listed in this book were confirmed at press time. We recommend, however, that you call establishments to obtain current information before traveling.

**INSIDERS' GUIDE**®

Copyright © 2006 Morris Book Publishing, LLC.

All rights reserved. No part of this book may be reproduced or transmitted in any form by any means, electronic or mechanical, including photocopying and recording, or by any information storage and retrieval system, except as may be expressly permitted by the 1976 Copyright Act or by the publisher. Requests for permission should be made in writing to The Globe Pequot Press, P.O. Box 480, Guilford, Connecticut 06437.

Insiders' Guide is a registered trademark of Morris Book Publishing, LLC.

Selected photos courtesy of Lee Sandstead (pp. 48, 57); The Green-Wood Cemetery (p. 82); Joe Petrocik (p. 115); Christopher Brooks (pp. 135, 142); The Forest Lawn Group (pp. 270, 271, 274, 276, 277); and Frank Gillespie (pp. 289, 291, 293). All other photos by the author.

Library of Congress Cataloging in Publication Data

Brooks, Patricia, 1926–
  Permanently New Yorkers : final digs of the notable and notorious / Patricia Brooks. — 1st ed.
    p. cm.
  Includes index.
  ISBN 0-7627-3794-8
  1. Celebrities—New York (State)—Biography. 2. Celebrities—Tombs—New York (State)—Guidebooks. 3. Tombs—New York (State)—Guidebooks. 4. New York (State)—Biography. I. Title.
CT251.B76 2005
929'.5'09747—dc22                                    2005014771

Manufactured in the United States of America
First Edition/First Printing

# CONTENTS

*To the significant souls, lost and then found,*
*in New York's many Elysian fields.*

# ACKNOWLEDGMENTS

For their special kindness and helpfulness, I would like to recognize especially Janice Burnett of Forest Lawn Cemetery in Buffalo; David Logan and Marjorie Gilbert of Sleepy Hollow Cemetery, Sleepy Hollow; Susan Olson of The Woodlawn Cemetery, The Bronx; Ken Taylor of The Green-Wood Cemetery, Brooklyn; Judith Mitchell of Kensico Cemetery, Valhalla; Steven LaFrancois of Rockland Cemetery, Sparkill; and Frank Gillespie of Mount Hope Cemetery, Rochester.

Heartfelt thanks also to William J. Carew, superintendent of the Memorial Cemetery of St. John's Church, Laurel Hollow, Long Island, who trudged through the snow one freezing January day to guide me to hidden graves (and brush the snow off them). I appreciate especially the patience of Donna Coon at Pinelawn Memorial Park and Cemetery, who researched names and locations and then painstakingly marked maps to steer me easily through the labyrinth of Pinelawn's many acres in Farmingdale. Others whose help is much appreciated include John Koepp of Cemetery of the Evergreens, New Lebanon; David Landolfe of St. Agnes Cemetery, Lake Placid; Hugh C. Mac-Dougle, historian, Christ Church, Cooperstown; Diane Bassette Nelson of Lakeview Cemetery, Interlaken; and Susan Trien of the Strong Museum, Rochester.

Special thanks belong to friends Amy Browning and Pat Nivakoff for driving me on several of my grave adventures, and to Joe Petrocik for his personal memories and photographs of Truman Capote.

In the I-really-couldn't-have-done-it-without-them category, my abiding gratitude to my son Jonathan for his guidance through the thicket of popular music and certain of its icons and other biographic research; to my son Christopher and his wife, Catherine, for photographs of and research on several grave sites; to my son Jim for his encouragement and support of my project; and to my husband, Lester, for his good-humored patience with "yet another cemetery book" and his willingness to accompany me on my sometimes hazardous quests.

Words are inadequate in my appreciation of my longtime Globe Pequot Press editor Mary Norris, without whose confidence and judgment this book would have been difficult if not impossible. Her upbeat enthusiasm kept me going on days when the temperature above ground was almost as chilling as it must have been below. (One subzero January day on Long Island, my camera froze and my car's transmission died . . . but that's another story.) Thanks, too, to Sarah Mazer, also at Globe Pequot, for shepherding my manuscript through the copy editing process, all the while keeping her cool.

For some of the book's photographs, I am grateful to the following for their quick response to my requests for photographic assistance: Frank Gillespie, Christopher and Catherine Brooks, Joe Petrocik, and Lee Sandstead, who all supplied their own work; and Janice Burnett, Susan Olson, and Ken Taylor, who provided prints from their respective cemetery archives.

# INTRODUCTION

When I mentioned my research for a book about grave sites and graveyards, a friend responded, "What a weird idea! How ghoulish!"

Yet visiting cemeteries is neither a novel idea nor a creepy one. The expansive, nonsectarian rural cemeteries that were developed in the nineteenth century were intended to be "gardens of graves," pastoral settings where visitors could contemplate Nature as well as pay respects to departed family members or friends.

Until Mount Auburn in Cambridge, Massachusetts, opened in 1831, previous American burial grounds were private family lots, church burying grounds, or prosaic town plots. Mount Auburn was patterned on the famous French necropolis Cimetière du Pere Lachaise, which opened in 1804 and was the template for all the American rural, parklike cemeteries that followed.

Next came The Green-Wood in Brooklyn in 1838, Flushing Cemetery in 1853, The Woodlawn in the Bronx in 1863, and many others. New York State's topography, with its rolling hills, valleys, meadows, and sweeping vistas, favors a natural layout. This accounts for the many scenic cemeteries that dot the state, such as Kensico in Valhalla, Forest Lawn in Buffalo, Mount Hope in Rochester, Fort Hill in Auburn, and scores of smaller ones.

Such rural resting places were usually located at the edge of town or in the countryside, although cities have since infringed on many and even swallowed up a few. They were—and still are—notable for their Edenic beauty, idyllic for the dead, certainly, who now have leases in perpetuity on permanent rooms with views, but just as welcome to living visitors seeking comfort, solitude, and meditation.

Contemplation of nature is the raison d'état of many a cemetery visit. In fact, these rural burial grounds were parks before the concept of public parks existed. Wide roadways (to accommodate horse-drawn carriages), ancient trees forming canopies of shade over access roads, ponds, lakes, fountains, waterfalls, and a variety of flowering plants and trees—these are hallmarks of such arcadian nineteenth-century burial grounds. In the late years of that century, it was a Sunday custom to take a buggy ride to the cemetery to enjoy the views and the seasonal flowers and colors, and to admire the statuary and diverse tombs and monuments.

Unlike earlier graveyards, which were usually utilitarian rows of headstones with few embellishments (though some of the colonial stones had charming naive carvings), Victorian cemeteries were fraught with symbolism, which adds to our enjoyment of them today. Oak trees predominated—and still do—because they symbolize loyalty and faith. A stone hand carved over a gravestone meant "taking leave"; a granite tree stump or broken column signified a life cut short too young.

Visiting cemeteries is a time-honored tradition, and not just to pay respects to relatives or departed friends. The most famous tomb in the world is one of the great architectural marvels: the Taj Mahal in India, built in the seventeenth century by the ruler Shah Jahan in memory of his favorite departed wife, Mumtaz Mahal. Not only is the story one of history's most romantic, but the tomb itself is the sine qua non of majestic beauty. Other tombs are also major tourist attractions, notably the Egyptian pyramids in Cairo and Napoleon's grandiloquent tomb in l'Hôtel des Invalides in Paris.

Certain cemeteries are on tourist maps not just for what they are, but for whom they shelter. The roster at Paris's Pere Lachaise includes Oscar Wilde, Gertrude Stein, Molière, Frédéric Chopin, Maria Callas, Jim Morrison, and scores of other internationally known luminaries. The English Cemetery in Rome, on the agenda of many a literature major, shelters poets John Keats and Percy Bysshe Shelley. In London's Victorian Highgate Cemetery, the likes of Karl Marx and George Eliot are in repose (but not together). Buenos Aires's biggest attraction, it is said, is the grave of Eva Perón, wife of the dictator Juan Perón, at the ornate Recoleta Cemetery. And if you think tourists don't want to see Marilyn Monroe's final resting place, you haven't watched the tour groups swarming into Westwood Memorial Park in Los Angeles, heading for her simple wall crypt.

In our celebrity-driven age, it is small wonder that people track their heroes through life even unto their final homes. But that isn't the only reason we find cemeteries of interest. They provide a fascinating link between the past and the present. We may see a magnificent building, mausoleum, or sarcophagus, clearly the most important monument on the grounds. We then learn it houses an unfamiliar name, perhaps the most important man in town decades ago. Today he seems no more than a footnote to history or a bit player among better-known stars. Like Ozymandias, "King of Kings" in Shelley's poem, a monumental tomb built yesterday is no guarantee of immortality tomorrow.

While a famous name may be the magnet that draws us to a cemetery, we often linger because of the architectural monuments—opulent and often grandiose tombs in the style of Greek temples, Gothic chapels, or French châteaux, sometimes the work of famous architects—or the artful designs on gravestones. Those of the seventeenth and eighteenth centuries are especially enjoyable, with angels, skulls, and other graphic designs carved as reminders of what may lie ahead for us all.

Unusual epitaphs are another reason people are attracted to cemeteries. Almost irresistible are such posthumous messages as "Here lies John Yeast, Pardon me for not rising," or "Here lies the body of Emily White, She signaled left and then turned right," or "Here lies my wife, here lies she; Hallelujah! Hallelujee!"

Still another reason cemeteries can be so fascinating is that they are often more than the sum of their parts, as intriguing for their grounds, their natural wonders (lakes, ponds, springs, waterfalls, and the like), plantings, and statuary as for their occupants. No wonder that walkers, hikers, bird-watchers, and nature enthusiasts frequent cemetery grounds.

When it comes to cemeteries of beauty and variety, from simple antiquated graveyards to paradisial Valhallas, no state can top New York. When you add the names of the famous now gone, the range through the ages is incomparable. Presidents, pathfinders, inventors, captains of industry, jurists, generals, war heroes, traitors, labor bosses, religious leaders, revolutionaries, authors, actors, directors, dancers, musicians of all chords (classical, modern, jazz, and pop), eccentrics, roués, rascals, scoundrels, and lowdown crooks—all can be found throughout New York State, sometimes within a single cemetery.

With so many famous and infamous people crowding New York's past, it is almost impossible to include them all within a single book. As encyclopedic as possible, this one attempts to guide the reader to the state's various burial grounds where the greatest number of VIPs have found permanent homes. Locating them can be a pleasurable quest and, um, undertaking. If your favorite icon is missing, I hope you will let me know.

In addition to guiding you to various cemeteries, I have included brief biographic sketches, or "obits" (obituaries), about some of the most prominent permanent residents. There are more than 175 obits in all. In order to include as many people as possible, in a variety of professions, these obits are necessarily briefer than most lives deserve. How can you condense a life as rich and accomplished as Theodore or Franklin Roosevelt's, Susan B. Anthony's, Frederick Douglass's, or Alexander Hamilton's to 200 or 250 words?

Another pleasure of a graveyard visit is the discoveries. As you roam the paths, you may find someone from the past whose final whereabouts were unknown to you. Surprises are frequent. I found Hal Roach, the movie producer, in Elmira when I was searching for Mark Twain, and I uncovered (not literally) Nelson Algren in Sag Harbor while on a hunt for George Balanchine.

These unexpected discoveries have led me to list, under each cemetery included, the names, dates, brief IDs, and grave locations of many supporting players in residence, in case you wish to seek them out. Many are not household names today, but were movers and shakers in their time. You will find some 270 of them in the book.

To make this guidebook as helpful as possible, under each cemetery listing is a sidebar titled "Lunch Break." It includes suggestions of where to eat before or after your graveyard visit, in the event that you have traveled many miles and are unfamiliar with the area. Another sidebar after some obituaries is "House Call"—signifying that the individual's home is nearby and open to visitors. (In some cases a related museum, church, or other building of interest is featured.) If, for example, you see Harriet Tubman's grave in Fort Hill Cemetery in Auburn, you might like to visit her Auburn home. The address, phone number, and a few details about the house will help you plan your trip.

H. L. Mencken once said that a cynic is "someone who, when he smells flowers, looks for a coffin." When I see a few crosses or obelisks in the distance, I search for the cemetery, not cynically, but with great expectations. I know from experience that the odds are good that I will serendipitously find something of interest, either an unusual tombstone, a clever epitaph, or the presence of a celebrated name recovered from the past. What I really need is a bumper sticker that proclaims "I brake for cemeteries."

When I say that I hope to see you in the graveyard, don't take it personally. It's not a curse but a heartfelt wish that you, too, will find the same pleasure there that I usually do.

# CHAPTER 1

# Manhattan

*I*f we were to draw a map of areas in which the most celebrated New Yorkers are recouping for eternity, the map would sag heavily in New York City and its environs. That is perhaps inevitable, as through the centuries so many prominent people have lived and worked in this area. Some you may have forgotten, and some you may never have heard of (though they were famous in a long-ago era); others are personal heroes who evoke memories of times past.

# CHURCH OF THE HEAVENLY REST
*2 East 90th Street; (212) 289–3400*

This Episcopal church in truncated Gothic Revival style makes a perfect final domicile, as several of its permanent retirees have discovered. There is no cemetery, but a small columbarium in the basement is open to family members and some visitors.

Among the most illustrious residents in the columbarium is **Tanaquil LeClerq** (1929–2000), a superb ballet dancer, chosen by George Balanchine to be his prima ballerina (and fifth wife) in twenty-five of his ballets for the New York City Ballet Company. She fitted Balanchine's ideal of the perfect ballerina: tall, slender, with long legs and a graceful neck. Tragically, her dazzling career was cut short by polio in 1956, and she was wheelchair-bound for the rest of her life. In spite of this handicap, she persevered, teaching dance at the Dance Theatre of Harlem and writing two books. **Diana Lynn** (1926–1971), stage and movie actress, is also in the columbarium. She was featured in light movie comedies of the 1940s—*Our Hearts Were Young and Gay* and *My Friend Irma* among them—as well as several Broadway plays, including *The Moon Is Blue* and *Mary, Mary. Office hours: 9:00* A.M.–*5:00* P.M. *Monday–Friday. Restrooms.*

## LUNCH BREAK

For a pizza with parchment-thin crust and a garden array of toppings, try **Pintaile's Pizza** (26 East 91st Street; 212–722–1967), a minichain that fans swear by. **Joanna's** (30 East 92nd Street; 212–360–1103) is another good bet, a mite fancier, with northern Italian food and a pleasant garden. I also like **Sarabeth's** in the Hotel Wales (1295 Madison Avenue; 212–410–7335) for super brunches—real pig-out affairs.

## GLORIA SWANSON    1897–1983

*B*orn Gloria May Josephine Svensson in Chicago, Swanson was an actress who played one role with such bravura that most people who saw her in *Sunset Boulevard* assume that Norma Desmond really *was* Gloria Swanson. In many ways that's true. Her part in this Billy Wilder classic was of an aging silent-movie actress whose career was detonated by the "talkies." Desmond is proud, imperious, egocentric, and larger-than-life, the very stereotype of a fading movie star.

Swanson was an inspired choice for the role. At the time she made the movie (1950), her lengthy career was more or less washed up. In all she made fifty-two movies, beginning in 1916; all but eight were silent films. She basically retired in 1934, but tried to make a comeback several times. With *Sunset Boulevard* it worked (briefly), and she received an Oscar nomination—the third of her career—for her role. There were four films after that, ending with *Airport* in 1974 in which she played herself, a role she had down pat.

In the teens and twenties, Swanson was one of the biggest stars of the silent screen. She had many successes, including six films directed by Cecil B. DeMille. Her first lead was in a DeMille film, *Don't Change Your Husband*, which might have been prophetic. She was married six times (the first time to actor Wallace Beery).

A lengthy secret affair with Joseph P. Kennedy (father of President John F. Kennedy) proved more fortuitous than Swanson's marriages; it helped her produce two movies of her own. The second was *Sadie Thompson*, an early talkie, in 1928. It was a major hit, earning her an Oscar nomination for best actress. Her second nomination came the following year with *The Trespasser*. Swanson's vault is located on the left side of the wall in the rear.

## GENERAL GRANT NATIONAL MEMORIAL
*Riverside Drive and West 122nd Street; (212) 666–1640*

Everyone knows it takes having an out-of-town guest for New Yorkers to visit the Statue of Liberty, but even having guests in tow rarely leads natives to Grant's Tomb. America's largest, most grandiose mausoleum (no jokes, please, about "who's buried in Grant's tomb?") is so obvious on its roost above the Hudson River that after a while, one becomes accustomed to it. It becomes almost invisible when viewed day after day after day.

That's not what Ulysses S. Grant's widow, Julia, had in mind. She spearheaded the drive to build this colossal memorial to her husband. Ulysses had chosen New York as one of several preferred burial sites, and when mayor William R. Grace offered prime land, it was a done deal. Even so, it took twelve years to approve the design, raise the funds, and finish construction. All the while, the late president remained in a holding vault guarded day and night by soldiers. As time dragged on, the U.S. Senate passed a bill decreeing that Grant was to be buried in Arlington National Cemetery. Julia vociferously disagreed. The much-publicized argument spurred a final push of fund-raising, and the mausoleum was completed in 1897. At the dedication by President William McKinley, surviving members of Grant's troops, ambassadors from twenty-seven countries, and a million people lined the streets in tribute.

Was it worth the wait? Julia thought so. She insisted that she be buried there with her husband, side by side in separate ten-ton granite and white marble sarcophagi. Modeled on Napoleon's tomb in Les Invalides in Paris, this massive monument is crowned by a 150-foot-high cupola. From a portico, doors 16½ feet high open to views of the crypt. Among the artistic flourishes are niches with busts of five generals who served with Grant and mosaic murals depicting Grant's military achievements. The shrine is manned by the National Park Service, and the knowledgeable rangers on duty give intriguing details about the president, his tomb, and the problems in building it. The theatrical entrance, via wide steps overseen by a belligerent-looking carved eagle, is on Riverside Drive and 122nd Street, next door to Riverside Church. *Open 9:00 A.M.–5:00 P.M. daily; closed Thanksgiving, Christmas Day, and New Year's Day.*

## LUNCH BREAK

For down-home Southern cooking at modest cost, try **Kitchenette** (1272 Amsterdam Avenue; 212–531–7600), located between 122nd and 123rd Streets. If you crave old-time Italian food at old-time prices, there's **Max** (1274 Amsterdam Avenue; 212–531–2221) at 123rd Street.

## ULYSSES S. GRANT  1822–1877
## JULIA DENT GRANT  1826–1902

Great generals do not necessarily make great political leaders, as our eighteenth president proved. As the general whose strategic battle and victory at Vicksburg divided Confederate forces and effectively won the Civil War for the Union, he was a man of action—hard-hitting, courageous, and brilliant. He proved a graceful victor, accepting Robert E. Lee's surrender at Appomattox on benign terms.

As president, Grant was a man of inaction—often befuddled, out of his depth, and unaware of or unable to deal with the chicanery of unscrupulous subordinates and fair-weather friends. Yet he was so popular with the public, as the general who won the war after other generals had failed to do so, that he was elected to two terms and came within sixty-six votes of being nominated for an unprecedented third term. Scandals plagued his presidency but didn't touch the Teflon-like Grant personally (sound familiar?).

As a youth in Ohio, Grant so hated working in his father's tannery that he developed a lifelong aversion to animal blood. (His meat had to be cooked so thoroughly, it was "practically charcoal.") A reluctant plebe at West Point, he graduated in the middle of his class, then fought under General Zachary Taylor in the Mexican War. In 1855 he retired to a mundane civilian life in Missouri, failing at farming and small business. His years of glory came later when, in his forties, he rejoined the army. His Civil War successes proved that people can, under stress, rise to the occasion.

After his presidency Grant joined a financial firm. Its subsequent bankruptcy left him penniless. By then he had developed cancer of the throat, probably exacerbated by his twenty-cigars-a-day habit. To recoup his losses and provide for his family, Grant began to write his memoirs. Finishing them became a race against death, which ended in a tie. Posthumously, the book earned nearly $450,000—a huge amount at the time, and enough to keep his beloved Julia and family solvent. The book survived Grant and his reputation, and it is read and enjoyed even today. Grant remained popular beyond death. Some 60,000 people marched in his funeral procession, with a million others lining black-draped Broadway. *Sic transit gloria mundi.*

Julia Grant was the daughter of a plantation owner near St. Louis, Missouri. She met Ulysses through her brother; the men were classmates at West Point. Julia's father disapproved of Grant because he was too poor, but Julia married him anyway. Despite all of their hardships and disappointments, they had a happy, devoted relationship. Julia called her years in the White House "the happiest period" of her life. A plain, stout, cross-eyed woman, she reveled in the attention, finery, and good living that accrues to a First Lady. Her tenure coincided with the most opulent period in American history up to that point, and Julia loved every minute of it. At the same time, she was devoted to her husband and later fought to preserve his memory and days of glory.

## ST. BARTHOLOMEW'S EPISCOPAL CHURCH
*109 East 50th Street and Park Avenue; (212) 751–1616*

In the lower rear of this beautiful Byzantine-style domed church, the simple Memorial Chapel has mottled-beige marble wall crypts along three sides. Names on the vaults are nearly impossible to read—what with the glare and the simple etching. In the top row of the wall opposite the altar, however, the third vault from the left bears the name Gish. Mother **Mary Gish** (1876–1942) gets top billing; next is **Dorothy Gish** (1898–1968), and on the bottom is **Lillian Diana.** To reach the chapel, go to the left side of the church (facing it) on 51st Street; halfway down the block is the entrance. *Chapel open 8:00 A.M.–6:00 P.M. daily. Restrooms.*

## LUNCH BREAK

The church has its own cafe—**St. Bart's** (109 East 50th Street; 212–888–2664). It couldn't be more convenient, and it has a pleasant, moderately priced New American menu. In warm weather the open terrace is delightful for crowd-watching on Park Avenue. If you crave something fancier, **The Four Seasons** (Seagram Building, 99 East 52nd Street; 212–754–9494) is just 2 short blocks away and is New York dining at its best.

## LILLIAN GISH   1893–1993

y all accounts, including Lillian's, her younger sister Dorothy was the natural talent in the family, with a flair for comedy. Both sisters were beautiful, but Lillian, with her perfect oval face, had a childlike innocence and was far more serious. "Dorothy got the happy side that God left out of me," Lillian often said.

Lillian worked from age nine—outlasting silent films and moving on to a sixty-year career in talkies and on the stage, radio, and television. At a graceful ninety-three years, she made her last movie, *The Whales of August*, with Bette Davis. Lillian grew from a star of silent melodramas like *Way Down East, Broken Blossoms, The Birth of a Nation,* and *Orphans of the Storm* into a genuine tragic actress. After the death of silent films, she appeared on stage in *Uncle Vanya, Hamlet* (at age forty-three she played a believable Ophelia), *Camille,* and *Crime and Punishment* (opposite John Gielgud). Later movies included *Duel in the Sun* and *The Night of the Hunter.* While Lillian had friendships with several men—believed by many to be platonic—she never married, claiming that she never "found a name I would rather carry than Lillian Gish." Clearly, she made it a distinguished one.

# ST. FRANCES CABRINI SHRINE

*701 Fort Washington Avenue; (212) 923–3536*

The shrine/chapel is located between Fort Tryon and West 190th Street, just 10 blocks from the George Washington Bridge. Mother Cabrini's final resting place is in a glass-sided coffin just below the altar, visible to visitors. There is also a display of memorabilia: personal items of St. Cabrini, photographs, and a video on her life.

The shrine is on property that Mother Cabrini bought in 1899 to build a girls' boarding school. The chapel is at one end of the building, which opened in 1930 as Mother Cabrini High School. On one wall of the chapel sanctuary are the words "Mother of Immigrants," a title that St. Cabrini was known by. An enclosed terrace at the end of the chapel affords a distant view below of the Hudson River. *Chapel open 9:00 A.M.–5:00 P.M. daily; closed major holidays. Mass celebrated 7:00 A.M. weekdays, 8:00 A.M. Saturday, and 9:00 and 11:00 A.M. Sunday.*

## LUNCH BREAK

Two attractive places to lunch are close by. **New Leaf Cafe** (Fort Tryon Park, Margaret Corbin Drive; 212–568–5323) offers tasty New American food in attractive park surroundings. Also near is **Hispaniola** (839 West 180th Street; 212–740–5222), featuring a mix of Nuevo Latino and Asian dishes in a comfortable duplex setting, with a soaring view of the George Washington Bridge.

## MOTHER FRANCES XAVIER CABRINI   1850–1917

The first American to achieve sainthood in the Roman Catholic Church, Mother Cabrini began life as Maria Francesca Cabrini in San Angelo, in northern Italy near Milan. Born to poor farmers, she was the youngest of thirteen children. From an early age she was attracted to the religious life. After becoming a nun she joined seven other sisters in founding the Missionary Sisters of the Sacred Heart of Jesus in 1880.

This brought Cabrini to the attention of Pope Leo XIII, who asked her to go to America in 1889 to attend to the religious needs of the many Italian immigrants there. She had hoped to go to China, but, ever obedient, she followed the Pope's mandate, "Not to the East, but to the West," and set sail for New York. Small and frail but fiercely resolute, she persuaded New York's

Archbishop Corrigan to assist her in founding an orphanage. With his help, she raised enough money to buy 450 acres along the Hudson. At first the nuns had to haul water from the river, but eventually—seemingly in answer to her prayers—a natural spring was found on the property.

This was the first of the forty-six orphanages that Mother Cabrini ultimately founded. Over the next twenty-eight years, she traveled throughout the United States, founding sixty-seven schools and many hospitals and missions. Many of her efforts were in New York, Seattle, New Orleans, and Chicago (where she died in 1917), but she also founded schools and missions in South American and European countries. Her great faith in the doable helped her to overcome obstacles like revolutions in South America, lawsuits in Italy, and an endless shortage of funds for her many projects. This dynamic, determined, God-fearing, genuinely religious woman packed scores of good works into her sixty-seven years. She died in a Chicago hospital that she had founded, felled by malaria that she had contracted in Brazil. Sainthood becomes her.

## ST. MARK'S IN-THE-BOWERY

*131 East 10th Street (at Second Avenue); (212) 674–6377*

Eclectic in style, with a soupçon of 1799 Georgian, an 1828 Greek Revival steeple, and an 1854 cast-iron Italianate porch, this appealing stone church reached its apogee in 1861 with James Renwick Jr.'s addition. Beginning in 1889, a series of beautiful stained-glass windows were added. Unfortunately, a fire in the 1970s destroyed much of the interior and the upper tier of windows. They have been replaced with modern designs, but the lower windows are still intact.

The land on which the church stands was deeded by Peter Stuyvesant to Trinity Church for use as a chapel. The chapel—St. Mark's—opened in 1799 as a separate parish, not an appendage of Trinity. The current St. Mark's is on the exact spot of Stuyvesant's own family chapel.

The graveyard is on both the right (east) and left (west) of the church. The east yard is rather cheerless, a combination of bare, hard ground and patterned pavings of red-brown brick and gray Belgian brick, punctuated by eleven old trees. The west yard, paved in patterns of pebbles and concrete, is more welcoming, with wooden benches and chairs in groupings, trees, and small shrubs. It functions as a community playground much of the year. In both yards, the graves are mostly vaults sunk into the ground. Many, dating back to

the early nineteenth century, are made of sandstone with their names eroded by time.

While there is just one famous person (Peter Stuyvesant) at rest here, there are many august names from New York history, like Schermerhorn, Lorillard, Livingston, Ingersoll, and Vandenheuvel. There are also several intriguing souls sheltering beneath their stones.

**Matilda Hoffman** (1791–1808; east yard, third stone on right, by front fence) is one. In the family vault marked MARTIN HOFFMAN, Matilda's claim to your attention is that she was Washington Irving's "intended"—a shy young girl, the daughter of a judge for whom Irving clerked. She contracted tuberculosis and died within two months. It is believed that Irving never recovered from her death. Regardless of whether that is true, he remained a lifelong bachelor.

At peace also is **Daniel D. Tompkins** (1774–1825; east yard, rear, just to right of walk), James Monroe's vice president from 1817 to 1825. His handsome bronze bust is in the west yard, facing the porch. **Nicholas Fish** (1758–1833; east yard, next to walk, beyond Stuyvesant) was a Revolutionary

War major and friend of Alexander Hamilton, for whom he named his son. The son later became secretary of state under Ulysses S. Grant.

Someone who found no peace within these ancient walls was **Alexander Turney Stewart** (1803–1876; east yard, empty vault), the proprietor of New York's first department store. Posthumously decried as "one of the meanest men who ever lived," his body was stolen from its vault 12 feet under, and a ransom note demanded $200,000. Eventually $20,000 was paid and the body was recovered and reburied (with, it is said, a burglar alarm) at the Episcopal Cathedral of the Incarnation in Garden City. The kidnappers were never caught, and the underground vault (grave 112, near the center) remains unoccupied—a dead end, so to speak.

Another missing person is **Commodore Matthew Perry** (1794–1858; west yard, John Slidell vault), who was here first, then transferred to Island Cemetery in Newport, Rhode Island.

The most famous of several statues on the grounds is the marble of the Native American *Lady of the Dew* (west yard; next to fence, midway). It was sculpted by Solon H. Borglum, whose brother Gutzon carved Mount Rushmore. Another of Solon Borglum's Native American figures, *Aspiration,* is to the left in the entrance porch. *Grounds open during office hours: 10:00 A.M.–3:00 P.M. Monday–Friday. Brochure/map $2.00; restroom. Office is on the second floor in brick building to the right and rear of the church's main entrance.*

## THOMAS ADDIS EMMET   1761–1827

Elder brother of Robert Emmet, the famous (or infamous, as his English rulers viewed him) Irish patriot, Thomas had a distinguished career, though it took a while to get it going. Born in Cork, Ireland, he was educated at Trinity College, Dublin, and Edinburgh University, where he studied medicine. Upon the death of an older brother who was a lawyer, Emmet abandoned medicine to study law and in 1790 became a member of the Irish bar.

Sympathetic to the cause of an Ireland free from foreign rule, he was at first a moderate. Then, as the British became more intransigent, he joined

## LUNCH BREAK

Right around the corner is **Koi** (175 Second Avenue at 11th Street; 212–777–5266), a quite good, moderately priced Japanese restaurant. There are several casual, less expensive spots in the vicinity, like the famous **Second Avenue Deli** (156 Second Avenue at 10th Street; 212–677–0606), which serves Jewish deli favorites (corned beef, pastrami sandwiches), and **Velselka** (144 Second Avenue at Ninth Street; 212–228–9682) which serves hearty borscht, pierogi, poppy seed cake, and other Eastern European specialties.

United Irishmen, a group considered traitorous by the ruling Brits. Like other leaders of the Irish rebellion, he was arrested in 1798, imprisoned in Scotland, and then exiled forever from the British Empire in 1802.

He first went to Paris, but upon hearing that his brother's uprising in Ireland had failed and that Robert had been hanged by the British, Thomas set sail for America. In New York he soon became a member of the bar, a highly visible and successful lawyer, and by 1812 the state's attorney general. A committed believer in liberty, he argued the case for freedom of African slaves seeking refuge in New York. He also took up Robert Fulton's cause as the inventor of the steamboat, defending him against the claims of others. Emmet's is the first flat grave, a red stone in the David S. Jones vault, in the ground to the right of the walk in the east yard.

## PETER STUYVESANT   1592–1672

The frowning visage on Stuyvesant's bust (which faces the entrance of the east yard) was carved in 1915 by Dutch artist Toon Dupuis as a gift from Queen Wilhemina of the Netherlands. It gives him the look of a stern person/leader/soldier. In fact, he was all three. Born in Friesland, Netherlands, Stuyvesant studied at Franeker, joined the military, and was sent to the West Indies. In an attack on the Portuguese colony of St. Martin in 1644, he was wounded and his leg had to be amputated. For the rest of his life, he hobbled on a peg leg ornamented with silver bands.

In 1645 Stuyvesant was appointed by the West India Company the director of New Netherland (later New York). For the following nineteen years, New Netherland and New Amsterdam, its capital, were his life. The last of the Dutch governors, he ruled with an iron hand and steely countenance, repressing Lutherans, Quakers, Indians, and the sale of liquor and firearms

with even-handed severity. "I shall govern you as a father his children," he told the Dutch settlers. An *authoritarian* father, he might have added

It was not an easy time to be in charge. The Swedes pressured Stuyvesant in Delaware, and he sailed down and overthrew the Swedish authorities there. He brutally suppressed three successive Indian uprisings (in 1655, 1658, and 1663). The English, whose colonies surrounded him, were not so easily pressured, and in 1664 he had to surrender New Amsterdam to Colonel Richard Nicolls. Scapegoated by the West India Company, Stuyvesant had one last hurrah—securing the right of free trade between England and Holland— before retiring to his sixty-two-acre farm, or *bouwerie,* from which the area and church take their name (Bowery).

Stuyvesant is not buried beneath his statue but is embedded in the church wall a few steps beyond it, on the east-yard side. Slate markers, one embedded inside and one on the outer wall, identify the spot. They read: "In this vault lies buried Petrus Stuyvesant late Captain General and Governor in chief of Amsterdam in New Netherland now called New York and the Dutch West Indies. Died Feby. A.D. 1672 aged 80 years." Those addicted to spirits said that he might not be buried at all. His servants insisted they heard his peg leg tapping around the farm; others claimed to have seen him, and still others swore that they heard him ringing the church bell. As busy as the area is today, it is probably safe to say that he is still snug inside his wall.

## ST. PATRICK'S CATHEDRAL

*Fifth Avenue and 50th Street; (212) 753–2261*

While the crypt, located beneath the altar of this imposing Gothic Revival cathedral, is rarely open to the public, the church's magnificent interior is worth visiting for anyone interested in burial sites. Beginning with **Archbishop John Hughes** (1797–1864), many New York cardinals and archbishops, "princes of the Church," have found lasting peace within these walls. Among the most prominent and probably the best remembered is **His Eminence John Cardinal O'Connor** (1920–2000), known for his Irish wit and blunt candor. He charmed even those who disagreed with his political stances on abortion and homosexuality.

The cathedral itself is the largest Roman Catholic one in the United States, begun in 1859 by James Renwick but not finished until 1906. Note the St. Michael and St. Louis altars, both from Tiffany and Company. *Open 7:00 A.M.–9:30 P.M. daily.*

## FULTON J. SHEEN   1895–1979

*K*nown first to laymen as the radio voice of *The Catholic Hour* and then as a television presence in a series called *Life is Worth Living* (which eventually had thirty million viewers), Sheen was respected in the church as a theologian, writer, and charismatic personality. His TV ratings at his peak topped those of Milton Berle.

For more than thirty years, Sheen was probably the most widely known name of any Catholic prelate in the country. With good humor, common sense, sound theology, and a mesmerizing voice, he used radio and then TV to inspire, educate, and convert listeners. (Among his many converts were Claire Booth Luce and Henry Ford II.) Sheen's talks were not always free of controversy. He had strong opinions on corporal punishment (for it), Freudian psychoanalysis (against it), and Communism (vociferously against it, to the point of supporting General Franco in Spain as a bulwark against Russian Communism).

While deadly serious about his religious beliefs, Sheen was not without humor. He once said that "Hearing nuns' confessions is like being stoned to death with popcorn." In receiving an Emmy Award for his television show, he credited "my four writers, Matthew, Mark, Luke and John." Other Sheenisms: "The big print giveth, and the fine print taketh away," and "Jealousy is the tribute mediocrity pays to genius."

In spite of all his learning and honors, Sheen endeared himself to supporters by brushing away his awards with comments such as these: "It's like being a Knight of the Garter. It's an honor, but it doesn't hold up anything," and "The proud man counts his newspaper clippings, the humble man his blessings."

Sheen's own beginnings were humble enough. He was born in El Paso, Illinois, the eldest of four sons of a farm family. He was baptized Peter John Sheen but was always known by his mother's maiden name, Fulton. He spent his early years at Catholic schools and then attended Catholic colleges; in 1912 he became a priest in Peoria. Postgraduate studies in theology led him on a fast career path to Catholic University, the University of Louvain in Belgium, the Sorbonne in Paris, and the Angelicum in Rome. At Louvain he was the first American awarded the Cardinal Mercier Prize for International Philosophy.

Sheen's conflict with Francis Cardinal Spellman, who had chosen him for the television talks, became so bitter that it had to be mediated by Pope Pius XII. The result: Spellman fired Sheen from the television show, and in 1966 Sheen became bishop of the Rochester, New York, diocese. When he resigned three years later, he said, "I am not retiring, only retreading." He spent another ten years preaching, writing, and attending to liturgical affairs, despite battling heart disease. In all he wrote sixty-six books and many articles. Admirers in the church are seeking his canonization. His current location is next to Cardinal Cooke and near Cardinal O'Connor.

## ST. PAUL'S CHAPEL AND CHURCHYARD
*Broadway and Fulton Street; (212) 602–0874*

Located across the street from what was the east side of the World Trade Center, St. Paul's is the oldest church in Manhattan (1766), the oldest public building in continuous use in the city, and the only building extant that was built by the British. It miraculously escaped damage from 9/11 and, in fact, served as a pivotal relief center for rescue and recovery workers at the WTC site. Exhibits from 9/11 are on the porch and inside, and memorial banners hang from the chapel balconies.

The interior is surprisingly light and airy, with rows of white Corinthian columns, cut-glass chandeliers above the center aisle, and pastel walls with white trim. Above the altar is *Glory,* a white baroque bas-relief by Pierre L'Enfant, the French architect who designed the city plan of Washington, D.C. Every U.S. president has visited and worshipped at this venerable Georgian-style chapel, except George W. Bush. (He still has time to make the record complete.) George Washington's pew is intact in the north aisle. He worshipped at St. Paul's when New York was the nation's capital and he was president.

Among several notables in the old churchyard is **George Frederick Cooke** (1756–1812; off the horseshoe-shaped path in rear right, near Vesey Street), an English character actor known for his portrayal of Richard III. His gravestone was paid for by the famous English actor Edmund Kean. Every ancient burial ground needs a resident ghost. The one at St. Paul's is Cooke, who wanders the grounds in search of his head; supposedly it was sold to pay his doctor's bills, with the skull later used in productions of *Hamlet*. Anyhow, it makes a good story.

Also in these serene environs is **John Holt** (1721–1784; south section 1, left of the chapel in the rear). Editor, publisher, and founder of the *New York Gazette* and another pre–Revolutionary War New York newspaper, this onetime mayor of Williamsburg, Virginia, was a patriot and agitator for freedom. *Grounds open during office hours: 10:00 A.M.–6:00 P.M. Monday–Saturday, 10:00 A.M.–4:00 P.M. Sunday. Map; restroom. Free classical music concerts many Mondays at noon.*

**LUNCH BREAK**

A great favorite is **Les Halles Downtown** (15 John Street; 212–285–8585), between Broadway and Nassau. It has terrific French bistro fare, reasonably priced.

## GENERAL RICHARD MONTGOMERY  1738–1775

*P*erhaps the most auspicious person in St. Paul's burial ground is a man who served two armies bravely. Montgomery was born in Ireland and educated at Trinity College, Dublin. In 1756 he joined the British army, following a long Montgomery family tradition. He saw plenty of action in the Seven Years War against the French, fighting them in Louisburg, Ticonderoga, Montreal, and later in Martinique and Havana. In 1772 Montgomery left the army, swearing that he would never marry nor wear a uniform again. He moved to New York, where he broke the first vow within a year. He married well (Janet, a daughter of Judge Robert R. Livingston) and soon became critical of Britain's colonial policies.

In 1775 Montgomery was a delegate to the provincial Congress and became a brigadier general in the Continental army. Sent to Canada to replace Philip J. Schuyler as commander, he managed to capture Montreal. The next goal was tougher. Joining his forces (barely 800 rough, stubborn, and poorly trained citizen soldiers) with those of Colonel Benedict Arnold, Montgomery attacked Quebec. He was killed, and the attack failed. Arnold continued the siege for more than three months but finally had to withdraw.

Montgomery was interred in the Quebec garrison, but in 1818 he was moved to St. Paul's, where Congress erected a memorial to him. His final barracks are beneath the east porch of the chapel.

## STRAWBERRY FIELDS

*West 72nd Street at Central Park*

While not a burial ground, this beautiful three-and-a-half-acre teardrop-shaped site, near the southwest end of Central Park, is as much an object of pilgrimage as many a grave. Named for the song that John Lennon composed for the Beatles, the site is opposite the Dakota apartment house where Lennon lived—and died. Lennon's widow, Yoko Ono, donated the site in 1985. It is a quiet place for rest and contemplation as well as a lovely memorial to Lennon, with more than 160 types of plantings, including many strawberry plants (natch!). At the site is a memorial bronze plaque that bears the words "Imagine all the people living life in

> ### LUNCH BREAK
>
> For tasty hot dogs and juices, you can munch standing up at **Gray's Papaya** (2090 Broadway at 72nd Street; 212–799–0243). **The Boat Basin Cafe** (79th Street at the Hudson River; 212–496–5542) offers river views along with more leisurely lunching.

peace" (from Lennon's famous solo song "Imagine"). Underneath the quotation are the names of some 120 countries supporting that hope—or at least claiming to do so. A large circular Italian mosaic in the pavement with the word "Imagine" in the center reinforces Lennon's wish. Loyal Lennonites gather at the site on the dates of Lennon's birth (October 9) and death (December 8), and on many other days of the year.

## JOHN LENNON   1940–1980

What would popular music be today if John Lennon hadn't met Paul McCartney in June 1957 and started playing music with him? We'll never know because, as the cliché goes, the rest is history. After collaborating in a band called The Quarrymen (that's when George Harrison joined them), which then became Long John & the Silver Beatles, they dropped all but "The Beatles." With the addition of Ringo Starr on drums, The Beatles went on to shake up not only popular music, but world culture and politics as well. With their identical schoolboy suits and matching haircuts, they made teenage girls swoon and teenage boys want to form a rock band.

Their impact still resonates. Consider just one year—1964. In April the group held all five top spots on the U.S. singles music charts (a first) with "Can't Buy Me Love," "Twist and Shout," "She Loves You," "I Want to Hold Your Hand," and "Please Please Me." That same month, Lennon's first book, *In His Own Write*, was published. *A Hard Day's Night*, The Beatles' first movie, made with director Richard Lester, came out that year. *Help!* followed a year later. Then in 1967 Lennon played a part in Lester's *How I Won the War*.

The nominal leader and most outspoken member of The Beatles, Lennon was known for his wit and sarcasm. In 1966, when he said in an interview "We're more popular than Jesus now" and "I don't know which will go first, rock 'n' roll or Christianity," he released a firestorm of fury in the United States, with sporadic Beatles boycotts and organized burnings of Beatle albums in towns across the nation. Lennon later apologized. Throughout his career he said and wrote many widely quoted lines, like "Part of me suspects that I'm a loser, and the other part of me thinks I'm God Almighty" and "If you tried to give rock and roll another name, you might call it 'Chuck Berry.'" No line was more quoted than "All we are saying is give peace a chance."

In 1967 The Beatles' *Sergeant Pepper's Lonely Heart's Club Band* was released at No. 1 in Britain and the United States. It is widely considered by both critics and fans to be the seminal rock-and-roll record of all time.

Lennon's first marriage (in 1962) was to Cynthia Powell, whom he'd met in art school. A son, Julian, was born the next year. The marriage ended in 1968, after John became involved with Yoko Ono, an avant-garde artist whom he met at one of her exhibits. Many link Lennon's relationship with Ono (they married in Gibraltar in 1969) with the breakup of The Beatles—he brought her to recording sessions and allowed her input in how songs were recorded, causing resentment among the other band members—but Lennon vehemently denied that assertion. Whatever the reasons, the group officially disbanded in 1970.

Lennon and Ono released three albums on their own even before The Beatles broke up: *Unfinished Music No. 1: Two Virgins* (1968), *Unfinished Music No. 2: Life with the Lions* (1969), and *The Wedding Album* (1969). After the band's breakup Lennon and Ono had several other successful releases, notably *Give Peace a Chance* (1969) and *Instant Karma* (1970). The early 1970s were times of turmoil, and the Lennons were active critics of U.S. involvement in the Vietnam War. In 1971 the couple settled in New York City, and shortly after, Lennon's album *Imagine* found critical and commercial success. Then came the birth of Sean Taro Ono Lennon in 1975, Lennon's five-year semiretirement to become a "house husband," and in November 1980 the release of *Double Fantasy*, his final album.

A month later, on December 8, Lennon was gunned down outside the Dakota by Mark David Chapman, a deranged fan who had been hiding in the shadows. Within minutes Lennon was dead. Immediately after his death, *Double Fantasy* was No. 1 in both the United States and the United Kingdom. His line "Life is what happens while you are busy making other plans" seems almost too ironic to bear.

## TRINITY CHURCH CEMETERY & MAUSOLEUMS
*770 Riverside Drive; (212) 368–1600*

Trinity, the oldest active cemetery in Manhattan, is divided into two parts—east and west of Broadway between West 153rd and West 155th Streets. The larger, older portion (or "wing") is built into a precipitously steep hillside, from Broadway's west side, sloping down to Riverside Drive. The main entrance is halfway down the hill on West 153rd Street, with another entrance at the lower end of West 155th. The other wing is directly across Broadway, east to Amsterdam Avenue. The entrance to this second wing is on Amsterdam Avenue. This section surrounds the lovely late Gothic Revival Church of Intercession, which is *not* connected to Trinity.

The Trinity cemetery property, on twenty-four acres, was bequeathed by one of its most illustrious lodgers, John J. Audubon. It has a grand vista, high above the Hudson River, and is ornamented with elms, oaks, pines, and shrubbery. The cemetery is at its prettiest in late spring, when rows of purple irises contrast with the gray headstones, monuments, and sarcophagi. Audubon must have loved the hilltop location; it is part of the thirty-five acres he bought and named "Minnie's Land" for his wife. (Minnie, meaning "mother" in Scots, was what their children called Lucy Audubon.) A bronze plaque at the southeast corner marks this as a historic spot, where some of the fiercest fighting occurred on November 17,

### LUNCH BREAK

The immediate neighborhood offers little but fast-fooderies, like MacDonald's, Subway, and Chinese takeouts. But 11 blocks farther north is a branch of the **Dallas BBQ** minichain (3956 Broadway; 212–568–3700), which offers gargantuan portions of tasty chicken 'n' ribs. Nothing fancy, but certainly filling.

1776, during the Battle of Washington Heights in the Revolutionary War.

The cemetery came into being in 1843. Its obelisks, mausoleums, statues, vault markers, and monuments are old and substantial, representing charter members of New York's high society. One resident is here accidentally. **Alfred Tennyson Dickens** (1845–1912; main cemetery's northeast corner at West 155th and Broadway), son of Charles Dickens and godson of Alfred Lord Tennyson, died suddenly while in New York planning his father's centenary celebration. *Grounds open 8:30 A.M.–4:30 P.M. daily. Office hours: 8:30 A.M.–4:30 P.M. Monday–Friday. Map; restrooms.*

## JOHN JACOB ASTOR   1763–1848

Astor seems like one of those true-blue Anglo-American names. But Jacob, the first American Astor, was actually born in the village of Walldorf near Heidelberg, Germany. As a young man he spent four years in London working in an uncle's piano and flute factory. At twenty he sailed for New York. On the voyage a fellow passenger urged him to get into the fur-trading business, advice he was quick to take. Shrewd, hard-working, thrifty, and ambitious, Astor had made a fortune within six years—the largest fortune of any American up to that time. In 1808 he established the American Fur Company to compete with the British fur monopoly in Canada; soon he had trading posts from the Great Lakes to the Pacific Ocean, with the main depot at the mouth of the Columbia River in Astoria, a town he founded in what later became Oregon.

By standards of the day, Astor was a tycoon, shipping cargos of furs in his own vessels to Hawaii and countries as far as China and India. He also had a hand in many other American pies, speculating in government securities and snapping up real estate all over New York. After 1834, when he sold his fur company, Astor spent his remaining years managing his many business interests. It was said that he was obsessed with money. Even as he lay dying, Astor reportedly urged one of his agents to collect the overdue rent from an indigent widow.

When he died, Astor's fortune was estimated at $30 million. Part of his legacy was a $400,000 bequest to build a library. It first was called the Astor Library and later became part of the New York Public Library. If you are coming from the West 153rd Street entrance, the Astor family vault is on the left side of the curve in the road.

# JOHN JAMES AUDUBON   1785–1851

When you think Audubon you think birds, and that's as it should be. But Audubon's life was more complicated that that. He was born in Haiti, the illegitimate son of a French naval officer and planter. As a kid he loved drawing birds but hated school, especially the military school his father sent him to for a year. At seventeen he was studying in France with the great painter Louis David, and the next year he was shipped off to New York for a career in business.

This went nowhere, but Audubon cut quite a swath. He could dance, shoot, ride, and fence; he was tall and handsome; and he spoke with a French accent. No wonder he attracted Lucy Bakewell, the pretty daughter of a Pennsylvania farmer. When they married, she encouraged him to concentrate on what he did best: paint birds. His life's work would become drawing and cataloguing the birds of North America. This task entailed endless travel and the money needed to sustain it. To raise the funds, Audubon gave drawing lessons, painted portraits, and even attempted several ill-fated business ventures.

Audubon's frequent travel was laced with all kinds of adventures and long separations from his loving wife, who also taught to support their family. In six years Audubon had accumulated enough bird paintings to make a book, but he couldn't get anyone in America to publish it. In England the beauty, skill, and precision of his work was quickly recognized in both artistic and scientific circles. *The Birds of America*, his greatest volume, was printed in parts by subscription. For the next thirteen years Audubon shuttled back and forth between London and New York, overseeing publication, completing more bird paintings, and writing the text with the help of William MacGillivray. In 1839 the book in four volumes was finally completed, with 435 hand-colored folio plates and an index. It was so successful that it was followed by *Ornithological Biography*. Audubon's financial future was secure.

That year the family settled in New York permanently. Audubon prepared a smaller version of his first book and began a major new enterprise, *Viviparous Quadrupeds of North America*. With only one volume completed in 1847, his powers rapidly declined. He died four years later. But through his beautiful drawings and skillful prose (abetted by MacGillivray and John Bachman), Audubon opened a whole new natural world to scores of readers.

The Audubon grave is located to the left behind the Church of Intercession, near the West 155th Street fence. It is marked by a Celtic cross beautifully "embroidered" with bas-reliefs of birds on one side and animals on the other; on the front of the base is a bust of the artist himself with his name below it.

## ELIZA BOWEN JUMEL   1769-1871

Some people are known for the company they keep. Madame Jumel is best known for the company she *married*—especially her third husband, Aaron Burr. By the time they married, Burr was a rather pathetic seventy-eight-year-old (she was sixty-one) and not a catch by anyone's standards. Only days after the wedding in 1833 he invested a large sum of her money—and lost it. Convinced that he had married her for her fortune (probably true), Jumel filed a complaint against him; they separated, and the divorce was granted September 14, 1836, the very day that Burr died. Jumel lived thirty-five years longer.

In her youth Jumel was a real beauty. She eloped at age seventeen from her foster home in Newport, Rhode Island (her mother had died at sea, giving birth to Eliza, on a ship traveling between France and the West Indies), and married (or perhaps not, gossips said) Colonel Peter Croix, a British officer. They lived in New York, and Eliza became a quick favorite of New York society at that time. Her looks, brains, wit, and indiscretions made her the notorious darling of many distinguished men, causing tongues to wag and her reputation to sink. Whether she was a courtesan is one of many murky questions about her life.

After Croix's death the young widow (or courtesan—gossips again) moved to Paris and married Stephen Jumel, a wealthy French wine merchant. Before you could ask "*combien ça coute?*" she spent half his fortune. After the couple moved to New York, she proved a shrewd investor and recouped most of the fortune she had dissipated. Her small, austere mausoleum is built into a hillside beside the curving drive that winds from the entrance of the cemetery down to the office. The name JUMEL on the top of the facade identifies it.

## CLEMENT CLARKE MOORE   1779–1863

*F*irst in his class at Columbia College, professor of Oriental and Greek literature, Hebrew and biblical scholar, writer of treatises, translator of the Roman poet Juvenal, Renaissance man in his knowledge of religions, languages, poetry, and politics—all for naught! Clement Moore's position in American history now seems to center on an indiscretion he committed when he was forty-three. In 1822 he composed a poem for his six children that was published the following year in the *Troy Sentinel*. It quickly became a classic, read and recited by children down through the ages. The poem? *A Visit from St. Nicholas*.

Moore—the only child of an heiress (Charity Clarke) and the Episcopal bishop of New York, rector of Trinity Church, and president of Columbia (Dr. Benjamin Moore)—had a privileged childhood. His family estate covered land that now ranges from 18th to 24th Street, between Eighth and Tenth Avenues. His entire professional life was devoted to scholarship.

At age thirty Moore compiled the first Hebrew dictionary in the United States. He did not expect his fame to rest on the images conjured by "not a creature was stirring, not even a mouse" or "visions of sugar-plums danced in their heads" or even "he had a broad face and a little round belly, that shook when he laughed like a bowlful of jelly." While his poem created the image we have even today of St. Nicholas, or Santa Claus, Moore didn't acknowledge his authorship of it until he was sixty-five years old. His long, productive life ended in his summer home in Newport, Rhode Island, just before his eighty-fourth birthday. No, 'twas not the night before Christmas, but July 1863.

It has been a Christmastime ritual since 1911 for families to visit Moore's current residence with a wreath for his grave. A candlelight procession ends

with the church's minister reciting Moore's famous poem. The grave is behind the office, to the right of Riverside Mausoleum, down a sloping grass bank, just in front of the high stone wall protecting the cemetery from Riverside Drive. The modest gray granite sarcophagus and individual gravestones are hospice to seven Moores: Clement, his wife, four daughters, and a son.

## TRINITY CHURCHYARD
*Broadway at Wall Street; (212) 368–1600*

To many who work downtown, this hallowed graveyard (which is older and smaller than its sister on Riverside Drive) is the ideal place to spend a quiet lunch hour resting on a bench, munching sandwiches, or reading. Slightly elevated above street level, surrounded by a spiked cast-iron fence and gate, and sitting under a gnarled shade tree in a zone of grassy silence, barely removed from the roar of traffic and buzz of crowds, Trinity induces a surprisingly unearthly feeling. It is a welcome islet of greenery contrasting with the nearby concrete canyons.

The church and cemetery were built in 1697 on a burial site that held the remains of seventy-five Algonquin Indians, who had been killed in a 1643 battle with the Dutch. The early church fathers were not always welcoming, at least not to African Americans. At its beginning, the church decreed that "no Negroes be buried within the bounds and limits of the Churchyard of Trinity Church . . . as they will answer to it at their peril."

Trinity hasn't been an active burial ground since 1822. It doesn't seem possible, but in 1840 a historian estimated that some 160,000 deceased people resided there—a number equal to New York's entire population that year. Today visitors drop by as much for the churchyard's colonial history and historic residents as for its soulful silence.

The enclosed graveyard is to the north and south of the old Episcopal Trinity Church, the third church on the site, which was built by Richard Upjohn in Gothic Revival style and consecrated in 1846. Its 280-foot-high steeple was a beacon to ships from 15 miles away. The sandstone church itself—with its stained-glass side windows (some of the oldest in the United States), fifteenth-century Italian altarpiece, monument rooms, and interesting small museum—is well worth a visit. Compact as Trinity is, there is much to savor.

> ## LUNCH BREAK
>
> If you like Mexican food, **Chipotle** (2 Broadway; 212–344–0941) is great for a quick, easy-on-the-wallet meal. For something fancier there's **14 Wall Street** (14 Wall Street; 212–233–2780), located in J. P. Morgan's former thirty-first-floor apartment. It is popular for "power lunching" and its exhilarating views, and it has heady prices to match.

The grave that garners the most attention is that of Alexander Hamilton, but there are other distinguished full-timers here, including Revolutionary War officers, delegates to the Continental Congress, and U.S. senators and congressmen.

Two inhabitants are men who felt strongly about freedom of the press long before there was a First Amendment—or even an independent country and constitution to write a first amendment *for*. **William Bradford** (1660–1752; north churchyard, near right side of the church) printed the first newspaper in the United States, the *New York Gazette*, and is considered the father of the American press. **John Peter Zenger** (1697–1746; unmarked), a publisher, printer, and archrival of Bradford, was also an advocate of an independent press.

Another tenant is **James Lawrence** (1781–1813; left of the church in the south churchyard), captain of the *Chesapeake*. His ship was locked in combat with the British frigate *Shannon* in the War of 1812. As the wounded

Lawrence lay dying, he said to his men, "Don't give up the ship!" Sharing his grave is **Augustus C. Ludlow** (1792–1813; same as Lawrence), his second-in-command.

Also in these compact environs is **Francis Lewis** (1713–1803; north churchyard, opposite the side door), a Welshman and the only signer of the Declaration of Independence who is buried in Manhattan. A 39-foot-high, four-sided monument at the center of the path in the north churchyard was designed by architect Thomas Nash and honors **Caroline Webster Astor** (1830–1908), whose "digs" are actually uptown with other Astors in Trinity Cemetery.

Some of the oldest tombstones beg to be rubbed (now a forbidden pastime), like the puff-cheeked, stern-looking, bewigged face on the stone of **Anthony Ackley,** who died in 1782. His grave is on the northeast Broadway corner. The most ancient stone in any New York City graveyard belongs to **Richard Churcher,** who died at age five in 1681. The much-deteriorated stone bears an hourglass with wings and below it a skull and crossbones. It is in the lower edge, next to the path, of section 2 in the north churchyard.

Take time to admire the various statuary, especially the full-length bronze of **John Watts** (1749–1836; section 26 in the south churchyard). In wig and gown, with parchment scroll, he looks every bit the proper jurist, which he was—as the first judge of Westchester County in 1806. *Grounds open 7:00 A.M.–5:00 P.M. Monday–Friday, 8:00 A.M.–3:00 P.M. Saturday, 7:00 A.M.–3:00 P.M. Sunday. Office hours: 7:00 A.M.–6:00 P.M. Monday–Friday, 8:00 A.M.–4:00 P.M. Saturday, 7:00 A.M.– 4:00 P.M. Sunday. Map; daily services; no stone rubbing allowed. Free guided tours of the church and museum offered daily at 2:00 P.M. and by appointment.*

## ROBERT FULTON   1765–1815

*B*rilliant and mercurial, Fulton was a man who did many things well. Inventor, visionary, artist, engineer, and statesman—if he lived today, he would be a candidate for a MacArthur "genius" grant. At an early age, this penurious Pennsylvania native was apprenticed to a Philadelphia jeweler, but he soon decided that his future lay in portraiture and landscape painting.

Intending to study with expatriate artist Benjamin West in London, Fulton sailed for England in 1787. He painted for seven years with some success but then shifted his focus to engineering. He soon invented a system of lockless canals. Before long he was in Paris, wrote a book on canal navigation, and constructed a submarine boat, the *Nautilus*. His other inventions included machines for making ropes, spinning flax, and sawing and polishing marble. Everything seemed to challenge him to improve it.

Fulton's major accomplishment, for which history remembers him, was using steam to propel a boat. He had the vision to realize how essential steam navigation would be to American progress. In 1807, with Robert R. Livingston, he built the *Clermont*, a steamboat that plied the Hudson River between New York and Albany; it was the first steamboat service in the world. Fulton and Livingston secured a navigation monopoly for a maximum of thirty years. In 1814–15, at the request of the U.S. government, Fulton constructed the *Fulton*, a thirty-eight-ton vessel with central paddle wheels. It was, in effect, the first steam warship. Who knows what other ideas might have germinated in later years if Fulton had not died at age forty-nine.

His sarcophagus resides in the Livingston family plot, in section 7 (halfway down the back path, at the edge) of the north churchyard. A monument honoring him is in the south churchyard, section 1c.

## ALBERT GALLATIN   1761–1849

Among immigrants who helped shape the young United States was this Swiss man from Geneva who served the new government as financier and diplomat. Gallatin served all of the first six U.S. presidents in one capacity or another. Called "the nation's banker," he was secretary of the treasury for thirteen years, first under Thomas Jefferson and then under James Madison. During that time he arranged the financing for Jefferson's purchase of the Louisiana Territory and for its exploration. His savvy use of federal

funds made possible new roads and canals, enabling goods to be shipped from one state to another.

So significant was Gallatin's work that when Lewis and Clark discovered the three rivers that form the Missouri River, they named them after Jefferson, Madison, and Gallatin—the three men they considered the most important at the time.

Earlier in his long life, Gallatin served briefly as representative and senator from Pennsylvania, where he had settled. During the Whiskey Rebellion of 1794, he helped keep the nation together in its first test. Later his diplomatic skills helped negotiate the end of the War of 1812. He also served as envoy to England and minister to France. Retiring from government service in 1817, Gallatin became president of the National Bank of the City of New York and was a founder of New York University.

Gallatin's imposing sandstone sarcophagus, designed by Richard Upjohn (who also built the church), is near Fulton's in section 7, the farthest end of the north churchyard.

## ALEXANDER HAMILTON  1757–1804

We tend to view our founding fathers with rosy lenses, but they were men with both virtues and weaknesses. No one illustrates this better than Hamilton, the youngest of the fifty-five framers of the U.S. Constitution, a lieutenant colonel, and an aide-de-camp to General George Washington.

As Washington's treasury secretary, Hamilton put the infant American republic on a sound financial keel, promoted the establishment of a national bank, founded the Bank of New York, and did everything possible to strengthen the federal government. Later President Thomas Jefferson, a Hamilton foe, asked treasury secretary Albert Gallatin to check the archives to "uncover the blunders and frauds of Hamilton," Gallatin's predecessor. Gallatin did so with gusto and then reported his findings to his boss: "I have found the most perfect system ever formed. Any change in it would injure it. Hamilton made no blunders, committed no frauds. He did nothing wrong." Strong words from a longtime foe and rival.

Hamilton's intellect was huge, his courage and integrity beyond reproach. He was an immigrant (a native of the British West Indies), a lawmaker, a soldier, and, most importantly, an economist. At the same time, he meddled in every branch of government, intrigued behind Washington's back, quarreled with John Adams and Thomas Jefferson, and sometimes let personal rivalry interfere with public policy.

Yet in 1800, when the presidential election between Jefferson and Aaron Burr ended in a tie and went to the House of Representatives, Hamilton supported Jefferson (whom he disliked) as the lesser of evils, believing that Burr was dangerous and ill-equipped to be president. Later Hamilton worked successfully to keep Burr from becoming the governor of New York. Burr's response was to challenge Hamilton to a duel, an "offer" he couldn't refuse.

Less than three years earlier, Hamilton had given his twenty-year-old son, Philip, advice on dueling that proved prophetic. He told Philip, according to a newspaper account at the time, that "dueling is honorable, but killing is immoral. Therefore young Hamilton should waste his shot." He did so and was killed.

So what happened after Burr's challenge? The duel took place at Weehawken, New Jersey, on July 11, 1804. Hamilton deliberately missed Burr on his first shot. But Burr wasn't playing the same game. Burr's first shot hit his foe in the stomach, mortally wounding him. Hamilton died the next day at age forty-seven. He left behind a widow, seven children, and, ironically for a savvy moneyman, insufficient funds to provide for them.

Hamilton's odd sarcophagus, with an urn at each of the four corners, has a stone pyramid rising from the center. It is at the far edge of the circular path in the south churchyard, section 1c, on the left side of the church, near Rector Street.

# CHAPTER 2

# The Bronx

*T*here are two cemeteries in the Bronx known for their famous residents—each very different from the other, and both worth visiting because they reveal the final dwellings of some of New York's all-time superstars.

# ST. RAYMOND NEW CEMETERY

*East 177th Street and Lafayette Avenue; (718) 792–1133*

Actually there are two St. Raymond cemeteries, the Old and the New. Both Catholic cemeteries, they are related but are not contiguous. The old smaller one, no longer in use, dates back to 1875 and is located at East Tremont Avenue and Whittemore Avenue (718–792–2080). Among a crew of U.S. congressmen, Civil War officers, and Congressional Medal of Honor recipients, the most distinguished inhabitant is **Father Francis Patrick Duffy** (1871–1932; section 9, range 99, grave 10). Canadian-born, he was ordained at Catholic University in Washington, D.C., in 1896 and taught ethics and psychology at St. Joseph's Seminary in New York. In 1914 he became the chaplain of the famous "Fighting 69th" Infantry Regiment, an Irish-American unit that endured some of the most brutal fighting of World War I—at Lorraine, Champagne-Marne, Meuse-Argonne, and elsewhere. Always at or near the front lines, Father Duffy received the Distinguished Service Cross and Distinguished Service Medal, among other awards for bravery. He and his unit were immortalized in the 1940 movie *The Fighting 69th*, starring Pat O'Brien as the priest.

The *new* St. Raymond's—near the water, with a view of the Bronx-Whitestone Bridge—broke ground in 1953. It is a vast and somewhat dispiriting necropolis, with rows and rows of similar-size headstones along wide oak-tree-lined drives. Its major asset: It is so carefully laid out that particular graves are easy to find. Within each section, the graves are designated by "range" numbers, and each headstone base is etched with plot and grave numbers. Other cemeteries would do well to emulate this model system.

Sometimes it seems as if the entire graveyard should be jumping after hours, given that so many singers and musicians are in subterranean residence. **Jackie Jackson** (1941–1997; St. Matthew section, range 19, grave 26) is here. As a songstress with the Chantels, her hits included "Maybe" and "I Only Have Eyes for You." Here also is **Guadalupe Yoli** (1939–1992; St. Matthew section, range 7, grave 88), known as "La Lupe" and the "Latin Judy Garland" because of her voice and lifestyle (drug and money problems, multi-romances, and popularity with gay fans). She was a Cuban salsa singer who accompanied Tito Puente, the top Latin performer of all time. The very popular **Hector Lavoe** (1946–1993), a salsa star of the 1950s known as "El Cantante," used to be here but recently was reinterred in Puerto Rico.

St. Raymond's is home on the ranges to many performers: **Angela Martin** (1942–2004; Our Lady of Hope mausoleum, crypt 364, unit F-U), actress, ventriloquist, and singer with Frank Sinatra, Tony Bennett, and others; **Merlin Santana** (1976–2002; Holy Cross section, range 19, grave 48), feature actor in television and films; **Luis "El Maestro del Cuatro" Silva** (1910–2003; Holy Cross section, range 19, grave 86), a musician who played a version of guitar known as "el cuatro"; **Henry James "Red" Allen** (1908–1967; St. Anne section, range 16, grave 52), composer, actor, and jazz musician who played with King Oliver, Louis Armstrong, Fletcher Henderson, and others; and **Anthony DeMassi** (1933–1991; St. Matthew section, range 11, grave 76), sometime actor in television and movies, best known as a longtime bodyguard for David Bowie.

**LUNCH BREAK**

Next door to the old St. Raymond and a few blocks from the new cemetery is a convenient place for pizza, **Louie** (3178 East Tremont; 718–931–4248), which also serves dinner.

**Anthony "Fat Tony" Salerno** (1911–1992) may not have been the worst of the handful of mafiosi seeking eternal rest at St. Raymond, but he was certainly the most notorious. Surprisingly, after his long life of crime, he died of natural causes at age eighty-one, while still in prison. If you care to visit, he is in section 16 of the mausoleum (range 1, plot 3, grave 1). *Grounds open 8:00 A.M.–4:00 P.M. daily. Office hours: 8:00 A.M.–4:00 P.M. Monday–Friday, 9:00 A.M.–noon Saturday; closed major holidays. Map; restroom.*

## BILLIE HOLIDAY 1915–1959

*W*ith a soulful, jazzy contralto that was so recognizable and arresting it could stop conversation in a crowded room, Billie Holiday sang of optimistic love ("Our Love Is Here to Stay") and thwarted love ("But Not for Me"), of hope ("I Wished on the Moon"), suicide ("Gloomy Sunday"), and racism ("Strange Fruit"). Even when despair and drugs slurred the words, she kept on singing.

Hers is one of the saddest stories in the history of jazz. Born Eleanora Fagan Holiday, she was the illegitimate child of a teenage mother. Holiday ran errands for a bordello in her native Baltimore as a young girl, was raped at age ten, and quit school after fifth grade. Her mother moved to New York and Billie later joined her, but Billie was arrested for prostitution at age fifteen and jailed on Welfare Island for four months. At some point she discovered that

she had a voice that people would pay to hear, and by the early 1930s, she was recording with Benny Goodman, Count Basie, Red Norvo, and others. Saxophonist Lester Young dubbed her "Lady Day," which stuck as a lifelong nickname.

The 1940s and 1950s were a seesaw—up (great fame and success) and down (marriage to a drug addict who got her hooked, too). A drug bust for heroin led to a year in a federal penitentiary. Once released, Holiday continued to suffer the racial indignities endemic to that time, such as having to ride the service elevator in fancy hotels where she was the featured performer. She married again; then there were more drug charges and finally premature death from kidney problems and cardiac arrest.

"She died of everything," one obituary reported. A proud, intense woman, Holiday was a unique interpreter and improviser of jazz for the ages. "They Can't Take That Away" from her. Here, with her mother, **Sadie Holiday Fagan** (1896–1945), in the St. Paul section (range 56, plot 29, grave 1), "Comes Love" or at long last peace.

hen Frankie Lymon and the Teenagers skyrocketed on to the pop
music scene in 1955, they dazzled and flared, then fizzled out
almost as fast. They were a Harlem doo-wop vocal quintet whose
squeaky-clean teenage image—Frankie was fourteen, the others all under sixteen—made them appealing to both white and black audiences. In their letter sweaters, with their smoothed-back hair and sweet-sounding harmonies,
the Teenagers rose to the top of
the music charts. What took
them there were Lymon's
youthful tenor voice and his
smash hit song "Why Do Fools
Fall in Love?".

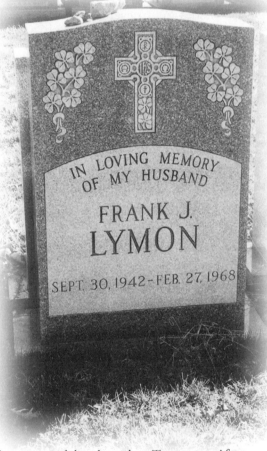

They were too young, and
fame came too fast. Lymon left
the group and went solo—but
then his voice changed. He
married three times, was
seduced by drugs (goodbye
schoolboy image), and died of a
heroin overdose at age twenty-
six. His great, if short-lived, talent landed him in the Rock and
Roll Hall of Fame. Later, "Why
Do Fools Fall in Love?" was
featured in the movie *American
Graffiti* and revived by Diana
Ross. To whom did the royalties belong? It turned out that
none of Lymon's wives was
legally married to him, and the
authorship of the song was hotly contested by the other Teenagers. After
lengthy litigation, royalties now go to the two surviving group members, Jimmy
Merchant and Herman Santiago. The doo-wop beat goes on. Frankie, may you
rest in peace in the St. Anthony section, range 13, grave 70.

# THE WOODLAWN CEMETERY

*Webster Avenue and East 233rd Street; (718) 920–0500*

One of the most out-of-this world, heavenly residences in New York is in the Bronx. The planners of this rural cemetery intended it to be so back in 1865 when the first "guest" arrived. The 400 acres (more than 20 city blocks) of undulating hills and meticulously landscaped banks are virtually an arboretum, which was the plan from the start.

As New York burst its seams in the mid-nineteenth century, with city cemeteries full to overflowing, a group of forward-looking planners turned north to find more space. The Bronx River Valley was a natural locale, with easy access to the railroad line for funeral corteges and a woodland exquisitely suited to the hereafter. So in 1863 the land was purchased, soon to be sculpted into a rural cemetery in the mode of Mount Auburn in Cambridge, Massachusetts, and The Green-Wood in Brooklyn.

Thanks to the founders' foresight and planning, The Woodlawn today is arcadia, one of the three most beautiful postmortem habitats in the country (in my opinion). The grounds are stippled with some 3,000 trees of forty-six different species. These include many rare specimens, like the European cut-leaf beech, umbrella pine, white pine, golden rain tree, Kentucky coffee tree, hackberry, katsura, cork tree, and a giant white oak that is more than 240 years old. Trees attract birds: Some hundred species have been spotted twittering in the trees; bathing in the ponds, waterfalls, and lakes; and calling their winged colleagues.

From its beginnings, The Woodlawn was much sought after by fashionable New Yorkers in search of a permanent state of grace. The roll call reads like a more egalitarian version of Mrs. Astor's "Four Hundred," with noblemen and nouveaux riche, philanthropists and philanderers, cultural royalty and robber barons, tycoons and tyrants. Today there are more than 350,000 inhabitants in this silent city.

Many of the numerous stately mausoleums (there are about 1,200 of them), built for prominent "lifers," are architectural wonders, the work of Richard Morris Hunt; McKim, Mead & White; James Renwick; James Gamble Rogers; and Louis Comfort Tiffany. Note the splendid dwellings of **William A. Clark** (1839–1925; Oak Hill, Central Avenue, section 84), Montana senator and patron of Washington's Corcoran Gallery of Art; **Herman Armour** (1837–1901, Chestnut section), head of Armour and Company, meat packers; **Harry Helmsley** (1910–1997; Aster, north border, section 209), controversial hotelier and billionaire real estate broker; **Collis P. Huntington** (1821–1900; Magnolia), entrepreneur, land developer, and railroad magnate; and **Jules S. Bache** (1861–1944; Whitewood), founder of J. S. Bache and Company, financier, and art collector, whose mausoleum was modeled after the temple of Isis at Phylae, Egypt.

Included on the residents' list are dancers like **Irene** (1893–1969; Parkview) and **Vernon Castle** (1887–1918; Parkview), a celebrated ballroom dance team of the early twentieth century. **Antoinette Perry** (1888–1946; Hickory Knoll) is there, too. The Tony Award (the theater version of the Oscar) was named for this actress and director.

While jazz musicians are omnipresent, note these musicians as well: **Victor Herbert** (1859–1924; Whitewood), conductor and composer of popular comic operas, such as *Babes in Toyland*; and **Fritz Kreisler** (1875–1962; Butternut), the Austrian-born, world-famous concert violinist.

Athletes, too, are in these fertile grounds, like **Gertrude Ederle** (1906–2003; Arbutus, section 181, center of plot), the first woman to swim across the English Channel and the winner of three Olympics gold medals in 1924; **Frankie Frisch** (1898–1973; Birchhill), the "Fordham Flash," a baseball player with the New York Giants and St. Louis Cardinals; and **John Reid** (1840–1916; Lake), a Scotsman deemed the father of American golf. **Grantland Rice** (1880–1954; Oakwood, Alpine Avenue, section 93), one of the all-time great sportswriters and a Baseball Hall of Fame member, joins them. He is remembered for saying, "It's not whether you win or lose, it's how you play the game."

You can visit many industrialists and business leaders, including **Augustus Juilliard** (1836–1919; Sassafras), the textile magnate and philanthropist who endowed what became the Juilliard School of Music; **Samuel Kress** (1863–1955; Walnut), merchant, philanthropist, and art collector; **Roland H. Macy** (1822–1877; Crowngrove), founder of R. H. Macy's department store; and **J. C. Penney** (1875–1971; Pine), founder of the J.C. Penney chain of retail stores (his middle name was—no kidding—Cash).

Artists abound: **Alexander Archipenko** (1887–1964; Oakwood), a cubist sculptor; **James Montgomery Flagg** (1877–1960; Catalpa), the ubiquitous magazine illustrator who created World War I's famous recruiting poster "Uncle Sam wants you!"; **John Held** (1889–1958; Dogwood, Elder Avenue, section 116), whose illustrations of flappers encapsulated the Jazz Age;

**George McManus** (1884–1954; Parkview), creator of Maggie and Jigs in the *Bringing Up Father* comic strip; and **Joseph Stella** (1877–1946; Clover), an Italian-born futurist painter.

There are heroes: **Admiral David Farragut** (1801–1870; Aurora Hill), renowned for his defeat of the Confederate fleet at Mobile Bay and his order, "Damn the torpedoes! Full speed ahead!"; and **Isador** (1845–1912; Myosotis) and **Ida Straus** (1849–1912; Myosotis), who went down with the *Titanic*. He wouldn't leave until all women and children were in lifeboats; she wouldn't leave without him.

Two prominent Japanese men are domiciled at The Woodlawn. **Jokichi Takamine** (1854–1922; Heather) was called the father of modern biotechnology for developing the first commercial starch-digesting enzyme and for isolating adrenalin. Married to an American, he spent much of his life promoting friendly relations between his birth country and his adopted one and was instrumental in arranging the gift of cherry trees to Washington, D.C. One of The Woodlawn's most visited graves is that of **Hideyo Noguchi** (1876–1928; Whitewood), a bacteriologist who discovered many diseases but died of yellow fever while working on a cure for it. His grave site, a giant boulder in a woodsy setting, has an inscribed bronze plaque that reads, "Through devotion to science, he lived and died for humanity."

**LUNCH BREAK**

For lunch or dinner, **Rory Dolan's** (890 McLean Avenue, Yonkers; 914–776–2946) is convenient and moderately priced.

To reach the cemetery by train from New York City, take the Metro North train from Grand Central Station to the Woodlawn stop; the cemetery is a short walk away. *Grounds open 8:30 A.M.–5:00 P.M. daily. Office hours: 9:00 A.M.–4:30 P.M. Monday–Saturday. Map, restrooms. Friends of Woodlawn Cemetery (718–920–1469) offers special tours in spring and fall months at 2:00 P.M. on Saturday and Sunday. Modest fee; tours limited to forty people, so call the cemetery for reservations.*

## ALVA SMITH VANDERBILT BELMONT   1856–1933
## OLIVER HAZARD PERRY BELMONT   1858–1908

etween them, the Belmonts were top-heavy with provenances. Even though Alva's first husband, William Vanderbilt, was one of the world's richest men, he had to prove he wasn't just a parvenu by hiring Richard M. Hunt to build a $3 million mansion on Fifth Avenue—and then a "cottage" in Newport that cost, with lavish furnishings, $9 million. Three years after the latter palace was built, the Vanderbilts divorced and Alva married Oliver Belmont.

Oliver was the son of August Belmont, a megamillionaire who had to overcome his own nouveau riche status by marrying up—to Caroline Perry, daughter of Commodore Matthew Perry. The second-generation Belmont had all the proper credentials: St. Paul's School, the U.S. Naval Academy at Annapolis, member of the August Belmont and Company banking firm. In his own right he was a sportsman, horse-racing fan, newspaper publisher, and one-term Democratic congressman. Together, the Belmonts made quite a splash in New York society.

After Oliver's death, Alva became active in the suffragette movement. She wrote (with Elsa Maxwell) a suffragist operetta, *Melinda and Her Sisters* (best forgotten now); founded the Political Equality League; and became president of the National Woman's Party, a post she held for life.

As if this weren't enough, in later life Alva became an architectural designer and was one of the first women elected to the American Institute of

Architects. The Belmonts' ornate Gothic "cottage" at The Woodlawn, just inside the main gate in Whitewood (Whitewood Avenue, section 134), was modeled on the St. Hubert Chapel in Amboise, France, designed by Leonardo da Vinci. Nothing like thinking big.

## IRVING BERLIN  1888–1989

American history is full of rags-to-riches stories, but few are as stirring as that of Israel Baline, aka Irving Berlin, the youngest of eight children of a Russian Jewish family who emigrated to the United States when he was five years old. He had the usual Lower East Side Manhattan childhood and dropped out of school as a teenager to earn money for the family after his father's untimely death.

As a singing waiter who never learned to read or write music but had a good ear, Berlin was soon writing songs, both words and music. His budding career blossomed with "Alexander's Ragtime Band" in 1911 and his alliance with Flo Ziegfeld, who used Berlin tunes in all his revues. Other collaborations—with Victor Herbert, George M. Cohan, Vernon and Irene Castle, and others—were fruitful, too, and the songs danced from Berlin's pen.

Berlin could write any kind of popular song. Yet he could never play in any key but F-sharp. To overcome this handicap he had a piano specially constructed with a hand clutch to change keys. It is now in the Smithsonian Institution.

Berlin created the songs for a George F. Kaufman play, *The Cocoanuts* (1925), which starred the Marx Brothers. He also wrote songs for three Fred Astaire–Ginger Rogers movies in the 1930s: *Top Hat, Follow the Fleet,* and *On the Avenue.* These included such hits as "Cheek to Cheek," "I've Got My Love to Keep Me Warm," and "Let's Face the Music and Dance." With his steady work ethic and upbeat personality, Berlin left—after 101 years—a rich musical legacy that includes such classics as "Always," "Blue Skies," "God Bless America," "White Christmas," and "There's No Business Like Show Business," to cite just a few.

He was as true-blue on a personal level as in his work. Married in 1912 to Dorothy Goetz and widowed the same year (she died of typhoid fever), Berlin was heartbroken. It was sixteen years before he remarried, this time to a Catholic, Ellin Mackay, whose father bitterly objected. But the marriage proved a happy one. Berlin not only wrote songs glorifying the American dream, he seems to have lived it. His unassuming granite gravestone, flat in the ground, and that of his wife, **Ellin Mackay Berlin** (1903–1988), are bordered by pachysandra. They are in the Columbine section, directly facing Heather Avenue.

## NELLIE BLY    1864–1922

lizabeth Cochrane Seaman, who used the pen name Nellie Bly, was a woman's libber long before the phrase was created. She was born in Pennsylvania, spent much of her working life in New York City, and traveled extensively. The first woman reporter on the all-male staff of the *Pittsburgh Dispatch* (in 1885), she covered the effects of unfair labor practices on working-class women. This caused such a brouhaha, she felt the need to leave town and received an assignment to Mexico. There she exposed the contrasts between the wealthy and the poor and criticized the Mexican government. Bingo! There she went again: persona non grata.

Bly's next stop was a job on Joseph Pulitzer's *New York World*, where her first scoop was reporting on conditions in an insane asylum. To gain entry she posed as someone mentally ill. Her report led to a grand jury investigation of the asylum. She next replicated—and bested—the fictional *Around the World*

in Eighty Days by making the trip in seventy-two. This brought Bly universal fame and a ticket to write any story she wanted to cover— including interviews with famous and controversial figures and many more exposés. But after her marriage at age thirty-one to a wealthy seventy-two-year-old, Bly seems to have put her career on hold. Her record confirms her status as one of the great reporters of her day and a feminist in fact if not in name. Her memorial stone rests in the north edge of the Honeysuckle section, near Bainbridge Avenue.

## RALPH JOHNSON BUNCHE   1904–1971

Considered one of the most intelligent and principled U.S. diplomats of the past century, Ralph Bunche, a Detroit native, had a distinguished academic career before he joined the United Nations and became an undersecretary-general. A grandson of slaves, Bunche was an honors graduate of the University of California and a faculty member at Howard University. He earned a Harvard PhD and became the chief assistant for Swedish sociologist Gunnar Myrdal's book *An American Dilemma: The Negro Problem and Modern Democracy* (1944).

As an analyst in the Office of Strategic Services during World War II, Bunche became an expert on Africa. This led to a State Department job, and in 1947 he joined the United Nations as a mediator in territories under UN trusteeship. He negotiated a cease-fire between Arabs and Israelis after the first Arab-Israeli War, for which he was awarded the Nobel Peace Prize—the first person of color to achieve this honor. Although high-level positions in the U.S. government eluded Bunche because of race, he earned great recognition abroad for his UN work. Late in life he advised Martin Luther King Jr.; like King, he favored a peaceful resolution of American racial problems.

His small headstone and those of his wife, **Ruth Harris Bunche** (1906–1988), and daughter, **Jane Bunche Pierce** (1933–1966), lie in the Myosotis section, in front of a large rough-hewn granite memorial with the name BUNCHE engraved beneath two gracefully carved olive branches. Nothing could be more appropriate.

## GEORGE M. COHAN   1878–1942

Born in Providence, Rhode Island, Cohan really was a "Yankee Doodle Boy," as one of his most patriotic songs phrased it. From age seven he was one of The Four Cohans, a vaudeville company that consisted of him; his older sister, Josephine; and their parents. While Cohan was an actor, a singer, and a dancer, he also began writing songs for the little troupe at age thirteen. His first song hit was "Hot Tamale Alley" in 1895, and his musical comedy *The Governor's Son* came six years later. This was followed in 1904 by *Little Johnny Jones*, which featured "Give My Regards to Broadway" and "Yankee Doodle Boy."

Between 1901 and 1940 Cohan produced eighty Broadway shows and starred in many of them. "Over There," written in a burst of wartime fervor in 1917, quickly became *the* song of World War I and—along with "It's a Grand Old Flag"—won for Cohan a Congressional Medal of Honor. His patriotic spirit was highlighted in Jimmy Cagney's portrayal of him in *Yankee Doodle Dandy*.

Cohan's handsome Gothic mausoleum, designed by Louis Comfort Tiffany, has united the "Four Cohans" again. Note the altar (visible by peeking through the Tiffany windows) and ornamented bronze doors, which *always* sport a fresh American flag—courtesy of a veterans' group—and Cohan's congressional medal. On the doors in small print are the names COHAN and NIBLO (Josephine's married name)—rather discreet for show-business folks. The mausoleum faces Park Avenue at the edge of the Butternut section.

## MILES DAVIS    1926–1991

*I*n the second wave of jazz innovators, Miles Dewey Davis III was a standout. The son of well-to-do African-American professionals, he was born in Alton, Illinois, grew up in East St. Louis, and had a classical music education. As a child he studied the violin. Like a musical vacuum cleaner, he devoured the records of Louis Armstrong and other greats of that era, absorbed church music on visits to his grandfather in Arkansas, played with a New Orleans group while still a kid, watched Billy Eckstine direct a band featuring contemporary jazz, and sat in on trumpet with Dizzy Gillespie, Charlie Parker, Art Blakey, and others.

Listening to Gillespie and Parker, Davis knew he had to go to New York to get in on the new sound—bebop—so at age seventeen he enrolled at the Juilliard School. He soon dropped out, went to California, made friends with bassist Charles Mingus, and then formed a nine-piece band that included Gerry Mulligan and John Lewis. Davis's new jazz style drew on all his early musical influences, resulting eventually in his *Birth of the Cool* album (1949). A huge success at the Paris Jazz Festival was followed by a few dry spells, which led to a drug habit that Davis battled all his life.

During an off-drugs period in the mid-1950s, he produced some of his very best music—albums like *Milestones* and *Round About Midnight*—with arrangements by Gil Evans, who would become his lifelong collaborator, and a quintet that included John Coltrane, Paul Chambers, and Red Garland. His groups changed and regrouped, as did his style. "I have to change," he said. "It's like a curse."

Still the hits continued—*Sketches of Spain, Miles Ahead,* and Davis's much-acclaimed version of *Porgy and Bess. Kind of Blue* is the best-selling jazz LP of all time. By the end of the 1960s, influenced by Jimi Hendrix and rhythm and blues, Davis went electric and created what would become known as fusion, epitomized by the landmark *Bitches Brew*.

More ups and downs followed. From 1975 to 1980 he didn't play a note publicly, beset by poor health and a drug-use relapse. Then came two records that won Grammy Awards: *We Want Miles* and *Decoy*. At age sixty-five Davis died of respiratory failure, pneumonia, and the effects of a stroke. He had been married and divorced three times (one wife was actress Cicely Tyson), and he left behind a daughter, three sons, and several grandchildren.

Davis once said, "Sometimes you have to play a long time to be able to play like yourself." His constant musical improvement testified to that. At the narrowest point of the triangular Alpine Hill section, where Heather, Fir, and Knollwood Avenues meet, you can't miss the large, polished black granite, signlike memorial in front of his sarcophagus. It proclaims "In memory of Sir Miles Davis," with two measures from his composition "Solar" along the bottom of the sign and an oversize trumpet carved along the right-hand side. Under a huge shade tree, separated from other grave sites, Miles is alone again—resting up, no doubt, for Gabriel's final trumpet call.

## DUKE ELLINGTON   1899–1974

The career of Edward Kennedy Ellington—nicknamed "Duke" in school days, for his regal manner and stylish clothes—is proof that talent doesn't always burn itself out young. Born in Washington, D.C., to upward-striving parents who worked two jobs apiece to care for their family, Ellington was initially more interested in art and sports than in music, even though he had studied piano since age seven. At his high school graduation, he received the offer of a Pratt Institute art scholarship, but by then he was hooked on music, playing ragtime in local bands. This led to work with Elmer Snowden's

Washingtonians, a five-man combo that settled in 1923 at the Hollywood Club in New York.

Before long Ellington was the leader; the group doubled in size and was signed by the Cotton Club, the premiere jazz venue in the city. The Cotton Club years (1927 to 1931) made Ellington a "name," with the chance to play everything from dance music to blues to jazz instrumentals. His most fertile period musically—as composer and recording artist—was 1932 to 1942, which brought forth "Mood Indigo," "Sophisticated Lady," "It Don't Mean a Thing," and "Black and Tan Fantasy."

Billy Strayhorn joined the band in 1939 as arranger and second pianist and is considered the genius behind many of the band's later arrangements. His "Take the 'A' Train" became the band's theme song. Even though Ellington once said, "The wise musicians are those who play what they can master," he continued growing musically and expanded what was known as the "Ellington effect."

Carnegie Hall hosted performances of his large-scale "Black, Brown and Beige," "Harlem," and "Liberian Suite." Ellington also worked on full-length productions like *Jump for Joy*; film scores, including that for *Anatomy of a Murder*; and sacred music for Episcopal church services. He collaborated with John Coltrane, Charles Mingus, and other avant-garde instrumentalists. Probably the most prolific composer in jazz history— some estimate 2,000 compositions—the Duke was also a nice guy, a family man, and deeply religious, as the two stately, 8-foot-tall granite crosses at his grave site sug-

gest. Sheltering the grave is a huge Chinese paper maple tree. In the triangle that is the Wild Rose section, converging with Heather and Knollwood, his grave site squares off quietly against Miles Davis's flamboyant site across the road.

# JAY GOULD  1836–1892

The financial and audacious roguery of Gould and his buddy Jim Fiske make the savings-and-loan and Enron debacles of our age seem almost picayune. In an era of anything-goes finances, Gould epitomized the robber in the phrase *robber baron.* Born in Roxbury, New York, and brought up in Fairfield, Connecticut, he worked as a blacksmith, clerk, and surveyor. At age twenty-one, with savings of $5,000, he and another man opened a tannery in Pennsylvania. Through chicanery (a pattern he was to repeat throughout his life), Gould wrested control away from his partner. He then began speculating in small

railways. Gould, Fiske, and a third man, Daniel Drew, became partners in the directorship of the Erie Railroad. With a series of court-defying moves and outright bribery, they used stock-watering tricks to loot the railroad—and they got away with it.

Heady with their success, Gould and Fiske then manipulated the country's credit, export, and produce markets. They tried to corner the gold market, but this caused the panic of Black Friday (September 24, 1868) and brought an uproar of public outrage, which forced Gould out of the Erie Railroad. Nevertheless, $25 million richer, he turned westward, bought control of several other railroads, and ventured into other fields. He became part owner of the *New York World* newspaper, for example, and controlled the Western Union Telegraph Company. Called the "most hated man in America," Gould was both despised and feared. Coincidence or not, his stock rose by several points the day he died.

Money may not buy happiness, but for Gould it bought a magnificent hilltop mausoleum in the Lakeview section overlooking Hawthorne Avenue. It is a Greek temple with Ionic columns, sheltered by an enormous weeping beech tree (which in 1985 was designated one of the 113 great trees of New York City). Interestingly, Gould's name does not appear on the facade.

# LIONEL HAMPTON   1908–2002

*L*ongevity had little to do with the popularity of this "King of the Vibes," though living to age ninety-four didn't hurt. Hampton's career spanned almost eight decades of popular music. Through the years he jammed with virtually every star in the jazz pantheon, from Louis Armstrong, Dinah Washington, and Benny Goodman to Charlie Parker, Sonny Rollins, Charles Mingus, and Quincy Jones. In 1987 he performed with Frank Sinatra at Carnegie Hall; in 1997 he received the National Medal of Arts.

Most vividly remembered for his Benny Goodman years, Hampton began playing drums in a fife-and-drum band in Kenosha, Wisconsin, where he went to school. After his family moved to Chicago, he studied at a music school for newsboys and played in a newsboy band. He played everything he could get his restless fingers on—timpani, xylophone, orchestra bells, flute, and snare drum in the school marching band. At times in his long career, he led his own band; at times he played with small combos.

Hampton could create melodic wonders, as in his interpretations of "Dinah" and "Moonglow" with Benny Goodman. At other times he was pure ham, marching into the audience with his brass section or encouraging the audience to clap along with the music. This love of and excitement about performing made him a great entertainer, a role he played with verve throughout his life. When he was eighty-six years old, he jammed with musicians one-third his age; playing two-fingered piano, he outswung, outsoloed, and outlasted them all.

A lifetime of memories and jazz memorabilia went up in flames in 1997 when Hampton's apartment caught fire (caused by a lamp tipping over and igniting a bed). But "Hamp" persevered another five years. Today his final sojourn is in the Fir area, Knollwood Avenue, section 170.

## W. C. HANDY    1873–1958

William Christopher Handy, best known as the father of the blues, got his musical baptism early. Both his grandfather and father were ministers of the African Methodist Episcopal church in Florence, Alabama, where Handy sang spirituals and hymns every Sunday. He also listened to workers along the river lamenting their hard life in song.

From these influences Handy created a sound that was both soulful and hopeful, which he called "blues" and described as "the sound of a sinner on revival day." Of the forty blues tunes he wrote, the first—"St. Louis Blues," published in 1914— became the most famous. Other favorites are "Beale Street Blues," "Yellow Dog Blues," "Memphis Blues," and "Joe Turner Blues." Failing eyesight hardly lowed Handy down, as he continued to write songs, play trumpet, arrange and publish popular and religious music, and, oh yes, compile and write three books on the blues: *Blues Anthology, Treasury of the Blues,* and his autobiography, *Father of the Blues.* At his Harlem funeral, guess what was played? "St. Louis Blues," of course.

Handy's small, remote gravestone lies like an afterthought in the Cosmos section of The Woodlawn, close to the edge, near East 211th Street.

## COLEMAN HAWKINS   1904–1969

*H*awkins, or "Hawk," is something of an anomaly in the history of jazz. He didn't overdose on drugs or liquor, and he didn't die young or on poverty row. One of the greatest twentieth-century jazz saxophonists, he made the transition from jazz to bebop as smoothly as the notes he played, earning him the title "father of the tenor sax."

Maybe it started with his comfortable childhood in St. Joseph, Missouri. Both parents loved music, so he took piano and cello lessons, learning classical music, which he enjoyed his entire life (Johann Sebastian Bach was a special favorite). His discovery of the saxophone was the beginning of a lifelong romance. From age twelve he played part-time in local dance bands, but when

Fletcher Henderson, leader of a Big Band in the 1920s, beckoned, Hawk's jazz career really took off.

After eleven years with Henderson's band—enlivened by late-night Harlem jam sessions— Hawk spent a five-year sabbatical touring Europe, where his work was wildly appreciated. While there he developed an interest in the whole European cultural scene—art, theater, and, of course, music. Back in New York he started his own nine-man band. In 1939 he recorded "Body and Soul," which remains one of the all-time great singles in the history of jazz, influencing every generation—and every sax player—since.

In 1944 Hawkins made some records in Chicago that have been called the beginning of bebop. He dismissed such claims, never wanting to be pigeonholed musically. Although the public's interest in jazz declined in the 1950s, Hawkins continued to record and perform into the 1960s. The words at the bottom of his granite headstone read, "Always in our hearts." To anyone who hears his liquid sax, that's certainly true.

## CHARLES EVANS HUGHES  1862–1948

ughes's long and distinguished career had modest beginnings in Glens Falls, New York. As an adult, this Brown University and Columbia Law School graduate was quick to succeed, first as a law professor at Cornell University, and later as investigative counsel for several New York State agencies. In 1906 he became governor of New York and initiated far-reaching reforms, resigning to serve on the U.S. Supreme Court. In 1918 Republican Party leaders persuaded him to challenge Woodrow Wilson for president. It was a close election, but Hughes lost.

Later, as Warren Harding's secretary of state, he negotiated important arms treaties. Hughes returned to the Supreme Court in 1930 as chief justice, proving to be wise, fair-minded, and honorable. Though he disagreed with many New Deal programs, he sustained the Wagner Labor Relations Act, a centerpiece of Franklin Roosevelt's legislation. Hughes's views on freedom of the press and civil rights were ahead of his time. His final chambers can be found in the Elder section, nudging Elder Avenue.

## BARBARA HUTTON  1912–1979

he phrase "poor little rich girl" might have been custom-tailored to Barbara Hutton. Granddaughter of F. W. Woolworth and daughter of the man who founded the E. F. Hutton brokerage firm, little "Babs" was a chubby, lonely child with a nanny but no friends. Her father ignored her, her mother may have committed suicide (the medical records mysteriously disappeared), and Hutton believed that no one loved her nor ever would. She may have been right. When she was twelve, she inherited $28 million from her grandparents' estate. Her father invested it, and by twenty-one, when Hutton came of age, she had $50 million to play with.

That was the beginning of her search for love and acceptance, a hunt that led to seven marriages, mostly to fortune-hunting men, many of them minor European nobility. Only one marriage—number three, to Cary Grant—seems to have been a love match, but it didn't last either. One marriage was notorious for its cynical brevity: After fifty-three days, Hutton and playboy Porfirio Rubirosa separated, and he was $3.5 million the richer. Anorexia, a custody battle over her only child, bouts with depression, alcohol and drugs—these were the tabloid outlines of Hutton's life. Her son's 1972 death in a plane crash (at the age of thirty-six) may have pushed her over the edge: She died five years later, bedridden and with only $3,500 left of her enormous fortune.

Hutton reclines now, along with her grandfather, in the Woolworth faux-Egyptian mausoleum she had ridiculed as the "pyramid." It faces Central Avenue in the Pine section.

## FIORELLO LA GUARDIA   1882–1947

Funny, scrappy, and bursting with self-confidence, the "Little Flower"—as La Guardia was called—was the perfect fit for New York and New Yorkers, who elected him mayor three times, beginning in 1933. He had substance as a reformer against the corrupt Tammany Hall machine, which had dominated city politics for decades. La Guardia—short (barely 5 feet) and stout—is best remembered for the time, during a newspaper strike, when he read comic strips to kids on the radio.

More significantly, he was scrupulously honest and boasted (relentlessly) of many real accomplishments: cleaning up the slums, building parks, creating public housing and airports, revising the city charter, and developing a civil service free of politics. He had reason to boast—these were big accomplishments for any man, little or not. His ambitions for higher office were cut short in 1946 by the cancer that quickly killed him.

The most colorful of four New York City mayors at The Woodlawn, La Guardia faces Alpine Avenue in the Oakwood section. His simple, elegant, pale pink headstone features an engraved little flower.

## BAT MASTERSON   1854–1921

William Barclay Masterson, known by everyone as "Bat," had what may have been the most unusual career path of anyone in these historic grounds. After all, there weren't many people *anywhere* who went from a life of action in the West—as a buffalo hunter, sheriff, peace mar-

shal, killer of dangerous outlaws, and gambler—to a career as a sportswriter for a New York newspaper at age forty-nine. Masterson did and seems to have been successful at it. No one today thinks of him as a writer, remembering him instead as one of the good guys of the West, known for bravery and a cool head. These served him well in 1878 when he captured a notorious bandit, Dave Rudabaugh, and later killed two outlaws after they had gunned down his brother, the acting marshal of Dodge City.

Bat's granite headstone in the Primrose section states, "Loved by everyone." Rudabaugh might have argued about that, but not President Teddy Roosevelt, who appointed Masterson a federal deputy-marshal in 1905. He gave up that job two years later because it interfered with his sportswriting at the *Morning Telegraph*, where he eventually became sports editor. Masterson died at his desk with his pen in hand (but without boots on his feet).

## HERMAN MELVILLE   1819–1891

The blank scroll with a quill pen engraved on Melville's rough-hewn granite headstone (in the Catalpa section, under a giant oak tree)—covered with bas-relief ivy—is unnerving. It suggests either nonproductivity on the author's part or nonrecognition by the public. The first is anything but true, the latter partially so. In the first eleven years of his life as an author, Melville was extraordinarily productive. Based on his true-life adventures with cannibals in the South Seas, he wrote *Typee* (1846), which brought him instant fame. *Omoo* followed the next year, and in quick succession came *Mardi, Redburn, White-Jacket,* and, in 1851, *Moby Dick*—deemed a failure at the time but now considered his masterpiece.

More was to come. *Pierre: or The Ambiguities, Israel Potter, The Piazza Tales,* and *The Confidence Man* were all written by 1857. Then followed a dry spell and relative obscurity. But let's turn the page back to the beginning:

HERMAN MELVILLE
Born August 1, 1819
Died September 28, 1891

Melville came from distinguished stock on both sides of his family, with roots traceable to thirteenth-century Scotland. Both his grandfathers fought in the American Revolution, but his immediate family hit hard times. Melville left his New York City home at age seventeen to go to sea as a cabin boy. Then came nearly four years of wandering the world on the whaler *Acushnet*, which provided rich material for writing.

When his later books did poorly, Melville worked as a customs inspector for nineteen years, during which time his literary reputation sank out of sight. At his death in 1891, he left unfinished *Billy Budd*, his "last writes," as it were. Though incomplete, the book ranks with *Moby Dick, Typee,* and *Omoo* among his major works. Don't call him Ishmael; call him genius. To the right of Melville's headstone is that of his wife, **Elizabeth Shaw Melville** (1822–1906).

## ROBERT MOSES   1888–1981

During his reign (there's no other word for the forty-four years he spent as New York's major builder, mover, and power magnate), Moses was despised by some, respected by others. It's possible that no other unelected public servant has ever wielded such power in the United States. From 1924 to 1968 he reshaped New York into the city it is today, like it or not. As the parks commissioner he was the master builder responsible for most of the city's highways, bridges, and redevelopment projects in the twentieth century. Yet he was not an architect, not an engineer, not a planner.

He *was* a dynamo: energetic, tireless, bold, and creative. He understood politics, political manipulation, and how to yank the right cords in order to get things done. Arrogant and abrasive, he was also a great administrator.

The list of Moses's projects is impressive: Bronx-Whitestone, Throgs Neck,

Triborough, and other bridges that link the five boroughs; the Brooklyn-Battery Tunnel; Shea Stadium; Lincoln Center; the New York Coliseum; the United Nations; Co-Op City; and the 1939 and 1964 World's Fairs. Then there were the scores of highways, public-housing developments, and parks and more than 600 playgrounds.

On paper, all of these achievements sound astounding—and many were. But the costs were high: $27 billion, more than 250,000 people evicted from their homes, and neighborhoods demolished. Replacement housing for the poor, who were evicted so Moses could build his highways, was cheap and shoddy. The money that went into the highways robbed the city coffers of funds to modernize the subway system and failed to create a cohesive transportation system.

A man with a huge *edifice* complex, Moses rarely admitted he was wrong and would do almost anything to have his way, bulldozing any politician who got in his path. Yet he began life more idealistically. With excellent education credentials that included Yale, an MA in political science from Oxford University, and a PhD from Columbia, with a dissertation on the civil service system, he entered public service to do good—and he did.

But somewhere along the way, his ego wrestled with his public spiritedness, and the ego won. Robert Caro, author of *The Power Broker*, the definitive tome on Moses, calls him America's greatest builder but notes that "It would be impossible to say that New York would have been a better city if Robert Moses had never lived. It is possible to say only that it would have been a different city." No one can argue with that. Moses's grave is in the Iris area, Van Courtlandt Mausoleum, on West Border Avenue, section 212.

## THOMAS NAST   1840–1902

Nast amply demonstrated the power of the pen in *Harper's Weekly* in his savage caricatures of Tammany Hall and its political head, William "Boss" Tweed. Nast's attacks eventually contributed to the downfall of Tweed's machine and the man himself. When Tweed escaped from jail and fled to Spain disguised as a sailor, he was identified by non-English-speaking Spanish authorities solely from Nast's precise drawings.

Nast came by his fury at political corruption *nast*-urally. The son of a liberal German immigrant, he inherited his father's sense of justice. This, combined with superb draftsmanship, made his work famous throughout New

York. As a Radical Republican, he was such a staunch supporter of Abraham Lincoln and the Union that Lincoln called him "our best recruiting sergeant." A Nast cartoon in 1864, titled "Compromise with the South," depicted Columbia weeping at a grave labeled "Union heroes in a useless war" while a Union amputee shakes hands with a healthy Confederate soldier. It was so widely reprinted that some credited it with helping Lincoln win reelection.

Nast drew in a careful, detailed style, with bold cross-hatching, which suited perfectly his strong sense of black and white, good and evil. He is credited with creating the symbols of the political parties: a donkey as a Democrat (first drawn in 1870) and an elephant as a Republican (1874). His rendering in 1863 of Santa Claus as a jolly, roly-poly fellow in a fur-trimmed suit is the prototype still in use today.

Nast began his career at age fifteen at *Frank Leslie's Illustrated Newspaper*, after producing a sample drawing for Leslie full of details and humor. After a variety of drawings of prizefights in England, battles in Sicily, and other assignments, he homed in on politics, which quickly became his forte.

Eventually the *Harper's Weekly* management changed, and Nast's drawings lost their bite and went out of style. He tried to return to his first love, historical painting, without much luck. Freelancing didn't pay the bills of his large family, so in 1902 he accepted President Theodore Roosevelt's offer to serve as consul general in Guayaquil, Ecuador. Within a few months Nast died there of yellow fever, but it took four years for his body to be returned to New York and The Woodlawn. His tenancy nowadays is in the Birch Hill section, beneath a granite headstone with these stinging words: "He who practices teaching is crucified."

## JOSEPH PULITZER    1847–1911

The annual Pulitzer Prizes perpetuate a name that otherwise might be buried in journalism archives. But Joseph Pulitzer is worth remembering as someone who brought an independent, politically fearless approach to newspapers. Hungarian-born, Pulitzer thirsted for adventure despite a poor physique and bad eyesight. No army in Europe would take him, so at age seventeen, he sailed for the United States and promptly enlisted in the Union army. After four skirmishes, he was mustered out. A job at a German newspaper in St. Louis was the beginning of his life's work—buying, publishing, and editing newspapers.

First came the *St. Louis Dispatch*, which became the highly successful *St. Louis Post-Dispatch*, and then a move to New York and the purchase of the *World*, which was also a winner. Espousing workers' rights, taxation of luxuries and inheritance, reform of the civil service, and punishment of crooked officials were all part of Pulitzer's editorial creed. The brief newspaper war between Pulitzer and William Randolph Hearst led to sensationalistic reporting on both sides, smudging Pulitzer's sterling image. But later, under his personal guidance, the *World* became again a respected and accurate newspaper, making its owner wealthy in the process.

His will established a school of journalism at Columbia University and a series of awards "for the encouragement of public service, public morals, American literature and the advancement of education." Thus the Pulitzer Prizes were born and continue to be coveted by writers. Their namesake now rests in the Evergreen section, near Central Avenue.

## ELIZABETH CADY STANTON   1815–1902

The wife of an ardent abolitionist lawyer, **Henry Brewster Stanton** (1805–1887), Elizabeth Cady Stanton had her consciousness raised when female delegates were excluded from the floor of a World Anti-Slavery Convention in London in 1840. First she got mad, and then she got even. She went home and, with Lucretia Mott, organized America's first women's rights convention, which was held in 1848 in Stanton's hometown, Seneca Falls, New York.

At the convention she presented a woman's bill of rights that outlined the inferior position of women—in government, church, the law, and society—and introduced resolutions demanding redress, including voting rights. That same year Stanton helped secure passage in New York State of a law giving married women property rights. Two years later she joined forces with Susan B. Anthony on the issue of women's suffrage. For the next forty years they worked together, with Stanton writing on the subject and Anthony organizing the movement. By the end of the Civil War (after the birth of her seventh child), Stanton was able, as a woman of affluence, to work full-time for the movement as president of the National Woman Suffrage Association, a position she held until 1893. Articulate, argumentative, sometimes abrasive, and always dedicated, she remains an inspiration to feminists everywhere.

The 1830 Elizabeth Cady Stanton House (see House Call) was her home from 1847 to 1862 and is open to the public, with much of her memorabilia on display. Closer at hand is her sizable last domain, just off Central Avenue in the Lake section, near Woodlawn Lake. Stanton is domiciled on the Stanton plot with her husband and other family members.

## F. W. WOOLWORTH    1852–1919

*F*or a man who made millions from plebian merchandise, Frank Winfield Woolworth developed extremely patrician tastes. A farm boy who failed as a dry-goods salesman, he latched onto a merchandising idea that made him so much money that when he died, he left a fortune of $65 million. It was simple, as good ideas often are: selling fixed-price merchandise of all kinds at 5 cents per item. Woolworth soon boosted that to 10 cents, developed a chain of 5-and-10-cent stores, and had merchandise produced in bulk exclusively for his chain.

His success enabled him to build a fifty-six-room Italian Renaissance mansion on Long Island, sleep in a bed that had belonged to Napoleon, and have solid gold fixtures in his bathrooms. In 1913 he paid $13.5 million (cash) to erect his Woolworth Building—the tallest skyscraper of its time—in lower Manhattan. At his death there were more than 1,000 stores in the Woolworth chain.

In the Pine section, facing Central Avenue, you can't miss Woolworth's Egyptian Revival mausoleum, with two busty sphinxes "guarding" its doors. This final pied-à-terre was designed by John Russell Pope, architect of the Jefferson Memorial in Washington. When it came to his personal comfort, Woolworth never thought small.

## HOUSE CALL

The **Woolworth Building** in Manhattan (233 Broadway), at Park Place near City Hall Park, is Woolworth's legacy. It was the world's tallest building until 1930, when the Chrysler Building overtook it. This superb neo-Gothic wonder was designed by Cass Gilbert. As a commercial enterprise, the building now has tightened security, but it is possible to step inside to look at the splendor of the Byzantine mosaic ceiling, gold-leafed cornices, and other elegant details in the lobby. Architecture buffs love it.

# CHAPTER 3

# Brooklyn

*T*here are many cemeteries in Brooklyn, some with notable full-time lodgers, but all are over-shadowed by the sheer number of famous residents at one of America's greatest burial grounds: The Green-Wood. Still, any ardent seeker of lost persons will be interested in some of the other habitats noted herewith. Many of them can be found within an "island" of seventeen cemeteries that melt together in a cluster bordering Brooklyn and Glendale, Queens.

As Staten Island boasts only one "celebrity cemetery," I have included that listing at the end of this chapter. The Moravian Cemetery in New Dorp is located on the southeast part of the island and is most easily reached via Brooklyn's Verrazano Bridge.

# CYPRESS HILLS CEMETERY

*833 Jamaica Avenue; (718) 277–2900*

This expansive, nonsectarian burial ground, the largest of a group of seventeen adjoining cemeteries, was founded in 1848. It seemingly knows no county boundaries—sprawling from its entrance in Brooklyn into the Glendale area of Queens in the rear, and accommodating its share of celebrated New Yorkers. Within the confines of the cemetery is Cypress Hills National Cemetery, which opened in 1864. It is the final home of 21,000 veterans (from the War of 1812 through World War II) and their spouses.

A variety of headliners can be found on these placid grounds, which are dotted with pines, locusts, and other trees. One is actor-comic **Victor Moore** (1876–1962; Cypress Hills Abbey mausoleum, special section 15, crypt 3, aisle NN). He began in vaudeville, appeared frequently on Broadway, and ended as a comic character actor in dozens of movies. His physique (short, bald, and pudgy); his voice (creaky and quavering); and his perfect timing made any role he played memorable. One such role was the hapless vice president Alexander Throttlebottom in the stage musical *Of Thee I Sing*.

World-famous Dutch-emigrant artist **Piet Mondrian** (1872–1944; Crescent Knoll, block 51, grave 1191), a modern abstract painter, resides here. His small granite stone in the ground is relatively anonymous, considering his international reputation. Mondrian is known for his sparse, cerebral geometric paintings of straight black lines and squares on white canvas, with small patches of vibrant primary colors; his unique style is easily recognizable and viewable in museums all over the world. Also on the premises is **James "Gentleman Jim" Corbett** (1866–1933; Cypress Hills Abbey, crypt 76, aisle JJ), a San Francisco–born boxer and heavyweight champion of the world from 1892 to 1897.

These sloping grounds also shelter two notable musicians. Most remembered today is **James Hubert "Eubie" Blake** (1883–1983; section 11, lot 98, grave 1), a jazz pianist and composer who wrote more than seventy-five songs, including "Bugle Call Rag," "Boogie Woogie Beguine," and "Memories of You." His best-known song—"I'm Just Wild About Harry" (1921)—was written with Noble Sissle. **Joshua "Josh" White Sr.**

## LUNCH BREAK

There is nothing in the immediate vicinity, but a few blocks away is the gemütlich **Zum Stammtisch** (69-46 Myrtle Avenue, Queens; 718–386– 3014), which serves authentic German dishes in abundant portions, at reasonable prices.

PIET MONDRIAN
1872 — 1944

(1908–1969; section 18, Maple View east, grave 219) was a blues and folk singer, a guitarist, and a popular performer in cafe society nightclubs in Greenwich Village during the 1930s and 1940s. His big hit was the folk-pop tune "One Meatball." *Grounds open 8:00 A.M.– 4:30 P.M. daily. Office hours: 8:00 A.M.– 4:00 P.M. Monday–Friday, 8:00 A.M.–1:00 P.M. Saturday. Map; restrooms available.*

## JACKIE ROBINSON   1919–1972

The title of *I Never Had It Made,* the autobiography of Jack Roosevelt Robinson, couldn't be more accurate. Robinson, born in Cairo, Georgia, had to work hard every step of the way. In doing so, he broke Major League Baseball's rigid color bar, established himself as one of the major players of his day, and opened the clubhouse door to generations of African-American baseball players who followed him. No mean accomplishment.

To help him make the leap from the Negro League, Robinson had considerable athletic talent and was a good hitter and a superb base stealer. He was the first athlete at UCLA ever to earn letters in four sports—baseball, basketball, football, and track—*in the same year.* Robinson had something even rarer than natural ability: true grit and a strong will. He needed both to withstand racial taunts from white fans in big-city ballparks, physical abuse from players on opposing teams, the gibes of unfriendly sportswriters, and the petty nastiness of some of his own teammates. But Branch Rickey, general manager of the Brooklyn Dodgers, chose well in 1947 when he selected Robinson to be the man who could handle the pressure of breaking the odious color code. Overcoming all the taunts and demeaning tricks, Robinson won the Rookie of the Year award.

With Robinson on base, the Dodgers won six pennants in his ten big-league seasons. In 1949 he won the National League's Most Valuable Player award for his batting average of .342, 124 runs batted in, and 37 stolen bases. Near the end of his career, when he was traded to the Giants, Robinson retired rather than play for the Dodgers' fiercest opponent. In 1962 he was elected to baseball's Hall of Fame.

This major-league man died much too early—at age fifty-three—from complications of diabetes. His staunch, upright gray granite headstone, with "A life is not important except in the impact it has on other lives" and his signature etched in the stone, lies secluded between two little evergreens. It is in section 6, lot west half of P, grave 8, at the corner of Peace and Jackie Robinson Way, directly across from Memorial Abbey. His son, **Jack Roosevelt Robinson Jr.** (1946–1971), resides next to him.

## ARTHUR ALFONSO SCHOMBURG   1874–1938

*P*uerto Rican–born (to a freeborn black midwife from the Virgin Islands and a German-Latino father), Arthur Schomburg called himself an *Afroriqueno* (black Puerto Rican), though much of his postschool life was spent in New York, where he moved in 1891.

When he was in fifth grade in Santurce, Puerto Rico, a teacher asserted that blacks had no history, no successes, and no heroes. This sparked a life-long quest to prove such ignorance and prejudice wrong. In the process Schomburg uncovered scores and scores of rare documents, unpublished books and letters, and other items that eventually led to a research center of black history (see House Call), of which he was the curator. Schomburg's scholarship and enthusiasm influenced many young African Americans to pursue studies and careers in black history. "The American Negro," he once wrote, "must rebuild his past in order to make his future . . . History must restore what slavery took away."

Just as interested in black Caribbean history, Schomburg was active in the liberation movements of Cuba and Puerto Rico. Later he was an active presence and influence in the literary movement known as the Harlem Renaissance. He lies in section 15, Locust Grove, division 2, block 10, grave 13785.

## HOUSE CALL

**The Schomburg Center for Research in Black Culture** (515 Malcolm X Boulevard at West 135th Street, Harlem; 212–491–2200) includes a free research center (in a 1905 building designed by McKim, Mead & White, with a 1990 annex) under the aegis of the New York Public Library. One of the world's largest archives of black history, the center has more than five million items—books, rare manuscripts, photographs, art, films, recordings, and artifacts documenting black culture and heritage—plus changing shows (free). Of special interest to seekers of buried treasure, the ashes of Harlem Renaissance poet **Langston Hughes** (1902–1967) are secreted under the floor, just below an engraving of one of his poems.

## MAE WEST   1893–1980

One wonders how Mae West would have fared if she lived in the current "anything goes" age. She managed in a straitlaced era of strict screen censorship to make a career—that spanned seventy-six years—based on double entendres and broad sexuality. As she once said, "It isn't what I do but how I do it. It isn't what I say but how I say it and how I look when I do it and say it." With her sexy strut, tight-as-skin gowns, smirk, and insinuating lines, like "Come up and see me sometime . . . when I've got nothin' on but the radio," West was almost a send-up of sexuality. In fact, one

of her best quips—and she was famous for them—was "I believe in censorship. I made a fortune out of it."

West's clever one-liners could make up an entire book. Among the gems: "When I'm good I'm very good, but when I'm bad I'm better." "To err is human—but it feels divine." "I'm the lady who works at Paramount all day . . . and Fox all night." "Too much of a good thing . . . can be wonderful." Some quips were scripted for her movies.

West's career began when she was seven and won a gold medal for competing in an amateur talent competition at the local Brooklyn vaudeville house. Before long she was acting in stock companies, and by 1911 she was on Broadway with Al Jolson. That was the year of her short-lived, first and only marriage to Frank Wallace, a song-and-dance man with whom West had teamed up in vaudeville. In 1926 she began writing her own plays, which showcased her particular talent and persona. The titles say it all: *Sex, The Wicked Age, Pleasure Man, The Constant Sinner,* and *Diamond Lil.* In some ways, West *became* Diamond Lil.

The lady was indefatigable—on the stage and, so the gossip went, in her private life. She played every medium in a seemingly endless career: nightclubs, movies, stage, radio, television, records. Her costars included Cary

Grant (twice, in *She Done Him Wrong* and *I'm No Angel*); W. C. Fields; John Huston; and, in her last film, when she was eighty-five, Timothy Dalton (*Sextette*, 1978). During World War II West was so popular that the British Royal Air Force named an inflatable life jacket after her. It isn't hard to guess why.

Her best film moments were with Fields, who was the perfect foil. In later years, with her overblown hourglass figure, platinum hair, and stylized delivery, West seemed almost a caricature of herself—the aging zoftig broad. She's bedded down now, so to speak, in the imposing Memorial Abbey mausoleum, which is kept locked.

## FRIENDS RELIGIOUS SOCIETY OF PROSPECT PARK BROOKLYN QUAKER CEMETERY
*Prospect Park; (718) 596–4839 or (718) 768–8298*

On the southwest side of spacious 525-acre Prospect Park, with its numerous attractions, is this private Quaker cemetery of hills, maple trees, and simple Quaker headstones, tucked behind locked gates. It was a burial ground long before there was a park in the vicinity. Unless you are a Quaker, are accompanying a Quaker, or have some special clout, this cemetery is pretty much off-limits to the general public.

### LUNCH BREAK

**Franny's** (295 Flatbush Avenue; 718–230–0221) is located between Prospect Place and St. Mark's Avenue. It offers delicious crisp-crusted, artisanal pizzas from a wood-fired, brick-walled oven. For a tad more ambience, there's **Bistro St. Mark's** (76 St. Mark's Avenue; 718–857–8600), with French bistro fare at reasonable prices and a rear garden for warm-weather dining.

## MONTGOMERY "MONTY" CLIFT   1920–1966

One of twin sons of an Omaha, Nebraska, banking family, Clift discovered Broadway early, appearing in *Fly Away Home* when he was just thirteen. It whetted his appetite for acting. He spent the next ten years in New York doing Broadway shows before he headed west in 1948 to play in *Red River*, a western with John Wayne.

Westerns and other macho films were not really his forte. In his many starring roles in Hollywood, handsome Clift usually played sensitive, often troubled young men with great conviction, perhaps because he was one himself. Depressed about his homosexuality in an era when gay men remained in the closet (especially when they were movie icons), he became addicted to alcohol and pills. Even so, he rang up Oscar nominations in such films as *A Place in the Sun, From Here to Eternity,* and *Judgment at Nuremburg.*

During the filming of *Raintree County* in 1957, his car hit a tree so hard that Clift's face was smashed almost irreparably. It took extensive plastic surgery to reconstruct it sufficiently for him to resume his movie career. Two hits followed: *The Young Lions* with Marlon Brando and *Suddenly Last Summer* with Clift's good friend Elizabeth Taylor. While shooting *Reflections in a Golden Eye* in 1966, he died in bed of occlusive coronary heart disease at age forty-six. His surroundings, in this tranquil place, are far more peaceful than in his stressful life. Clift's simple granite grave marker was the work of John Benson, who designed the dramatic grave site of John F. Kennedy in Arlington.

## THE GREEN-WOOD CEMETERY

*Fifth Avenue and 25th Street; (718) 768–7300; www.greenwoodcemetery.org*

Located about 10 blocks south of Prospect Park, The Green-Wood was modeled after Mount Auburn in Cambridge, Massachusetts, and was the third of America's so-called rural cemeteries that became popular in the mid-nineteenth century. Many cemetery connoisseurs consider it the nirvana of all burial grounds.

The Green-Wood opened its gates to permanent inhabitants in 1840. Eventually it was coveted (and still is) as the life-after-death home for ambitious New Yorkers, who loved its isolated splendor and hilltop location. Although the Brooklyn below was much smaller then than it is today, resident spirits can still see the Brooklyn Bridge, with distant views of New York Harbor and the Statue of Liberty.

Designed by David Bates Douglass, this lofty city of the dead is an earthly delight of trees, ponds, four small lakes, streams, and 20 miles of serpentine roads and paths. Its 478 acres are home to rabbits, raccoons, possums, hawks, snipes, woodcocks, and hosts of migrating birds. The majestic Gothic Revival main gate, which includes the offices, was designed in 1861 by Richard Upjohn (who is also buried here), the architect of Trinity Church and other landmark buildings. The 1911 chapel by architects Warren & Wetmore (who

designed Grand Central Terminal) is a pure delight, inspired by English Gothic styles.

Aside from the architectural gems, this sepulchral Eden has dozens of notable funereal images, so meaningful to Victorians, that grace many tombs: a granite tree trunk or broken column (signifying a life cut short), hearts entwined, shrouded stone figures in mourning, swords in their scabbards, a carved hand on a tombstone (taking leave). At The Green-Wood one can find them all.

Birds are in daily residence, too—about 200 species of them. Some nest, like the black-crested night heron, rock dove, and great crested flycatcher; others fly over, such as the glossy ibis, snow goose, and red-shouldered hawk. Common, uncommon, and occasional, birds are part of The Green-Wood's naturalness, which adds to its paradisial appeal to strollers and hikers alike.

When The Green-Wood first opened, its success was not a slam dunk. Permanent occupants had to be ferried over from Manhattan (there was no Brooklyn Bridge yet). Something was needed to build instant prestige for the new cemetery. The solution of some early marketing genius was to transport **DeWitt Clinton** (1769–1828; section 108, lot 8325) from Albany to The

Green-Wood. The builder of the Panama Canal and former New York governor had been at his posthumous rest in Albany for some thirteen years when he was moved. This may have been the first time a politician moved his headquarters *after* death. In any case, the ploy worked. Before long, people could hardly wait to get in.

The roll call of spirits at The Green-Wood, which currently tops 600,000, reads like a roundup of America's highest achievers. The following is a sampling. Among many famous painters and other artistic types are **Asher Durand** (1796–1886; section 60, lot 1053), a landscape painter of the Hudson River school; **George Bellows** (1882–1925; section 24, lot 478-479), an artist of the Ashcan school; **William Merritt Chase** (1849–1916; section 68, lot 1739), a painter best known for portraiture; lithographer-artists **Nathaniel Currier** (1813–1888; section 108, lot 8325) and **James Merritt Ives** (1824–1895; section 53, lot 6801) of Currier & Ives fame; and furniture designer **Duncan Phyffe** (?–1786; section 78, lot 9034).

Architects are tenants, too. Among them are English-born **Richard M. Upjohn** (1802–1878; section 118, lot 366), who built many famous churches in the English Gothic style and was a founder of the American Institute of Architects; **John Frazee** (1790–1852; section 186, lot 19577), who designed many monuments at The Green-Wood; and **James Renwick Jr.** (1818–1895; corner of Sassafras and Vine Avenues), the architect of St. Patrick's Cathedral, the Smithsonian Institution, and Washington's Corcoran Gallery.

That's just the beginning. The vast tree-graced grounds are also peopled by the shades of industrial leaders, including **Elias Howe Jr.** (1819–1867; section H, lot 19967), inventor of the sewing machine, who came to rest beneath his own bust after being reinterred from Cambridge Cemetery in Cambridge, Massachusetts; and **Edward Robinson Squibb** (1819–1900; section 5, lot 17568), founder of Squibb Pharmaceuticals (now Bristol-Myers Squibb).

If there is music in the air, it may be emanating from the imposing Steinway mausoleum, the domain of **Henry Steinway** (1797–1871; section 46, lot 15388), founder of the piano manufacturing company, whose permanent manse has room for 200 family members (only 70 or so are in residence so far).

Economist **Henry George** (1839–1897; section P, lot 29673), who favored a single tax on land to support government, is here. Social arbiter **Ward McAllister** (1835–1895; section 74, lot 29325), who coined the phrase "The 400" to define New York's society leaders, has his own approved residence at The Green-Wood.

A personal favorite is the simple retreat of **Townsend Harris** (1804–1878; section 99, lot 7615), a diplomat, scholar, and ambassador to Japan who negotiated the first trade agreement between that country and the United States. His memorial consists of two flat, square black stones, with markings in both Japanese calligraphy and English, inserted at the edge of a large set of flat white blocks. Next to one stone are polished Japanese pebbles (as in a classic Japanese garden) with a miniature tree in the center and a white pagoda beside it.

Five of Theodore Roosevelt's immediate family members are in residence, all near one another in section 51, lots 10267, 10270, and 10273. The group includes his parents, **Theodore Sr.** (1831–1878) and **Martha Bullock Roosevelt** (1835–1884); an uncle, **Robert Barnwell Roosevelt** (1829–1906); a great-uncle, **James Roosevelt I** (1795–1875); and TR's first wife, **Alice Hathaway Lee Roosevelt** (1861–1884), who died of Bright's disease the same day his mother died of typhoid fever.

Also present is **James Gordon Bennett** (1795–1872; section A, lot 8100), the legendary editor-publisher of the *New York Herald*, who initiated the practice of hiring foreign and war correspondents.

There is no exit here for many of the thespian residents. On stage are **Frank Morgan** (1890–1949; section 168, lot 14447), a character actor forever remembered as the Wizard in *The Wizard of Oz,* and his actor brother **Ralph Morgan** (1882–1956), who helped found the Screen Actors Guild and was twice its president. Both rest in the Wuppermann family plot (their real last name). English-born **Laura Keene** (1827–1873; section 182, lot 21444), a popular actress who was on stage at the Ford Theatre when Lincoln was shot, eventually found her way to The Green-Wood. Almost everybody who was anybody did.

**LUNCH BREAK**

Restaurants abound along Fifth and Seventh Avenues north and south of The Green-Wood. In Park Slope, **Belleville** (350 Fifth Avenue at Fifth Street; 718– 832–9777) has sassy French bistro food. **Cocotte** (337 Fifth Avenue at Fourth Street; 718–832–6848) offers French–New American food in cozy surroundings.

There are enough members of nineteenth-century local baseball teams for a game on this field of dreams. Most of the names in this arboreal clubhouse are forgotten now, but they include **Jim Creighton** (1841–1862; section 13, lot 11005), baseball's first star, who swung so hard at a ball that he ruptured his bladder and subsequently died; and **John B. Woodward** (?–1896; section 72, lot 10915), who played outfield on Brooklyn's Excelsior team and later became a Civil War general. Journalist **Henry Chadwick** (1824–1908; section 31, lot 8919), dubbed "the father of baseball," pioneered the sport's statistics, notably box scores and batting averages; his imposing column is crowned with a granite baseball, complete with classic stitching. It is fitting to find **Charles Hercules Ebbets** (1859–1925; section 129, lot 35567) still in Brooklyn. President of the Brooklyn Dodgers, he gave his name to the much-revered (though long gone) Ebbets Field.

The Green-Wood attracts all types, even some shadowy ones, like crime boss **Albert Anastasia** (1902–1957; section 182, lot 38325) of "Murder Incorporated" and mafioso hit man **Joey Gallo** (1929–1972; section 12, lot 40314). But enough about them. *Grounds open 8:00 A.M.–4:00 P.M. daily. Office hours: 8:00 A.M.–4:00 P.M. Monday–Friday; closed holidays. Map $3.00; restrooms available. Three major groups conduct tours; call the office or check the Web site for names and descriptions.*

## JEAN-MICHEL BASQUIAT 1960–1988

When he burst onto New York's art scene, which was desperately seeking something new and different, Basquiat seemed a natural— an untrained ghetto-bred graffiti artist with great ability. The truth was something else: He was a middle-class Brooklyn kid whose Haiti-born father was an accountant. From age four Basquiat liked to paint and showed an aptitude for it. To encourage him, his Puerto Rican mother took him to museums to see professional works by modern artists. Basquiat responded to art but not to school, dropping out for good at seventeen.

Basquiat began doing graffiti with a friend—not the usual run-of-the-subway stuff, but vibrant murals with clever commentary. Shrewdly, he painted where his work would have maximum impact: on walls outside art galleries, night-clubs, and other places where influential people gathered. He was soon dis-covered and quickly became the poster boy of the New York art scene. Working in the neo-expressionist style, Basquiat combined paint with graph-ics and cartoon elements. By the time he was twenty-four, his paintings were in museum shows and selling for $25,000. His face adorned magazine covers. Andy Warhol was his new best friend.

By then Basquiat had a $2,000-a-week drug habit, from which Warhol tried to wean him. It worked briefly, but a few months before Basquiat's twenty-eighth birthday, he was dead of a heroin-cocaine overdose. Whether he is regarded as a tragic figure of art or just a footnote depends on how time treats his work. He painted fast and furiously, leaving a sizable body of paint-ings in less than ten years. In one year alone—1982, when Basquiat was twenty-one—he painted most of his best work, but much of the later work was repetitive. As art critic Robert Hughes noted, "It did not develop." Even so, Basquiat has had a number of posthumous shows, including one in 2005 at the Brooklyn Museum. Permanent reputation or not, there's no question that this painter had talent. Basquiat's grave is in section 176, lot 44603.

## HENRY WARD BEECHER 1813–1887

ecause of a presumed illicit affair with one of his parishioners, Beecher is remembered today by many as the Jimmy Swaggart of the nineteenth century, the epitome of religious hypocrisy. But this popu-lar Brooklyn clergyman was in some ways more a Billy Graham, revered by all who heard his sermons. The Beechers were a family descended from Puritans, and young Henry was destined early for the ministry. His father, Lyman Beecher, was a Connecticut cleric, and his sisters were Harriet Beecher Stowe and Isabella Beecher Hooker, both social reformers.

Henry was an emotional, sensitive, sometimes unstable young man who took a long time to find his niche. When he did, it was as a reformer, not a conventional minister. His sermons, lectures, and antislavery speeches, deliv-ered in a rich, sonorous voice, soon brought him attention far beyond his Brooklyn-based Plymouth Congregational Church parish.

Now about that affair. The "injured" husband (who had a reputation himself as a rake) charged Beecher with adultery and sued, demanding $100,000 in damages. The trial lasted six months, was tsk-tsked and chuckled at all over the country, and ended with a hung jury (nine for acquittal, three against). Some eighteen months later, a council of Congregational churches examined the charges and vindicated Beecher.

Did he or didn't he? When two of his lawyers came to consult with him on a Sunday, he told them, "We have it on good authority that it is lawful to pull an ass out of the pit on the Sabbath day. Well, there never was a bigger ass or a deeper pit." Though he retained his popularity with church members and continued to lecture on public affairs, Beecher's legacy remains spooked by the scandal. In his final vicarage—section 178, lot 11776—the headstone that Beecher and his wife share reads, without a touch of irony, "He thinketh no evil."

## LEONARD BERNSTEIN   1918–1990

*I*t might be a stretch to call Leonard Bernstein the Leonardo de Vinci of music, but he was certainly multitalented—as a composer of both classical music and musical comedy, and as a conductor, pianist, author, and music educator. Piano lessons as a child, glee club at Boston Latin School, and a music major at Harvard were all preparation for a career in music. College friendships with Dimitri Mitroupoulos, Adolphe Green, and Aaron Copland later boosted Bernstein's career.

For fifteen years he led a series of *Young People's Concerts* on television, explaining with obvious gusto how various instruments worked in musical compositions. Bernstein was also a masterful, if flamboyant, conductor. He led the New York Philharmonic from 1958 to his death, the first American-

born and -trained conductor to lead a major U.S. orchestra. He composed *Kaddish*, a symphony, and *Trouble in Tahiti*, a modern opera, but he probably will be remembered best for his scores for three Broadway musicals: *Wonderful*

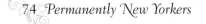

*Town, West Side Story* (a smash hit), and *Candide* (not a smash, but arguably the richest of all).

Off the podium Bernstein led almost as complicated a life. Though he was married to Chilean actress Felicia Montealegre for twenty-seven years and had three children with her, Bernstein was widely, if discreetly, known for his homosexual affairs. Yet here Felicia and Leonard are together again, side by side, in a quiet space bordered by ivy and punctuated by evergreens and rhododendrons, on Liberty Path, at the pinnacle of The Green-Wood (section G, lot 43642). The music you may hear in this serene retreat is the twitter of birds.

## GEORGE CATLIN   1796–1872

As the fourth of fifteen children, Wilkes Barre–born Catlin was trained as a lawyer. But in the early 1820s he witnessed a group of American Indians arriving in Philadelphia and knew he had found his calling. He later described his impressions: "a delegation of some ten or fifteen noble and dignified-looking Indians, from the wilds of the 'Far West' . . . equipped in all their classic beauty . . . tinted and tassled off, exactly for the painter's palette."

Wanting to see Indians in their natural habitat, he visited St. Louis to meet General William Clark (famed for the Lewis and Clark expedition), who took him to visit Plains Indians. In six years (1830–36) Catlin visited fifty tribes, traveling by steamer and a horse named Charley. In one year alone, 1832, he notched more than 2,000 miles and eighteen tribes. The year he started out marked the passage of the federal Indian Removal Act of 1830, pushing Indians off lands east of the Mississippi. He soon realized that the Indian habitats and old customs were, little by little, being destroyed and that the only way they could be preserved was by painting them.

In time, Catlin had done more than 500 paintings. He called them his "Indian Gallery" and, to make money to pay for his work, toured many cities with them and Indian artifacts, to little avail. Taking the works to Europe, where they had a better reception, helped him for a while. But by 1852 he was bankrupt and had to sell his entire collection. Joseph Harrison, a Philadelphia industrialist, bought and then stored it in his factory.

Meanwhile, Catlin lobbied a friend at the Smithsonian Institution in Washington, D.C., who invited him to exhibit what little of his work he still possessed in the Smithsonian "castle." Eventually Harrison's widow donated

the vast "Indian Gallery" to the Smithsonian. It is a treasure trove, both artistically and historically, recording in vivid colors a people and way of life long vanished. Catlin was prescient when he wrote about his paintings, "phoenix-like, they may rise from the 'stain on a painter's palette,' and live again upon canvass, and stand forth for centuries to come, the living monuments of a noble race." Without Catlin, records of some of these tribes would be written on the wind. His own record, his grave, is in section 60, lot 718.

## PETER COOPER    1791–1883

One of the Gilded Age's most successful businessmen and megamillionaires, Cooper was an inventor as well as an industrialist. He designed and built America's first steam locomotive, undertook the laying of the first Atlantic cable, and even invented—would you believe it?—jello. His enterprises were many: an iron foundry, a glue factory, real estate, railroads, insurance. He had done all this as a working-class kid with less than a year of formal schooling. As a boy, he learned carpentry, hat making, carriage building, and beer brewing. With all his successes, only one thing bothered him: He couldn't spell.

It was this embarrassment that led to what was the most substantial long-term accomplishment of his life. Believing that education should be "as free as water and air" and that children of the poor and immigrants should have the chance to study and learn, Cooper devoted the last thirty years of his life to making it possible. Thus Cooper Union was born. It was his goal to provide a free technical education for working-class children and women and to provide a forum for public opinion. Since 1859 Cooper Union has educated thousands of artists, architects, designers, and engineers. Some legacy for a man who couldn't spell! His final address is section 97, lot 3932.

## HORACE GREELEY   1811–1872

*T*oday the name Horace Greeley means little more than his quote, "Go West, young man, go West!" In his heyday, as editor of the *New York Tribune* (1840 to 1860), he exercised a voice for morality and integrity and was known for his clear, impeccable writing style. In editing the *Tribune*, New Hampshire–born Greeley wanted it to be, in his words, "removed from servile partisanship." Indeed it set high standards with its straight news reporting. There was no room on its pages for scandals or police-blotter stories.

Greeley was opposed to monopoly and class dominance, and as an abolitionist he was against any compromise with slavery. He bolted the Whigs and joined the new Republican Party. Bitten by the political bug, Greeley ran for office early, often, and usually unsuccessfully, though he did serve in the U.S. Congress for three months in the late 1840s. Efforts to get elected to the Senate failed, and as he became more involved in politics, his influence on the *Tribune* declined. While he supported General Ulysses S. Grant for president, he

soon became disappointed in Grant's policies and in 1872 ran against him as a splinter party candidate.

Despite his personal popularity, intensive campaigning, and rousing rhetoric, Greeley was demolished in the election, winning only six states. He called himself "the worst beaten man who ever ran for high office." To add to his despair, another man had assumed control of the *Tribune*, leaving Greeley editor in name only. This news, his exhausting campaign—waged in poor health to begin with—and the death of his wife just before the election may have tipped him over the edge: He died insane within the month, a tragic ending to a full, constructive life. He can be found at peace now in section 35, lot 2344.

## LOLA MONTEZ   1818(?)–1861

Whatever Lola wanted, Lola got—usually. First she wanted to be an actress, so she changed her real name of Eliza Gilbert to the more exotic moniker Lola Montez. The only problem was she couldn't act. So then she became a Spanish dancer (though Irish, born in Limerick in either 1818 or 1821, depending on which source you consult). Again, there was that little problem of no talent.

She soon learned her real talent lay in lying—down. And for years she reclined with the best of them: several English lords, the czar of Russia, the viceroy of Poland, Alexandre Dumas, and a cast of, well, if not thousands, then more rich and famous men than you could shake a tambourine at. Her sexual exploits became so legendary that Victorian wags called her "La Grande Horizontale."

What made Montez famous, or infamous, were two affairs, first with pianist Franz Liszt and later with King Ludwig I of Bavaria. Her jealousy, bad temper, and tendency to violence eventually wore down Liszt's patience. To escape her, the story goes, he locked her in their hotel room and skedaddled, leaving money at the desk to pay for the furniture she would break in her temper tantrum.

Ludwig was so bewitched by Montez that he built her a palace and paid her allowance from the state treasury. Before long, she was ruling him and Bavaria. Austrian Prince Metternich was so distressed by some of Montez's actions (in Ludwig's name) that he tried to bribe her to leave Bavaria and later organized riots against her. "I will never abandon Lola," the doddering Ludwig said, and indeed he didn't. Instead, *he* had to abdicate.

Montez left town, too—and eventually ended up in California during the gold rush, owning a saloon in the frontier town of Grass Valley. Finally she could dance without being booed off the stage. The rough 'n' ready miners loved her. So did every politician and newly minted millionaire within miles.

Larger than life for so long, Montez ended smaller: schizophrenic, delusional, and a pauper in New York, finally dying of a stroke in a cheap boarding house. Neither of her two children claimed the body. Not much of a journey's end for a woman who had danced her way through millions, Bavarian crown jewels, and a fortune in gold leaf. While it lasted, it was one heck of a run. Montez now lies, *permanently*, in section 8, lot 12730.

## SAMUEL F. B. MORSE   1791–1872

ew people have two careers as disparate as art and science, but Samuel Finley Breese Morse managed both brilliantly. Born in Charlestown, Massachusetts, he was the son of preacher Jedidiah Morse, who was famous in his own right as a geographer. Young Morse was an indifferent student at Yale, turned on by only two things: portrait painting and the development of electricity. After college he decided to go to England to study art, to his parents' dismay.

Settling in New York City in 1825, he quickly became a known and popular painter; he helped found the National Academy of Design and became its first president. He tinkered with inventions, patented a marble-cutting machine, and even dabbled in politics, running unsuccessfully for mayor and Congress. A chance conversation on an ocean voyage (to continue his art studies in Europe) reignited his interest in electricity, especially the newly discovered electromagnet, and changed the course of his life for good.

Morse didn't invent the first practical electromagnetic telegraph (that honor apparently belongs to Joseph Henry of Albany, working independently in 1830–31), but he perfected the apparatus on which the modern telegraph is modeled. Working with two partners, Alfred Vail and Leonard Gale, Morse made models, molds, and casts, and in 1836 he came up with a model that worked. The following year he took out a patent and petitioned Congress for funds for further experimentation. After six frustrating years trying to raise money elsewhere, he was awarded $30,000 by Congress to construct an experimental telegraph line between Washington, D.C., and Baltimore.

Success came on May 24, 1844, when Morse sent this message from the

U.S. Capitol to Baltimore: "What hath God wrought!" With these words he became a household name. Three years later Morse successfully defended his claim in court to officially be called the inventor of the electromagnetic recording telegraph. His invention not only made him a rich man, but also sped up the modern age. To communicate with him, visit section 25, lot 5761.

## HOUSE CALL

Morse's octagonal Italianate villa with a four-story tower, **Locust Grove** (370 South Road, Route 9, Poughkeepsie; 845–454–4500), overlooks the Hudson River and lovely gardens. Morse bought the property in 1847, after he was widowed but before he remarried. The house contains his paintings and others by John James Audubon and contemporaries. For anyone intrigued by the inventor and his diverse interests, the villa is well worth a special trip or detour.

## LOUIS COMFORT TIFFANY   1848–1933

This artist-businessman came by both his creative and mercantile skills naturally. His father, Charles Lewis Tiffany, was a silversmith and jeweler who founded the style-setting Tiffany & Company. Son Louis first wanted to be an artist. He studied with noted painter George Inness but soon found his métier in a handcraft—glassmaking. At a time when to most craftsmen clear stained glass was the sine qua non of the art form, as it had been for centuries, Tiffany wanted to create something different. Influenced by William Morris and the Arts and Crafts movement in England, he turned his artistic impulses to creating a new process of making opalescent glass. It was a major breakthrough.

In 1885 Tiffany founded his own glassmaking company, and a few years later he went beyond making windows to all kinds of glass products—bowls, vases, lamp shades, sculptural *objets*—in "favrilé," the distinctive iridescent style that he invented. Tiffany products became the rage. His signature lampshades (combinations of different-colored leaded, stained glass) became so popular that they almost lapsed into a cliché.

Some years after his death, the demand for Tiffany lamps and windows declined, but his work was so special, so luminous and distinctive, that he has now—all these decades later—resumed his reputation not as a craftsman, but as an artist. You have only to see the sun shining through a Tiffany window,

with all its subtle color tones and delicate range, to understand how unique and remarkable his achievement was.

Today his work is almost beyond price. New York's Metropolitan Museum of Art has a special Tiffany section. Laurelton Hall, the house he designed and built in Oyster Bay, Long Island, in 1904, was demolished. That's the bad news. The good news is that many of its windows and other Tiffany *objets d'art* have found their way into museums around the United States.

Considering the splendor he created for others, Tiffany's final habitat, in section 65, lot 619, is relatively modest.

## WILLIAM MARCY "BOSS" TWEED   1823–1878

You might not expect the son of a Scottish chair-maker to become— before he was forty—the most influential man in New York. From teenage apprenticeships as a saddler and then bookkeeper, young Tweed graduated to volunteer fireman. Then he wangled a job as an assistant alderman. Soon he worked himself into the inner sanctum of Tammany Hall, the power base of the Democratic Party, and in 1860 he became chairman— the boss—of Tammany's central committee, a position that controlled all nominations and appointments.

At a time when money "talked," people paid the "Boss" generously for jobs, favors, access, and the passage of bills. He opened the gates for the Brooklyn

Bridge project to proceed and, as his reward, accepted $40,000 in stock. Tweed's influence was exposed constantly by political cartoonist Thomas Nast in *Harper's Weekly*, yet his popularity grew, based on his larger-than-life personality (big, boisterous, full of wit and *bonhomie*) and his patronage and generosity to the poor. Eventually the greed became too egregious, and a member of the Tweed gang blew the whistle.

Many of his fellow rogues escaped abroad, but Tweed was tried and convicted, sentenced to twelve years in jail, and fined $12,750. Both punishments were reduced on appeal. Released after a year in prison, he was rearrested, tried in a civil suit, and ordered to recover all the money—$6 million—that he and his chums had stolen from the state. He couldn't do so and was reincarcerated, but so casually that he was able to escape. Tweed skipped to Cuba and then sailed to Spain disguised as a sailor. A Nast cartoon likeness alerted Spanish authorities, who shipped him back to New York and jail. The Boss confessed his crimes, thinking he had a deal for freedom with the local lawmen and politicos. But he was double crossed in the end and banished to prison, where he subsequently died.

There have been worse rogues in public life (recently, too). By all accounts, Tweed, brazen as he was, was also amiable and open-handed, which may be why so much of the money he filched during his ten-year reign—estimated to be between $30 million and $200 million, no one knows for sure—was dissipated. After all, he had a wife, eight children, several mistresses, numerous cronies, and an appetite for lavish meals at Delmonico's. The rather eccentric-looking, sprawling homestead of Tweed and his family (in section 55, lot 6447) isn't ostentatious, but it's not bad for a last hurrah.

## HOUSE CALL

The **Tweed Courthouse** (52 Chambers Street, Manhattan) was Tweed's most outrageous scam. It was supposed to cost New York $250,000 but ended up at consuming $13 million, due to graft and overruns. The solid-brass elevators, for instance, turned out to be brass-plated. It was finished the year Tweed was caught (1871) and was the scene of his first trial and sentencing. Long half-empty, the recently renovated building is now used by the Board of Education. Pop inside to see the WPA murals in the lobby.

# HOLY CROSS CEMETERY
*3620 Tilden Avenue; (718) 284–4520*

Beyond the double arched stone entrance gate, on both sides and in the rear of the steepled Chapel of the Resurrection, is the ninety-six-acre cemetery, which dates back to 1849 (predating the chapel by six years). When a cholera epidemic swept Manhattan, burials within the city limits were forbidden. So New York bishop John Hughes bought land for a burial ground from a farmer in the town of Flatbush. Holy Cross was developed at the geographic center of Kings County and was intended to serve the entire area. Since then, the cemetery has been the final domicile of some 725,000 people.

Beneath the chapel is a catacombs, home to some of the pioneer priests of the diocese. The tree-stippled grounds are divided into sections named after saints like St. Peter, St. Bernard, and St. John. Throughout are monuments topped with crosses or religious sculptures, obelisks, and the graves of many religious leaders, along with some surprising laymen. Among them are **Quentin Reynolds** (1903–1965; St. Peter's, range E, #16), a journalist and World War II correspondent; **"Terrible Terry" McGovern** (1880–1918; St.

John's, range A, #55), a colorful, aggressive champion prizefighter; **William Russell Grace** (1832–1904; St. Peter's, ridge A, #1-4), head of the W. R. Grace steamship line and the first Catholic mayor of New York; and **Willie Sutton** (1901–1980; St. Stephen's, range G, #19), a Depression-era bank robber and frequent prison escapee (known for his disguises). When asked why

**LUNCH BREAK**

Good for Italian food is the casual **La Trattoria** (187 Avenue U; 718–648–0334). Locals also recommend **China New Star** (22 South Flatbush Avenue; 781–338–9085), which has decent Chinese fare.

he persisted in robbing banks, Sutton's reply was "because that's where the money is." *Grounds open* 8:00 A.M.–5:00 P.M. *daily. Office hours:* 8:30 A.M.–4:30 P.M. *Monday–Friday,* 9:00 A.M.–1:00 P.M. *Saturday. Map; restroom.*

## JAMES "DIAMOND JIM" BRADY   1856–1917

*I*f you seek a clear distinction between a gourmet and a gourmand, have a look at Jim Brady's life. A self-made salesman and speculator who made about $12 million (in the pre–income tax era) in railroads by the time he was forty-five, he spent much of the rest of his life on two passions: diamonds and food. (A third was women, especially showgirls; Lillian Russell was his best-known sweetheart.)

The diamonds, estimated to be worth $2 million, were everywhere: on his ties, his vests, his cufflinks, his rings, and even his walking stick. He reputedly gave Russell a gold-plated bicycle with handlebars covered in mother-of-pearl and spokes adorned with rubies and sapphires.

The food Brady consumed was just as opulent—the best, most luxurious that New York in the Gilded Age could supply. For lunch he might consume two lobsters, deviled crabs, clams, oysters, and beef, finishing off with two or three (whole) pies. Dinner might start with an appetizer course of two or three dozen oysters, six crabs, and several servings of terrapin soup and then continue with entrees of two whole ducks, six lobsters, a sirloin steak, two terrapins, and vegetables. Dessert was often a platter of pastries and a two-pound box of chocolates. Brady's only known healthy habit: orange juice. Even with it, he overindulged, drinking a gallon with most meals.

The proprietor of Charles Rector's, a favorite Brady restaurant, called Brady "the best twenty-five customers I ever had." He was exceedingly generous to friends and acquaintances, and obviously restaurateurs were happy to see Brady arrive, usually with a freeloading entourage in tow. He loved giving lavish parties and dinners.

Fat as he was, Brady lived longer than one might expect. Still, much of his later life was plagued with the results of his constant excesses: diabetes, high blood pressure, and heart and urinary troubles. His prostate was swollen considerably beyond normal size; his stomach was six times larger than a normal person's. When Brady died, of complications from his many diseases, he willed much of his estate to Johns Hopkins and New York Hospital, to establish medical institutes in his name. The tall black granite stele marking his grave is in Select, ridge 8, #15.

## GILBERT "GIL" HODGES   1924–1972

A Hoosier lad from Princeton, Indiana, Hodges became—and still is— an icon to New York baseball fans, loved for his modesty and just plain niceness. None of his teammates recall ever hearing him swear. He had a brief debut in October 1943, as a Brooklyn Dodger, before he was drafted; he spent the next two years of World War II as a U.S. Marine, ending up on Okinawa with a medal for bravery. Typically Hodgian: He didn't mention the medal to his wife for three years.

Returning to the Dodgers in 1947, he played well and hard for them in Brooklyn and later in Los Angeles after the team moved west in 1958. As his career wound down, he played briefly for the New York Mets, the Washington Senators, and then the Mets again. As a sterling first baseman, Hodges won three Gold Gloves for excellence, played in seven World Series, and ended his career with 370 home runs.

It was later, as a manager, that he performed a miracle that endeared him for all time to New York's non–Yankee fans: He turned around a hopeless Mets team and in 1969 led them past the Chicago Cubs to a National League pennant and their first World Series title. That year they were indeed the "miracle Mets," and the popular, congenial Hodges was their miracle manager.

Who knows how many more baseball miracles might have been in his future? While golfing before spring training in 1972, he fell dead from a heart attack. Amazing Mets. Amazing Gil. Amazing grace. From the cemetery entrance, take the first left (before reaching the office), then turn left again to a circle. Hodges's red granite headstone is near the curb on the right side of the circle, in St. Catherine's, ridge B, #191.

## MORAVIAN CEMETERY

*2205 Richmond Road; (718) 351-0136*

Even before the first Moravian church was built in 1763, there were graves on this halcyon land. British soldiers were buried here (from the days when soldiers were stationed on Staten Island), and several gravestones go back to 1740. At first there were just five and a half acres. Little by little more land was bought or deeded, and now there are 113 acres of knolls, valleys, manicured grounds, and lakeside views.

The address of this cemetery, now nonsectarian, is a favorite of islanders. In addition to the beatific natural surroundings, there are four mausoleums awaiting kingdom come. A Moravian church with columns and portico, built in 1845 by the Vanderbilt family, is at the cemetery entrance, across from a 1763 white Dutch colonial church that serves as the cemetery office.

**Stephen Hinsdale Weed** (1831–1863; section O, lot 281), a Civil War brigadier general killed in action at Gettysburg, and **James J. "Truthful Jim" Mutrie** (1851–1938; section 17, subdivision B, lot 16), a Major League Baseball manager, are on the grounds. Note the cenotaph by Augustus Saint-Gaudens in honor of **Robert Gould Shaw** (1837–1863), the heroic Union colonel who commanded the all-black 54th Massachu-

> ### LUNCH BREAK
>
> **Lento's** (New Dorp Lane; 718–980–7709), off Richmond Road, is famous for its thin-crust pizzas, which are its raison d'être.

setts Volunteer Infantry in the Civil War. (Matthew Broderick and Denzel Washington star in *Glory*, the 1989 movie version of the story.) Shaw was buried in a mass Union grave at Fort Wagner, Charleston, South Carolina.

The biggest "bankable" name in this peaceful nirvana is Vanderbilt. Unfortunately, the Vanderbilts are as exclusive in the afterlife as in life: Theirs is a cemetery within the cemetery, closed off by gates from the general public. Within their forbidden terrain, several generations of the socially prominent and financially successful clan have permanent residences in the Vanderbilt mausoleum, beginning with the patriarch, **Cornelius Vanderbilt** (1794–1877), who founded New York Central Railroad and made a fortune in shipping and railroading. His son **William Henry Vanderbilt** (1821–1885), also a railroad man and financier, resides in proximity. So do two of William's sons, **Cornelius Vanderbilt II** (1843–1899), a noted financier, and **George Washington Vanderbilt** (1862–1914), an art collector and connoisseur. GW's private estate, Biltmore—a French Renaissance château on 100,000 acres in Asheville, North Carolina—is one of America's most famous and prized properties.

One of Moravian's most famous guests-to-be will not, mercifully, be arriving any time soon, but Martin Scorcese (1942– ), the director of *Raging Bull, Mean Streets, Taxi Driver,* and scores of other memorable films, has bought a plot here. May it remain empty for years to come. *Grounds open 8:00 A.M.–6:30 P.M. daily. Office hours: 9:00 A.M.–4:00 P.M. Monday–Friday. Map; restrooms.*

# CHAPTER 4

# Queens

Queens has a number of cemeteries where people of fame, fortune, and sometimes ill-fame and no fortune reside unto eternity. Here they are, listed alphabetically by town and, if there are several burial grounds within one town, also alphabetically by cemetery.

## ST. MICHAEL'S CEMETERY

*72-02 Astoria Boulevard; (718) 278–3240; www.stmichaelscemetery.com*

On almost ninety sprawling acres, this old cemetery belongs to St. Michael's Episcopal Church, on Manhattan's Upper West Side. The cemetery began in 1852 on a scant seven acres, designed to accommodate the poor. Through the years it has grown, and it now has eight mausoleums and space available to other churches and institutions. In the older sections are permanent retreats for late-nineteenth- and early-twentieth-century immigrants.

### LUNCH BREAK

Across the street from St. Michael's is **Jackson Hole** (69-35 Astoria Boulevard; 718–204–7070), which offers good burgers, generous portions, and reasonable prices.

Aside from the most famous resident within the confines, Scott Joplin, is another accomplished person: **Granville T. Woods** (1856–1910; range 3, plot 5, grave 144), an African-American inventor (sometimes called the "black Edison") whose creations mostly related to the railroad industry. Gangster **Frank Costello** (1891–1973; Costello mausoleum, section 15, row 1) also has taken refuge on the premises. Once known as the "Prime Minister of the Underworld" because of all the police and politicians he had paid off and who were beholden to him, Costello died of natural causes in his own bed. Later his crypt was broken into and the corpse disturbed. Sounds as melodramatic as his life. *Grounds open 8:00 A.M.–6:00 P.M. Monday–Friday, 9:00 A.M.–6:00 P.M. Saturday and Sunday. Office hours: 9:00 A.M.–4:30 P.M. Monday–Friday, 9:00 A.M.–3:00 P.M. Saturday, 10:00 A.M.–2:00 P.M. Sunday. Map; restrooms.*

## SCOTT JOPLIN    1868–1917

The simple gravestone, flush to the ground in row 2 (plot 5, grave 5), says "American composer" after Scott Joplin's name. Such modesty merely hints at the accomplishments of this once-obscure man, to whom full recognition came sixty years after his death.

The son of a former slave and free black woman, Joplin grew up in Texarkana on the Texas-Arkansas border. His early interest in music prompted a neighbor to give him lessons on the piano, violin, and horn. By the time he was eleven, Joplin was performing complex pieces and composing his own. At age twenty he left home and became an itinerant musician, playing saloons, brothels, pool halls, picnics, and fairs in cities and towns along the Mississippi River.

In Sedalia, Missouri, several key events occurred: Joplin met his future wife, studied music formally at a local black college, and began working with sophisticated rhythms and chords. While in Sedalia he composed "Maple Leaf Rag," which became a sheet-music best seller, earning him a small, steady income in royalties.

Later Joplin settled in St. Louis, taught music, and continued composing: "March Majestic," "Sunflower Slow Drag," "Elite Syncopations," "Peacherine Rag," "Cascades," and "The Entertainer" were among his creations. Always fascinated by classical music, he wrote several operas, but it was his toe-tapping ragtime tunes that earned him lasting fame. In 1911 Irving Berlin published "Alexander's Ragtime Band," which Joplin claimed was stolen from "A Real Slow Drag" in his opera *Treemonisha*. But because of Berlin's name and wealth, Joplin decided not to sue.

Joplin died prematurely while in New York, and his work more or less died with him. It rose again, briefly, when jazz musicians revived ragtime in the 1940s. The real, permanent jump start came in 1973, when "The Entertainer" was featured as the theme song in the popular Robert Redford–Paul Newman movie *The Sting*. Voilà! A whole new generation of Americans discovered ragtime. This uniquely American musical form is a blend of African-American rhythms and European musical style. In 1976 Joplin received, posthumously, a Pulitzer Prize for his contributions to American music.

# FLUSHING

## FLUSHING CEMETERY
*163-06 46th Avenue; (718) 359–0100*

This sun-dappled graveyard rests on a quiet, seventy-five-acre oasis of trees, gentle slopes, and roadways in the middle of a highly populated area off Northern Boulevard in Queens. Of course, when it opened in 1853, Flushing was rural, like so many burial grounds that have been gobbled up by cities.

May and June are lovely months to visit Flushing Cemetery. Then it is abloom with weeping and Kwanzan Burgundy cherry trees, crab apple and pear trees, lilacs, magnolias, dogwoods, tree peonies, rhododendrons, and azaleas. The grounds are a virtual horticultural treasure, with almost 200 different exotic specimens, from weeping European beech, Chinese holly, Norway spruce, and black walnut to European larch, Japanese yew and hemlock, American elm, and seven types of maples.

A short walk straight ahead from the attractive Spanish colonial–style office (at the corner of 46th Avenue and Pidgeon Meadow Road) is Section A. At its corner is the poignant World Trade Center Memorial, with the twin towers etched into black granite at the center of the memorial. Benches in front are convenient for sitting, contemplating, and mourning. It is directly opposite a graceful old multitiered iron fountain.

The subterranean inhabitants in Flushing Cemetery are easy to locate, thanks to a clearly marked map and friendly, helpful office staff. These inhabitants include veterans of seven American wars, including the War of 1812. Also in residence is financier **Bernard Baruch** (1870–1965; section 8), who cultivated friendships with and offered free advice to five U.S. presidents (though there isn't much evidence that any of them took it). This is the last appearance of **Mae Robson** (1865–1942; section 9-F9), a popular stage and movie actress who played in *Dinner at Eight* and *A Star Is Born*, among many films of the 1930s; and **Vincent Sardi Sr.** (1885–1969; section 12), founder of Sardi's, a Broadway restaurant popular with theater and newspaper people.

## LUNCH BREAK

This area has many Asian restaurants. One of the best and most authentic is **Kum Gang San** (138-28 Northern Boulevard; 718–461–0909), known for its highly spiced Korean food and moderate prices.

In these same restful grounds is **Dr. Adam Clayton Powell Sr.** (1865–1953; section 9), born of slaves, who rose to found and become minister of the famous Abyssinian Baptist Church in Harlem. He was the father of controversial congressman Adam Clayton Powell Jr. **Hazel Scott** (1920–1981; section 9), a jazz pianist and entertainer and onetime wife of Adam Clayton Powell Jr., resides in the same plot with Powell Sr. and his wife, Inez. *Grounds open 8:30 A.M.–4:30 P.M. daily. Office hours: 8:30 A.M.–4:30 P.M. Monday–Friday, 8:30 A.M.–1:00 P.M. Saturday; closed legal holidays. Map; restrooms.*

# LOUIS ARMSTRONG   1900–1971

The scat singing and exuberant trumpet playing of Louis Armstrong are so pervasive on CDs, cassettes, and radio that it seems impossible to believe that he's been gone since 1971. This dynamic man, whose mouth shape and infectious grin gave him the nickname "Satchmo" (for "satchel mouth"), is the epitome of jazz. Notice that his nickname is even etched into his polished black granite headstone with a white trumpet on top (resting on a marble tasseled "pillow") near the road in section 9. The gravestone of his fourth wife, **Lucille Armstrong** (1914–1983), is to the right of his.

Even those who normally don't dig jazz dig Louie. His effervescent persona and incandescent playing—whether he was singing bouncy duets with Ella Fitzgerald or blasting out trumpet solos—were real. His raspy, ebullient renditions of "Hello Dolly" and "Mack the Knife" made these show tunes his own.

Armstrong's early life on the mean streets of Storyville, the red-light district in his hometown of New Orleans, included time at the Colored Waifs Home for minor brushes with the law. It was time he put to good use, learning several musical instruments and earning the chance to play in the home's marching band. Later he met Joe "King" Oliver, who helped hone Armstrong's natural raw talent. Then it was on to Chicago and New York, and wider recognition. Triumphant tours of Europe, Africa, and Asia followed, and the accolade "Ambassador of Jazz" was his for life.

Armstrong never stopped loving what he did—and it showed. He once said, "Anyone can steal anything but my applause," which may be why he never gave a lackluster performance. Satchmo was no saint marching in—he supposedly smoked marijuana daily most of his life and had other foibles—but he *was* one of the most extraordinary jazz artists of the twentieth century.

## HOUSE CALL

The redbrick **Louis Armstrong House** (34-56 107th Street, Corona; 718–478–8274) is like a moment in time preserved in amber. Now owned and maintained by Queens College and the New York City Department of Cultural Affairs, the house, where Louis lived for twenty-eight years and Lucille lived twelve years longer (until her death in 1983), is a National Historic Landmark and a must-see for jazz fans. It is situated in Lucille's middle-class childhood neighborhood and furnished in her personal style. Everything is authentic, including Louis's den as he left it, enhanced by his photographs, tapes, trumpets, and other memories. A forty-minute guided tour includes anecdotes about Louis and his life there. There are changing exhibits and occasional concerts.

## DIZZY GILLESPIE   1917–1993

*J*ohn Birks Gillespie earned his nickname, Dizzy, for his humor and sense of fun. You might think, though, that the name derived from the lightning speed with which he played trumpet, his syncopated rhythmic phrasing, and his great technical facility that carried listeners to Dizzy-ing heights.

As a fifteen-year-old in South Carolina, Gillespie won a scholarship to the Laurinburg Institute in North Carolina, where he studied music theory and harmony while sitting in with Southern dance bands. Trumpeter Roy Eldridge was his inspiration, but once Gillespie began playing professionally, he hooked up with his contemporaries—including Thelonius Monk, Oscar Pettiford, Kenny Clarke, and (later) Charlie "Bird" Parker—and began to develop the sound known as bebop. Most of the group had some classical music background and deep roots in the African-American musical tradition.

Bebop's rise brought about a new culture of hip talk and a "uniform" of horn-rimmed sunglasses, beret, and goatee, all Gillespie trademarks. But for all the external "look," Gillespie was a serious musician. He immersed himself in other cultures, synthesized jazz and Afro-Cuban rhythms, became the U.S. State Department's first jazz cultural ambassador abroad, performed at the White House for three presidents, launched a "Jazz-America" project for public television, and mentored younger musicians. All the while he was proving himself to be a dazzling jazz innovator. Many awards and honors and an autobiography, *To Be or Not to Bop: Memoirs*, followed before diabetes and pancreatic cancer stopped the bopping for good. His unmarked grave is in section 31, at the edge of the cemetery near the corner of 46th Avenue and Auburndale Lane.

## JOHNNY "RABBIT" HODGES   1906–1970

*O*ne of the all-time great jazz saxophonists, John Cornelius Hodges was born in Cambridge, Massachusetts, and began his musical career as a drummer and pianist. By his late teens he was playing with several different bands. He really made his name as a featured soloist with Duke Ellington from 1928 to 1951, and then from 1955 to his death from a heart attack in 1970. For a brief period (1951–55) Hodges formed his own band, but his golden years were after his return to Ellington. Hodges was no slouch on the soprano sax and clarinet, but it was the sounds he brought forth from

an alto sax that could melt the heart. One of his best solos, "Don't Get Around Much Anymore," is still soul-stirring.

Hodges's highly visible headstone rests at the end of section D. It bears his name, with the words "alto sax" underneath it, and a floral border and cross at the top, all engraved in gray granite. A granite bench with HODGES etched into it is nearby for seated contemplation. All that's missing is the music.

# GLENDALE

## MOUNT CARMEL CEMETERY
*83-45 Cypress Hills Street; (718) 366–5900*

Mount Carmel is one of a number of Jewish cemeteries that melt into each other in an area that might be called a postlife housing project, for there are seventeen cemeteries of various denominations side by side by side. Separated only by their fences and gates, they continue for miles on the Queens-Brooklyn line. Mount Carmel, founded in 1902, now has about 82,000 permanent boarders within its ninety acres.

Mount Carmel subtitles itself "cemetery of the American Jewish past," for the number of prominent Jews who have taken up residence on these hallowed grounds. Actors don't have a monopoly, but there are some famous ones enshrouded here. The Adler family is well represented (section F). Most famous is **Stella Adler** (1901–1992), who acted in movies and television but is best known as a teacher (Marlon Brando was a student) of the Stanislavsky "Method" style of acting. Her brothers were also in the business. **Luther Adler** (1903–1984) appeared in dozens of TV series and thirty-three films, including *The Last Angry Man, Voyage of the Damned,* and *Absence of Malice*; **Jay Adler** (1896–1978) did most of his acting work in television. Their father, **Jacob Adler** (1855–1926), was a famous actor in the Yiddish theaters of Second Avenue, and his wife, **Sara Adler** (1858–1953), starred in many Yiddish productions.

Comedians also find Mount Carmel hospitable territory. **Henny Youngman** (1906–1998; Kurlander/Youngman plot, block 9, lot 45) was the king of one-liners like "Take my wife—please." **George Tobias** (1901–1980; section BR-21) was a comic actor, memorable as Abner Kravits in the television series *Bewitched.* **Minne Marx** (1865–1929; section 2, block 10W, L-373) and vaudevillian **Samuel Marx** (?–1933; same plot) were the parents of the Marx Brothers.

Several Jewish gangsters have had their close encounters with eternity here, including mobster **Abraham "Kid Twist" Reles** (1907–1941; section 1, line 12, grave 23) and mob money man **George Weinberg** (1901–1939; section 2, block 8, line 11, grave 12), an associate of Dutch Schultz. Far better known was a *victim* of crime: **Leo Frank** (1884–1915; section 1, block E, path 41, lot 1035, grave 2). Frank, a northerner, was a factory manager in a little Georgia town when schoolgirl Mary Phagan was raped and murdered there. In a case cited for its miscarriage of justice, Frank was wrongly accused, tried, convicted, and lynched. Anti-Semitism and regional xenophobia figured in the charge and in the fact that three appeals, all the way to the U.S. Supreme Court, failed.

A recent Mount Carmel arrivé is **Bella Abzug** (1920–1998; Tanklefsky Society Grounds, section 1, block C, map 14, grave 28), a civil rights lawyer and onetime star of the New York Democratic Party. The first Jewish woman elected to the U.S.

## LUNCH BREAK

Nearby is the **Glendale Diner** (7108 Meadow Avenue; 718–366–8846), a handy spot for a quick bite of burgers, salads, and the like.

Congress, she represented two different districts (at different times, of course) and was famous for her outspoken liberalism and advocacy of women's rights, as well as her brusque personality, humor, and addiction to large-brimmed hats. *Grounds open 8:00 A.M.–4:00 P.M. Sunday–Friday. Office hours: 8:30 A.M.–4:00 P.M. Sunday–Friday. Restrooms.*

## SHOLEM ALEICHEM   1859–1916

Aleichem, whose name means "peace be upon you" in Yiddish, was born Solomon Rabinowitz in Pereyaslav, Ukraine. Educated as a teacher and rabbi, he was increasingly attracted to writing, first in Russian and Hebrew, but from 1883 on in Yiddish. At that time in czarist Russia, most Jews wrote in Russian and Hebrew. But Aleichem wanted to reach a larger audience than just the scholarly Jews who spoke and read Hebrew, namely the three million less-educated Russian Jews whose only language was Yiddish.

He became their spokesman, encouraging others to write in Yiddish. Considered one of the founding fathers of Yiddish literature, Aleichem himself wrote more than forty books in the language; among them were five novels, 300 short stories, many plays, and even children's stories (a first in Yiddish). Aleichem's writing style was well suited to a popular medium like Yiddish, combining folkloric tales and quiet humor with philosophical observations like "Life is a dream for the wise, a game for the fool, a comedy for the rich, a tragedy for the poor."

Most of Aleichem's stories deal with life in the *shtetel* among the poor Russian Jews of the late nineteenth and early twentieth centuries. His story "Tevye's Daughters," translated in 1949, led to the musical *Fiddler on the Roof.*

Aleichem left Russia in 1905, fleeing persecution. After settling first in Switzerland, he moved to New York in 1914 and died there two years later. As he wrote, "No matter how bad things get you got to go on living, even if it kills you." His funeral drew hundreds of thousands of Jews in a procession that stretched from Harlem across the Williamsburg Bridge into Brooklyn. A journalist in a Yiddish newspaper described the funeral as "a meeting place for the children of the entire Diaspora." In his will Aleichem requested burial in Kiev (impossible at that time) "among ordinary Jewish working folk," hardly possible in his elite final retreat. His large twin-towered memorial (in Workmen's Circle #2, section 1, block E, map 19A, line 35, grave 15, special enclave) is etched in Yiddish, as his readers would expect.

# MIDDLE VILLAGE

## ST. JOHN'S CEMETERY

*80-01 Metropolitan Avenue, corner of 80th Street; (718) 894-4888*

This Catholic cemetery, with its cheerful green and white sign, opened in 1880. Through the years it has been the final home of congressmen, politicians, and Congressional Medal of Honor recipients of the Spanish-American and Vietnam Wars, as well as **Charles Atlas** (1893–1972; St. John Cloister, unit 5, 3rd floor, section 1, crypt 1A/3A), famous as a physical fitness pioneer, and **Frank Christi** (1929–1982; section 45, range B, grave 126), a yeoman actor in many movies and television series.

Unfortunately, St. John's also seems to be the favorite final haunt of an extraordinary number of New York gangsters and crime-family members known for the company they kept—and possibly killed. It has been dubbed the Mafia Valhalla, not a nickname it boasts of. Many of their grave sites are not listed because of family objections, but you are free to search on your own. Hint: Many are in vaults in St. John Cloister.

Among the most infamous are **Joseph "Joe" Columbo** (1923–1978; section 36, range F, plot 2, grave 1), the Columbo family boss who was shot on the orders of the Gambino family boss; and **Carlo Gambino** (1902–1976; St. John Cloister), who ordered the Columbo shooting but died of natural causes. Other gangers here, in graves unspecified at their families' request, are **John Gotti** (1940–2002), head of the Gambino crime family in New York; **Carmine "Lilo" Galante** (1910–1979), mafioso boss of the Bonanno crime family and organizer of the "French connection" heroin pipeline; and **Vito Genovese** (1897–1969), called the "boss of bosses," who died in prison. Even **Charles "Lucky" Luciano** (1897–1962) is on his final lam here. The most infamous gang leader of the 1930s and the scourge of law enforcement, he died of a heart attack in the airport in Naples, Italy. *Grounds open 9:00 A.M.–5:00 P.M. daily. Office hours: 9:00 A.M.–5:00 P.M. Monday–Friday, 9:00 A.M.–1:00 P.M. Saturday. Map; restrooms.*

> ### LUNCH BREAK
>
> Less than a mile from the cemetery is **Bann Thai** (69-12 Austin Street at Yellowstone Boulevard, Forest Hills; 718–544–9999), a tiny oasis of authentic Thai food at reasonable prices. A find.

## ROBERT MAPPLETHORPE    1946–1989

eath makes strange bedfellows. Photographer Robert Mapplethorpe was controversial but certainly not a criminal. In fact, he was a brilliant photographer who had retrospective exhibitions at the Whitney Museum of American Art, the Philadelphia Institute of Contemporary Art, and elsewhere. What made him controversial was not his talent, which was widely acknowledged, but his subject matter. A homosexual, he reveled in photographing gay couples, often in *flagrante delicto* or sadomasochistic poses. His work was vilified as much as it was praised.

Born to a Catholic family in Long Island, Mapplethorpe left home at sixteen, studied at the Pratt Institute in Brooklyn, and then worked as a designer and staff photographer for Andy Warhol's magazine *Interview*. His fifteen minutes of fame came when he became a full-time photographer, specializing in close-ups of friends (such as singer Patti Smith), flowers, and homoerotic portraits. He was deadly serious about his work, saying "I want people to see my works first as art and second as photography."

Mapplethorpe died of complications from AIDS. His oblong granite headstone, etched with a cross, is shared with family members in section 48 (range B, lots 131-133).

# RIDGEWOOD

## BETH-EL CEMETERY
*80-12 Cypress Hills Street; (718) 366–3558*

Beth-El was opened in 1864 and is as private now as it probably was then. Visitors who wish to pay respects to this refuge's most famous resident will not find admission easy or automatic. Fair warning. *Grounds open during office hours: 8:00 A.M.–4:00 P.M. Sunday–Friday. Restrooms.*

## EDWARD G. ROBINSON    1893–1973

eel life bears little resemblance to *real* life, as the career of Edward G. Robinson so vividly demonstrates. In his breakthrough movie, *Little Caesar* (1932), this longtime character actor played Rico Bandell—a killer so vicious that he became a paradigm of the sneering, lip-curling,

**LUNCH BREAK**

There isn't much of interest in the immediate vicinity, but **Zum Stammtisch** (69-46 Myrtle Avenue; 718–386–3014), a reliable German old-timer, is only a short drive away.

steely-eyed, merciless movie mobster. In real life Robinson was a gentle pussycat, a soft touch for dozens of worthy causes. An art connoisseur, he amassed one of the world's finest private collections, which sold for $3.25 million in 1957.

Robinson's homely looks and short stature wouldn't automatically have spelled "actor," but as a family cutup, he loved being on center stage. While studying law at City College in New York, he realized that he really wanted to act and switched to drama school. It was there that he changed his name from Emanuel Goldenberg to the more euphonious Edward Robinson, keeping the G as his middle initial. A dazzling monologue from *Julius Caesar* won him a scholarship at the American Academy of Dramatic Arts, and he was on his way.

Vaudeville and stock-company work followed, and in 1915 Robinson landed a role on Broadway in a play called *Under Fire*. He got the part because it called for a multilingual actor and he spoke several languages, a legacy of his birth and early childhood in Romania. Many juicy stage roles followed, and in the early 1930s Robinson moved to Hollywood. After *Little Caesar* he was typecast, playing thugs and hard-hearted types.

In 1940 *Dr. Ehrlich's Magic Bullet* broke the mold, and from then on Robinson began to play a variety of roles, always with skill and gusto. Some of his best, psychological performances were in *The Sea Wolf* (1941), *Flesh and Fantasy* (1943), *Double Indemnity* (1944), *The Woman in the Window* (1944), and *The Stranger* (1946). After twenty-eight years of movie work, he returned to Broadway in Paddy Chayefsky's drama *Middle of the Night*. In all, he appeared in more than a hundred films and forty Broadway plays.

Robinson was to receive a special Oscar at the Academy Awards ceremony in March 1973 for his "outstanding contribution to motion pictures." But he died of a heart attack in January while making the movie *Sammy Going South*—a rare example, for such a good actor, of bad timing. His autobiography, *All My Yesterdays,* was published posthumously. Robinson's personal life was as complicated as his movies. In the 1950s he was accused falsely of being a Communist, but later exonerated. Then he was forced to sell his prize art collection as part of a divorce settlement with his wife of twenty-nine years, and his only son attempted suicide several times and had frequent brushes with the law.

Robinson's crypt is inside the stately colonnaded mausoleum that inexplicably bears the name GOODMAN.

## LINDEN HILL JEWISH CEMETERY
*52-22 Metropolitan Avenue; (718) 821–2279 or (212) 477–2800*

In the cemetery row that bridges Brooklyn and Queens, Linden Hill Jewish is one of the more compact, easy-to-navigate burial grounds. If you want information ahead of time, it is best to call the Manhattan (212) number. The cemetery office is manned by a superintendent who is not always in the office.

The most notable resident is probably **David Belasco** (1853–1931; mausoleum, path 33, plot 1080), the San Francisco–born director, playwright, and theater manager. After a long apprenticeship touring mining camps and boomtowns of the Far West, during which he learned every aspect of the theater, Belasco came to New York. It didn't take him long to become a major presence on Broadway, known for his role in developing realism and naturalism in the American theater.

Anyone who has ever shopped at Bloomingdale's (isn't that everyone?) might want to know that the founder of this great store is at Linden Hill: **Joseph Bloomingdale** (1842–1904; mausoleum, Grand Pathway, plot RL).

New York politicniks may remember fondly **Jacob Koppel Javits** (1904–1986; path 13, private plot 188), who had a long, distinguished career as a moderate Republican (when this wasn't an oxymoron). After serving as a lieutenant colonel in the Chemical Warfare Service in World War II, he went on to become a U.S. congressman, attorney general of New York, and a four-term U.S.

> ### LUNCH BREAK
> **Dee's Brick Oven Pizza** (104-02 Metropolitan Avenue, Forest Hills; 718–793–7553) serves reasonably priced, crispy-crusted, wood-fired brick-oven pizzas that attract big crowds.

senator from New York. *Grounds open 8:30 A.M.–4:00 P.M. (promptly) Sunday–Friday. Office hours: 9:00 A.M.–4:00 P.M. Monday–Thursday. Map posted outside; restroom.*

# LINDEN HILL UNITED METHODIST CEMETERY

*323 Woodward Avenue; (718) 821–6480*

Located on twenty-four acres, the cemetery was founded in 1945. Sometimes people confuse this Linden Hill and the Jewish Linden Hill. It does seem curious that Jewish-born Ferenc Molnar has a permanent home in Linden Hill United Methodist rather than its Jewish counterpart. Perhaps the driver of the hearse had the wrong address. *Grounds open 8:00 A.M.–4:30 P.M. Monday–Friday. Office hours: 9:00 A.M.–4:00 P.M. Monday–Friday, 9:00 A.M.–noon Saturday. Restrooms.*

### LUNCH BREAK

**The Fame** (69-67 Grand Avenue, Maspeth; 718–478–4676) is a simple luncheonette, but the food is satisfying.

## FERENC MOLNAR    1878–1952

Linden Hill's most famous lodger is Budapest-born Ferenc Molnar, whose domain is now section E, plot 55. A man of many parts, he was a novelist first, a war correspondent in World War I, and, most famously, a playwright. In 1936 he moved to New York, where he had a number of his plays published and produced. The two best known in English of his twenty-five plays, *The Guardsman* and *Liliom,* have been revived several times. Rodgers and Hammerstein's *Carousel* is a highly successful musical variation on *Liliom* (and has enjoyed many revivals). During the post–World War II Communist reign in Hungary, Molnar's plays were, if not officially banned, certainly not produced. Their frothy romantic themes and airy cynicism didn't suit the dead-seriousness of Communist Hungary.

## UNION FIELD CEMETERY OF CONGREGATION RODEPH SHOLOM

*82-11 Cypress Avenue; (718) 366–3748*

With seventeen cemeteries of various denominations adjacent to one another in this "island" that straddles Queens and Brooklyn, almost half of them are Jewish, including Union Field. Intimate and compact—no winding roadways, no swaths of green meadows, no brooks or waterfalls—Union Field is organized in grids, which makes it easy for a visitor to cover the entire area on foot. Family mausoleums dominate the limited grassy plots, and the tops of many

headstones bear the carved word MOTHER, FATHER, BROTHER, or SISTER. In signs, epitaphs, and other inscriptions carved on gravestones, Hebrew dominates the cemetery.

Small as it is, Union Field has its share of accomplished residents. The list begins with **Charles Frohman** (1860–1915; Maple Road). He was a successful theater producer and manager and a major presence on the New York theater scene for many years in the late nineteenth and early twentieth centuries. In 1892 he founded the Empire Theatre Stock Company, which is credited with launching the star system. Among the stars he managed were Maude Adams and Ethel Barrymore. In 1915 Frohman was on the *Lusitania* when it sank. His older brother, **Daniel Frohman** (1853–1940; Maple Road), also a theater manager, outlived him by many years, dying peacefully at age eighty-seven. Both reside with other family members in their own mausoleum.

### LUNCH BREAK

A few blocks away is **Zum Stammtisch** (69-46 Myrtle Avenue, Queens; 718–386–3014), reliable for old-fashioned German dishes served in a cheerful Bavarian-style setting, with robust portions and moderate prices.

On the negative side of fame—infamy—is gambler **Arnold Rothstein** (1882–1928; section 52, off Cedar Avenue), notorious for bribing White Sox baseball players in the 1919 Black Sox World Series scandal. He was murdered at age forty-six. *Grounds open 7:00 A.M.–4:00 P.M. daily except Saturday. Office hours: 9:00 A.M.–4:00 P.M. Monday–Thursday, 9:00 A.M.–3:00 P.M. Friday and Sunday. Map; restrooms.*

## ROY COHN   1927–1986

Life was promising for whiz kid Roy Cohn, whose family was prominent in New York judicial circles. He graduated from Columbia Law School at age twenty, passed the New York bar at twenty-one, and soon became the youngest assistant U.S. attorney of his day. His career seemed made when he was chosen as one of the prosecutors in the high-profile Julius and Ethel Rosenberg treason case, and then it was almost unmade by his association with U.S. senator Joseph McCarthy. As the Communist-hunting McCarthy's chief counsel, Cohn made waves all over Washington with his rambunctious romp through Europe with David Schine, another McCarthy aide. Ostensibly their "mission" was to uncover Communists in U.S. embassies, but most of their time was spent on high-handed confrontations, parties, and high jinks.

For the next thirty years, it was all downhill as far as Cohn's reputation with the public was concerned. Although he became a financially successful lawyer, with friends in high places in the Republican Party, he was considered by many to be an opportunist with elastic ethics. He became known by the company he kept and represented—much of it bad. Mafia bosses John Gotti, Carmine Galante, and Anthony "Fat Tony" Salerno and crime-family members Thomas and Joseph Gambino and Angelo Ruggiero were all Cohn clients.

Cohn was indicted three times in eight years for perjury, witness tampering, and other crimes, but was acquitted each time. Continuous charges of unethical conduct plagued him, and weeks before his death he was finally disbarred.

Throughout his career Cohn was a highly visible figure in New York's nightclub scene. Rumors of his homosexuality were rampant but vociferously denied. Even as he wasted away from complications caused by AIDS, he denied that he was gay and that his illness was AIDS-related. At that time AIDS was still relatively unknown. Cohn can be found in a small family mausoleum in the Maple Road section.

## BERT LAHR   1895–1967

enerations of young people know Bert Lahr only as the Cowardly Lion in the 1939 movie *The Wizard of Oz,* which is an evergreen on television. But delightful as he is in that role, it was just one of many achievements that ranged from burlesque and vaudeville to Broadway musicals and films. Irving Lahrheim, as he was born, dropped out of school at age fifteen, shortened Lahrheim to Lahr, and joined a juvenile vaudeville act. He soon moved up from second to top banana. His loose style, eye-rolling, and rubberlike facial expressions made him a master of visual comedy that appealed to lowbrows and highbrows alike.

In 1927 Lahr made Broadway, starring in such musicals as *Flying High, Hold Everything,* and *Life Begins at 8:40.* Broadway was really his forte. His broad gestures, double takes, slapstick, and expert comic timing were perfect on the big stage. Later in life he demonstrated greater range than might be expected of such a comic. Cast in Samuel Beckett's first New York production of *Waiting for Godot,* he showed a new sensitivity and, of course, his usual perfect timing. He again demonstrated his ability to play drama with a light touch as Bottom in a 1960s American Shakespeare Festival production of *A Midsummer Night's Dream*.

Lahr rests now in the sizable Lahrheim family plot in Central Avenue, halfway down path 5 on the right side, just before an andromeda bush. His flat, gray granite gravestone bears the etched words BELOVED HUSBAND AND FATHER, but to the multitude of *Wizard of Oz* fans, he will always be the lovable not-so-Cowardly Lion.

# WOODSIDE

## CALVARY
*49-02 Laurel Hill Boulevard; (718) 786–8000*

Straddling both Woodside and Long Island City, this august Catholic burial ground is the oldest and largest of four operated by the Catholic Archdiocese of New York. It was purchased in 1845 from the Alsop farm; the original 115 acres have been added to so that Calvary, with seventy-one subdivisions, now totals 365 acres. Two major highways, the Long Island Expressway and Brooklyn Queens Expressway, crisscross and intersect Calvary's sections, with Old (or First) Calvary on the west and New Calvary (divided into Second, Third, and Fourth Calvary) east of the intersections. The four sections are formally listed as St. Callixtus, St. Agnes, St. Sebastian, and St. Domitilla, to evoke memories of the catacombs in Rome, where the earliest Christian martyrs were buried. Scenically, First Calvary is the most intriguing of the four sections. That's where the St. Callixtus Chapel (1908) is, with bas relief carvings over its various entrances.

Some 1,750,000 now rest perpetually at Calvary, which offers sanctuary to people as diverse as Congressional Medal of Honor recipients, Civil War generals, U.S. senators, politicians, actors, and, yes, even crime figures.

Here lies **Patrick S. Gilmore** (1829–1892; section 10, plot 15, near main gate in First Calvary), known as the father of the American band, composer of "When Johnny Comes Marching Home," and bandmaster for the U.S. Army during the Civil War.

At least three star athletes rest at Calvary: **William "Wee Willie" Keeler** (1872–1923; section 1W, range 15, plot B, grave 5, First Calvary), baseball Hall of Famer; **Michael "Smiling Mickey" Welch** (1859–1941; section 4, range 17, plot 2, grave 6, First Calvary), one of the nineteenth century's star pitchers; and **Martin J. Sheridan** (1881–1918; section 45, plot 4, grave 1/16, First Calvary), four-time Olympic gold medalist for discus throw in 1904, 1906, and 1908 and shot put in 1908.

Calvary is also the final abode of **Mary Louise "Texas" Guinan** (1884–1933; section 47, plot F, vault, First Calvary), a silent-movie actress and later hostess at a New York speakeasy during Prohibition. Her trademark greeting was an exuberant "Hello, sucker!" Other actors at liberty here include **Patsy Kelly** (1910–1981; section 66, plot 40, grave 7, Fourth Calvary), a Broadway and movie actress who appeared in *Rosemary's Baby* and many other films; **Una O'Connor** (1880–1959; section 70, plot 46, grave 16, Fourth Calvary), who played in the horror films *The Invisible Man* (1933) and *The Bride of Frankenstein* (1935), as well as *Witness for the Prosecution* (1957), her last film; and **Arthur O'Connell** (1908–1981; section 34, row 7, range Q, plot 10/11, Third Calvary), a character actor who was nominated for a Best Supporting Actor Oscar for *Picnic* and *Anatomy of a Murder.* **Bert Wheeler** (1895–1968; section 47, plot 46, grave 29, Catholic Actors Monument, First Calvary), half of the old-time comedy team of Wheeler and Woolsey, is also present and accounted for, as is librettist **Lorenzo da Ponte** (1749–1839; section 4B, First Calvary), whose grave and commemorative monument are both near the road.

Father and son politicos are at peace here: **Robert F. Wagner Sr.** (1877–1953; section 55, plot 8, grave 18-19, Second Calvary), U.S. senator from 1927 to 1949, and **Robert Wagner Jr.** (1910–1991; the same), mayor of New York from 1954 to 1965 and U.S. ambassador to Spain from 1965 to 1966.

Saints and sinners—cemeteries sometimes produce strange bedfellows and certain ironies. **Giuseppe Petrosino** (1860–1909; section 22, plot 9K, grave 17/18, Third Calvary) was the New York Police Department's first Italian-American detective and an active battler against the pre-Mafia Black Hand, a crime organization that extorted money from Italian immigrants. In contrast to Petrosino, the most vicious Black Hand leader is also at Calvary in the same division: **Ignatius "Lupo the Wolf" Lupo** (1877–1947; section 35, same plot as gangster brother-in-law Ciro Terranova, Third Calvary). His reign of terror lasted from the late 1890s until he went to prison in 1909.

Other ignominious residents in their final hideouts are **Thomas "Three Finger Brown" Luchese** (1899–1967; section 69, plot 164, grave 13, Fourth

## LUNCH BREAK

With its Irish-American food, **Donovan's Pub** (57-24 Roosevelt Avenue; 718–429–9339) is a natural choice for a quick, moderate, casual lunch.

Calvary), a Mafia chieftain; **Paolo "Paul Kelly" Vaccarelli** (1876–1936; section 36, range 5, plot G, grave 20, Third Calvary), leader of the violent Five Points gang, which included Al Capone; and **Benjamin "Lefty Guns" Ruggiero** (1926–1994; section 15, plot 100, grave 19, Second Calvary), a hit man for the Bonanno crime family. *Grounds open 8:00 A.M.–4:15 P.M. daily. Office hours: 9:00 A.M.–4:15 P.M. weekdays, 9:00 A.M.–1:00 P.M. Saturday. Map; restrooms. Mass at 10:00 A.M. every Saturday in St. Callixtus Chapel. Office is located in Second Calvary at the corner of 49th Street and Laurel Hill Boulevard.*

## CARMINE DE SAPIO   1908–2004

"Doing well by doing good" might be the motto of this one-time political head of Tammany Hall, the Democratic political machine in New York City, which he revived after World War II. Back in the days when politicians were handpicked by the local political boss, De Sapio chose Robert Wagner Jr. as the mayoral candidate in 1953 and Averell Harriman for governor in 1954. Both men won.

De Sapio, son of Italian immigrants, worked his way up the ladder of the New York Democratic club system (a necessary process in the city during the 1940s and 1950s). To the surprise of many, he was more progressive than bosses tended to be. Though strong-willed and authoritarian, he supported the first African-American borough president and the first Puerto Rican district leader, and he endorsed rent control, the Fair Employment Practices law, and lowering the voting age to eighteen. That was the "doing good" part. By "doing well," De Sapio was accused of bribery and corruption. In 1969 he was convicted of petty bribery and went to prison. His perpetual home is a vault in the mausoleum, section 27, plot 42, Third Calvary.

## ALFRED E. SMITH   1873–1944

When Al Smith, popular four-term New York governor, was soundly defeated for president by Herbert Hoover in 1928, the common wisdom was that a Catholic could never become president. So widespread was this belief that no one challenged it—until 1960 when John F. Kennedy narrowly defeated Richard Nixon for the job.

Political losses are rarely the result of just one thing. In Smith's case, his pronounced New York accent played a part—it was so alien and urban to so many people in the more agrarian parts of America. His signature brown derby and incessant cigar, though droll signatures to New Yorkers, didn't help him in the South and West. Being part of the Tammany Hall political machine was another negative. And it was no plus in the heartland that his campaign theme song was "The Sidewalks of New York."

Alfred Emanuel Smith was born in the shadow of the Brooklyn Bridge and grew up poor on Manhattan's Lower East Side, selling newspapers to supplement the family income. At age twelve, he had to quit school when his father died to work from 4:00 A.M. to 5:00 P.M. (for $15 a week) at the Fulton Fish Market.

To many poor and striving people in the early twentieth century, Democratic politics meant upward mobility. Smith began his political career in 1894 and, partly because of his genial personality, moved up quickly to the New York Assembly in 1903, where he eventually became leader and then speaker in 1915. From there it was county sheriff, president of the board of aldermen, and finally governor in 1918.

As governor, his amiable style—he was known as the "Happy Warrior"—made it easy to work with Republicans in passing laws improving factory conditions and regulating child labor. An able administrator, Smith reduced state government while making it more efficient. After losing the Democratic nomination for president in 1924, he tried again; Franklin D. Roosevelt nominated Smith, and he won in 1928. Then came his devastating loss to Hoover. In 1932 Smith lost the Democratic presidential nomination to Roosevelt, which caused a breach in their relationship that was never totally mended. Whether Smith became more conservative or just bitter later in life, he favored Republicans over Roosevelt in the next two presidential elections (1936 and 1940) and was accused of trading in his derby for a top hat. The "Happy Warrior" had lost his smile. In his postpolitical career, he worked to erect the Empire State Building and later became president of the corporation that managed the skyscraper.

This governor's "mansion" now is located in section 45, graves 3 and 4, First Calvary.

# CHAPTER 5

# Long Island

Long Island is dotted with towns and villages whose peaceful, often tiny rural cemeteries sometimes harbor surprising residents—mega-stars who lived in the vicinity and found permanent shelter and anonymity nearby.

## CROOKED POND

*Widow Gavits Road, off Sagg Road*

Crooked Pond is not a cemetery, but a pond that is part of the local nature conservancy. It is roughly equidistant from Bridgehampton and Sag Harbor, situated about 1 mile down Widow Gavits Road. Past a house and kennels is a narrow lane that leads down to the pond. A car can travel halfway down before being stopped by a barrier; then it is a short walk to the pond. Next to the pond is a massive boulder with a bronze plaque attached. *Grounds open dawn to dusk daily.*

### LUNCH BREAK

Popular, casual, and inexpensive, the **Golden Pear Cafe** (2426 Montauk Highway; 631–537–1100) is a local favorite. It also has branches in East Hampton and Southampton.

## TRUMAN CAPOTE   1924–1984

*I*f Truman Capote were female, he might have been called a minx. He loved flirting, exchanging confidences, and stirring people up; he feasted on amusing gossip and *schadenfreude*. He might almost have stage-managed the finale to his own life. It went like this: Capote died in Hollywood at the home of Joanne Carson (ex-wife of the late Johnny Carson). She planned to bury Capote at Westwood Village Memorial Park in Los Angeles, but his friends from New York intervened. In a tug-of-war (almost literally) over his ashes, half were kept in LA and buried in a crypt around the corner from Marilyn Monroe's in Westwood (the celebrity-mad Capote would have loved that). The other half, in a brass box, returned to the Hamptons with Capote's longtime lover and friend Jack Dunphy.

For years the ashes remained on a shelf in Dunphy's house. After his death in 1992, friends of both men decided to relocate Capote and Dunphy's ashes, and in an informal ceremony they were scattered over Crooked Pond and immortalized with a plaque. Capote has top billing with a quote from his first novel, *Other Voices, Other Rooms*: "The brain may take advice, but not the heart, and love having no geography knows no boundaries."

Capote's life was as fraught with emotion as his death. His childhood was fodder for his career as a writer and poet. He was born Truman Streckfus

Persons in New Orleans to parents who divorced and abandoned him. He later took his stepfather's name, Capote. His early years were spent in Monroeville, Alabama, with eccentric relatives, about whom he later wrote affectionately in *The Grass Harp* and other stories.

*Other Voices, Other Rooms* was published when Capote was twenty-three years old, and he was quickly hailed for precocity and a southern gothic style (even though from age eight he lived in New York and Greenwich, Connecticut). Like a meteor, he flared from being a copyboy at the *New Yorker* to being the pet of rich, famous, and influential New Yorkers before he finally crashed. Although Capote had other successes, including two O. Henry Awards for short stories, much of his time was spent cruising on rich friends' yachts and lunching with them at fancy French restaurants. Tiny and gay, with a high, squeaky voice, Capote turned what could have been liabilities into social assets as a raconteur, confidante, and wit.

A major breakthrough in his writing style was *In Cold Blood*, a nonfiction account of a real murder. It has been called his best book; it certainly introduced a new style: nonfiction written as a novel. But then came *Breakfast at Tiffany's, A Christmas Memory,* and magazine articles in his more familiar style. Television talk shows, readings, and social extravaganzas (like his spectacular Black and White Ball) followed, concurrently with alcoholism, drug use, and nervous breakdowns.

When chapters from Capote's self-described Proustian novel-to-be, *Answered Prayers*, were published in *Esquire* and *New York* magazines, they rang the death knoll on his social life and, ultimately, his career. The chapters were a thinly disguised roman à clef about the socialites who had befriended and confided in him. They read the serialized chapters, were shocked at his perfidy, and dropped him faster than an envelope of anthrax. This was the beginning of a downward spiral that led to the revolving door of sanatoriums and finally to death from a liver disease complicated by drugs and phlebitis.

## POXABOGUE CEMETERY
*Corner of Route 27 and Sagg Road*

Tiny and secluded (yet part of Bridgehampton), this quiet burying ground, with a few graves dating to the 1700s, has one celebrated inhabitant: novelist **James Jones** (1921–1977), whose grave is easy to find in such a small place. A witness to the Japanese attack on Pearl Harbor, December 7, 1941, Jones was in military service at Schofield Barracks on Oahu at the time. After the war he put his army service to good use, writing over time a trilogy of war novels, which are his main literary legacy. The first, *From Here to Eternity* (1951), made the biggest splash and became a successful movie starring Burt Lancaster and Montgomery Clift. The other two, *The Thin Red Line* (1962) and *Whistle* (1978), were interspersed with other works. *Grounds open dawn to dusk daily.*

## LUNCH BREAK

Good restaurants are a given in the Hamptons. Relatively new is **Almond** (1970 Montauk Highway; 631–537–8885), a stylish place for good French bistro food at reasonable prices. **Bobby Van's** (Montauk Highway, Route 27; 631–537–0590) is a long-time favorite for steaks, chops, and other standards.

# EAST HAMPTON

## GREEN RIVER CEMETERY
*Old Accabonac Road, ⅓ mile off Old Stone Highway, on the right*

*Delightful* isn't a word that usually applies to cemeteries, but it fits this minuscule one that is surrounded by a white picket fence. Tiny—with a drive running through it shaped like a horseshoe, with a spur or handle at the north end—Green River occupies fewer than three compact acres. Until the early 1950s, when artists and writers began moving to the Hamptons, it was a thimble-size last resort for locals. But now it is such an A-list for East Hampton's artistic community that it is oversubscribed.

For the grave connoisseur, it is ideal: small, with mostly flat land shaded by towering trees, evergreens, and lovely plantings; easily walkable; and rich in discoveries. At almost every step you will uncover a recognizable artistic or literary name. Many of the grave markers are unique, reflecting their creative owners.

Facing Accabonac Road, the cemetery's old section (inside its horseshoe drive) is the last known address of such creative star power as **Jimmy Ernst** (1920–1984; headstone near the road, behind two low evergreens), a modern artist and the son of surrealist painter Max Ernst. Jimmy's stone reads "Artists and poets are the raw nerves of humanity. By themselves they can do little to save humanity. Without them there would be little worth saving." Also in residence: **James Brooks** (1906–1992; just northeast of Ernst), an abstract artist; and **Frank O'Hara** (1926–1966; near the rounded end of the horse-

shoe in the rear), a poet, art critic, and cofounder of the New York School of Poets and Playwrights, whose flat stone reads "Grace to be born and live as variously as possible."

Just outside the horseshoe on the right side is **Alfonso Ossorio** (1916–1990; near the drive), an abstract expressionist painter and patron of Jackson Pollock and other artists. He is immortalized by a round, polished black granite stone on a pedestal. Close by is **Harold Rosenberg** (1906–1978; just above the headstone of Ossorio), a modern art critic and friend of the de Koonings who coined the phrase "action painting" to describe their work and that of Pollock and others.

To the left of the horseshoe drive are painter **Abraham Rattner** (1895–1978; headstone at south end), whose unusual round, black granite gravestone has his signature etched into the front; **Elaine de Kooning** (1918–1989; just north of Rattner), an abstract artist and the wife of Dutch-born abstract expressionist Willem de Kooning, whose big flashy green bas-relief plaque on top of her headstone is the easiest of all to see; **Frederick Kiesler** (1890–1965; flat stone to the northwest of de Kooning), an Aus-

trian-American architect and artist; **Ad Reinhardt** (1913–1967; flat white marble stone next to the drive at the turn), famous for his postmodernist black paintings; and **Stuart Davis** (1892–1964; high black stele to the left of Reinhardt), a modern painter whose career spanned several artistic trends. His headstone reads "The artist is a cool spectator-reporter at an arena of hot events." **Stefan Wolpe** (1902–1972; natural boulder at northwest edge of old section) was a German-born composer of avant-garde music.

In the new section (north of the old) are other artistic types, such as Belgian-born, Yale-educated **Henry Geldzahler** (1935–1994; headstone to the left of the drive "handle"), an art critic and writer who was the modern art curator at the Metropolitan Museum of Art; and **Alan Pakula** (1928–1998; rear left, next to fence), a stage and movie director whose films include *To Kill a Mockingbird* and *All the President's Men*.

As you wander the grounds, you might serendipitously discover other familiar names such as **Fred Coe** (1914–1979), a television producer-director; **Pierre Franay** (1921–1996), a French chef, columnist, and food writer for the *New York Times*; and **Steven J. Ross** (?–1992), a telecommunications mogul and former CEO of Time-Warner. *Grounds open dawn to dusk daily. No office, but a map with directions to the cemetery is available at the Pollock-Krasner House (see House Call, page 123).*

## LUNCH BREAK

For a super prix fixe lunch, try the historic and attractive **Maidstone Arms** (207 Main Street; 631–324–5006), which also has comfortable rooms and cottages for overnight stays. To eat on the run, get a deli sandwich and fresh-made doughnuts at **Dressen's Excelsior Market** (33 Newtown Lane; 631–324–0465). If you are in the village for dinner or Sunday brunch, **Della Femina** (99 North Main Street; 631–329–6666) is *the* place for simple elegance and superb food.

## A. J. LIEBLING  1904–1963
## JEAN STAFFORD  1915–1979

What goes around comes around. For years after his death, Abbott Joseph Liebling, well known in his day for sharp reporting and lucid prose in the *New Yorker,* seemed to fall into the oblivion saved for second-tier writers. Liebling who? But several of his books have recently been reissued, which means a new generation of readers can appreciate this distinctive prose stylist.

Liebling, whose father worked in New York's fur district, was educated in the city until 1920, when just shy of sixteen, he went to Dartmouth. Though precocious, Liebling didn't last long enough to graduate—kicked out, he claimed, for skipping compulsory chapel. His next stop was the Columbia School of Journalism (which he called "a training school for future employees of the A. & P."). After finishing there he took his first newspaper job, at the *Providence Evening Journal*. His real journalism school, though, was the city room of Joseph Pulitzer's newspaper, the *New York World*. Later Liebling joined the *New Yorker*, where he wrote often about horse racing and boxing, both personal passions. He also loved writing about food—and had the waist-line to prove it. During World War II he was the magazine's war correspondent, filing reports from England, Europe, and Africa.

After the war Liebling began a column for the *New Yorker*, "The Wayward Press," which was both popular and insightful; many of the columns have been reissued in the book *Just Enough Liebling*. His much-quoted comment that "freedom of the press is limited to those who own one" still stings. His many books, as diverse as his interests, include *The Sweet Science* (about boxing), *The Earl of Louisiana* (about Huey Long), *Between Meals: An Appetite for Paris*, *Chicago: The Second City,* and *The Telephone Booth Indian*.

Jean Stafford and Liebling seemed an unlikely duo. He was a bona fide

New Yorker, a newspaperman, and Jewish; she was California-born, Colorado-raised and educated, a novelist, and a WASP. But the *New Yorker* brought them together—they met in London on assignment for the magazine. She wrote twenty-one stories for the publication, as well as several nonfiction articles.

Stafford was best known for three novels and many short stories. Her first novel, *Boston Adventure* (1944), was a best seller, and the following year she won a Guggenheim Fellowship and a $1,000 award from the American Academy and National Institute of Arts and Letters. Her second novel, *The Mountain Lion* (1947), is considered her best. Her third, *The Catherine Wheel* (1952), like the others, was laced with autobiographical elements. In 1970 Stafford received a Pulitzer Prize for her *Collected Short Stories*. Throughout much of her life she battled alcoholism and depression. An eight-year marriage to poet Robert Lowell was a total mismatch; while married, she spent almost a year at the Payne Whitney Clinic trying to cope.

When it came to marriage, Liebling and Stafford had three apiece. Theirs, which lasted only four and a half years until his sudden death from pneumonia, was by all accounts a happy one. When he died, she retired to his East Hampton house and continued writing. Though a writer's block kept her from fiction, she wrote several children's books, articles, and a nonfiction account of a three-day interview with Lee Harvey Oswald's mother, called *A Mother in History*, that was considered something of a coup. A stroke in 1976 left Stafford with aphasia. Impaired in speech and vision, she died three years later, probably a mercy.

Stafford and Liebling can be found side by side, their "his and her" slate headstones (each with an etched snowflake and fleur de lis) at the northernmost edge of the horseshoe in the old section, hugging the drive. His stone reads "Blessed—he could bless." Hers merely provides her birth and death dates.

## JACKSON POLLOCK    1912–1956

*P*ollock, born on a ranch in Cody, Wyoming, became the symbol of abstract expressionism, the leading art movement of the 1950s and 60s. His "action" or "drip" style of painting looked simple. His technique was to spread a large canvas on the floor and then splatter paint all over it. There was order in what he was doing—a lifetime of study went into it—but to the public it often elicited the comment "A child could do *that*." Not so.

Pollock studied with Thomas Hart Benton at the Art Students League and went first through a social realism phase, then surrealism, with his work finally evolving into the large squiggles of color that adorn museum walls today.

He struggled at first to sell his work, but patrons like Peggy Guggenheim, Betty Parsons, and fellow artist Alfonso Ossorio came to his rescue with financial and moral support. But no one could help him control his rage or chronic alcoholism, which ended only when Pollock lost control of his car and crashed into a tree, killing himself and one of two companions. Fame came too late for him to enjoy. **Lee Krasner** (1908–1984), a fellow painter and Pollock's long-suffering wife of eleven stormy years, kept the Pollock flame alive.

Pollock's marker is a gigantic, rough-textured boulder (hauled into place by Krasner and friends) with his signature engraved in bronze. In front of it is Krasner's smaller gravestone, which is almost as dramatic. She originally selected it for his grave but decided that he needed a larger tribute. Krasner, a well-respected abstract expressionist painter in her own right, remains forever in Pollock's shadow, just as the stone sizes are symbolic of their relationship and their careers. Both graves are located just above the north edge of the horseshoe drive, at the top of the old section.

## HOUSE CALL

Less than 2 miles away in "The Springs" is the **Pollock-Krasner House and Study Center** (830 Fireplace Road; 631–324–4929), consisting of Pollock's studio (with his original paint-splattered wood floor), the couple's plain frame house, and a reference library on modern American art. The house is open only by appointment Thursday through Saturday, May through October.

# EAST MARION

## EAST MARION CEMETERY

*Cemetery Road*

Venerable, with ancient, eroding gravestones, this North Shore country cemetery, near the tip of the northeast fork of Long Island, seems a surprising choice of final address for its most internationally famous resident, Mark Rothko. His simple grave, marked by a boulder, is something of an anomaly on this ancient turf. But then, life is full of such oxymorons. *Grounds open dawn to dusk daily.*

## MARK ROTHKO   1903–1970

One might think that the incredibly beautiful, intense color paintings of abstract artist Mark Rothko reflected a sunny, upbeat disposition. That was anything but the case. Rothko suffered from depression for many years, and after a long struggle ended his life in 1970, by slitting his wrists in his New York studio. Ironically, he was at the peak of his power and success, recognized as one of the most accomplished of the abstract expressionists. Rothko disliked the term, which encompassed the very different styles of a group of American abstract painters who peaked at the same time.

Rothko began life in Daugavpils, Russia (now Latvia), and emigrated to the United States with his family in 1916 when he was thirteen. He studied art at Yale and the Art Students League. As an adult he first worked in relative obscurity, teaching art to make a living while doing his own work at the same time.

Although he was featured in exhibits at the Whitney Museum of American Art, it wasn't until the tidal wave of abstract expressionism washed over the New York art scene in the early 1960s that Rothko became a major name in the art world. In the mid-1960s he was commissioned to create fourteen paintings for a chapel in Houston, Texas, that architect Philip Johnson built for art collectors John and Dominique de Menil. The somber works, all in varying tones of black, provide serenity to this restful ecumenical place, which is called the Rothko Chapel.

Turmoil followed Rothko even after death, when his daughter sued the Marlborough Gallery, which had represented the artist for years. Before killing himself, Rothko bequeathed some of his best paintings to his two children, anticipating that their sale would provide financial security to his heirs. Marlborough insisted that the paintings belonged to the gallery because it had long subsidized the artist under a special agreement. In the court case that followed, it turned out that the gallery had defrauded Rothko and his estate for years by underestimating the value of his work, and several Marlborough directors were found guilty.

Today Rothko's works are in almost every major museum in the United States. The artist's current habitat, on the left side of the cemetery, is very visible.

# FARMINGDALE

## PINELAWN MEMORIAL PARK AND CEMETERY
*2030 Wellwood Avenue; (631) 249–6100; www.pinelawnmemorialpark.com*

There are six cemeteries in a cluster in this section of Farmingdale, several of them Jewish. There is also Pinelawn National Cemetery, where some 315,000 veterans of the Spanish-American War through the Vietnam War share quarters, along with their spouses.

Just south of the National Cemetery is nonsectarian Pinelawn Memorial Park and Cemetery. "Park" is an apt name, given that it is so meticulously tended. It seems almost new, as burial grounds go, yet it has been open for more than a hundred years (since 1902). Over 131,000 spirits lie within its 900 acres—many of them in handsome, modern-looking mausoleums—arranged around gardenlike courtyards or atriums. Those permanent residents in the ground are in grassy rows along neat, well-manicured paths. Most of the ground "residences" have flat markers; there are few headstones, uprights, obelisks, or individual or family mausoleums.

The formal grounds are especially lovely in late spring, when there are floral bursts of azaleas, beds of tulips, and flowering trees, accented by towering columns, arcs, moongates, fountains, ponds, pools, and garden statuary. The office is located in a well-appointed information center, with extremely helpful personnel. There is even a Long Island Railroad station at Pinelawn.

Reclining in this serene, well-manicured setting is the prematurely arrived **Brandon DeWilde** (1942–1972; Garden of Normandie North, section 80, range 37, block 1, plot C, grave 53), wistful child star in the Broadway hit *Member of the Wedding* and in the movie *Shane*. His life's journey ended tragically at age thirty in a car crash.

At the other end of life's spectrum is habitué **Guy Lombardo** (1902–1977; Pinelawn Garden mausoleum, Forsythia Court, south gallery, row 65, tier C), the Canadian-born band leader and violinist. His musical style, considered hokey by younger listeners, was a perennial hit with older fans, many of whom wouldn't consider New Year's Eve complete without hearing his band on the radio from the Waldorf Astoria, ending the year with his signature "Auld Lang Syne."

Making another kind of music was **"King" Curtis Ousley** (1934–1971; Pinelawn Garden mausoleum, Forsythia Court, west gallery, row 15, tier D), known professionally as King Curtis. Popular during the 1950s and 60s, he was called "the king of R & B saxophone." While at the cusp of fame, he was fatally stabbed on the steps of his New York house.

## LUNCH BREAK

There are many delis and pizza parlors along Route 110, but for something with more élan, consider **The Oak Room** (Carlyle on the Green, Bethpage State Park; 516–501–9700), just a few miles to the west, overlooking Bethpage Black Golf Course. It is one of Farmingdale's better restaurants, known for its steak and seafood dinners. It is more casual at lunch with burgers, sandwiches, and salads.

Another full-time resident is civil rights leader **Roy Wilkins** (1901–1981; Heritage Garden III, section 70, block 3, range 11, plot R, grave 19), executive director of the National Association for the Advancement of Colored People (NAACP) from 1955 to 1977. Ballet dancer **Andre Eglevsky** (1917–1977; Alfred D. Locke Division, section 31, block 9, range 2, plot H, grave 241) is also enshrouded on the grounds, as is **Bob Eberly** (1916–1981; Garden of Remembrance, section 60, block 3, range 75, plot G, grave 76), a popular vocalist of the Big Band era, when he sang for the Dorsey Brothers. He was best known for his renditions, in Jimmy Dorsey's band, of "Tangerine," "Green Eyes," and "Amapola."

Volatile, dyspeptic Broadway producer **David Merrick** (1911–2000; Pinelawn Garden mausoleum, Heather Court, southeast gallery, tier B, row 501) took his final curtain call in Pinelawn's seraphic surroundings. He received eight Tony awards; his smash-hit shows, among almost one hundred that he produced, included *Gypsy, Oliver!, Hello, Dolly!,* and *42nd Street,* but his staffers called him "the Abominable Showman" because of his terrible temper. He was not well liked. *Grounds open 8:00 A.M.–5:00 P.M. daily. Office hours: 8:45 A.M.–4:45 P.M. Monday–Friday, 10:00 A.M.–5:00 P.M. Saturday and Sunday. Map; restrooms.*

## WILLIAM JAMES "COUNT" BASIE   1904–1984

Although Basie was born in Red Bank, New Jersey, and learned to play piano there, he was always identified with the Kansas City sound. That's because, after tootling around the vaudeville circuit in New York, he got a gig in Kansas City with Walter Page's Blue Devils and then joined Bernie Moten's Kansas City Band.

When Moten died in 1935, Basie formed his own band, a nine-piece group that he called Barons of Rhythm; it included drummer Jo Jones and tenor saxophonist Lester Young. By the time the group got an engagement at New York's Famous Door on 52nd Street, Basie had added six members, and the band began to swing with its own identity. Basie soon became so well known for his unique piano that he was called "Count," as a comparison to "Duke" Ellington himself.

In a field not known for longevity, the Count had a long, long run. He disbanded his own orchestra in 1950, thinking that the Big Band era was over. But two years later he was back, as indefatigable as ever, playing with other groups and backing up such performers as Sarah Vaughan, Frank Sinatra, Bing

Crosby, Tony Bennett, and Sammy Davis Jr. Throughout the 1950s, 60s, and 70s, his inimitable piano played on. Even as he battled poor health, the irrepressible Basie pounded those keys until his death at age eighty. His crypt in Forsythia Court is in the west gallery, tier D, row 15.

## JOHN COLTRANE  1926–1967

*I*t's hard to imagine how this original, protean musician, who changed his style and improvised so radically, could have packed so much great music into such a short life—especially given that, early on, his life was often interrupted by heroin use, a habit that John Coltrane acquired in his youth. It cost him jobs with Johnny Hodges and Miles Davis before he finally kicked the habit for good, in 1957.

Although Coltrane grew up in North Carolina, Philadelphia claims him. He studied briefly at the Ornstein School of Music and Granoff Studios and played alto saxophone in local clubs. After brief U.S. Navy service in Hawaii in 1945, where he made his first record with a group of other sailors, he returned to Philadelphia, riffed with local bands, and switched to tenor sax. In 1949 he joined Dizzy Gillespie's big band, staying with it until 1951. While with Gillespie he had his first solo on a recording in "We Love to Boogie."

Because of heroin the next few years were unsteady, though Coltrane continued to attract attention for his "angry tenor," as one reviewer called his style. In 1957 Coltrane joined the Thelonius Monk Quarter, but he returned to Miles Davis's group the next year (having been fired earlier), performing with the band at the Newport Jazz Festival. In 1959 Davis recorded a landmark album, *Kind of Blue*, with Coltrane on tenor sax. From then until his sudden death of liver cancer at age forty-one, Coltrane made scores of recordings.

He really broke through to popular success in the early 1960s with two albums: *Giant Steps* and *My Favorite Things*. The latter contained his signature song by the same name. The next few years produced a sixteen-minute improvisation called "Chasin' the Trane," the *Coltrane Jazz* album, and *A Love Supreme*, which earned him two Grammy nominations, one each for jazz composition and performance. Many original works were in the pipeline when Coltrane died; they were published posthumously, earning him more Grammy nominations. In 1981 he won a Grammy for best jazz performance, as a soloist on the *Bye Bye Blackbird* album, and in 1992 he received the Grammy Lifetime Achievement Award, twenty-five years after it might have done him some good. His simple, in-the-ground stone is located in Garden of Sanctuary, section 60, block 1, range 46, plot Q, grave 49.

# GREENVALE

## ROSLYN CEMETERY
*Route 25A; (516) 626–1908*

Back in the 1800s, when the burial ground opened, it belonged to the local Presbyterian church. Now Roslyn's eighteen acres are nonsectarian. Among many locals residing here are three authors who in their time were famous, but today sleep in near-oblivion. **William Cullen Bryant** (1794–1878) was a household name in the nineteenth century, praised for his poems "Thanatopsis," "Green River," and "To a Waterfowl," among many others. His dark granite stele is in the rear of the grounds on the left side. **Frances Hodgson Burnett** (1849–1924; right, near entrance) was a famous and widely read author of children's classics, including *The Little Princess, Little Lord Fauntleroy* (a statue of him is nearby), and *The Secret Garden* (still a favorite of young girls). **Christopher Morley** (1890–1957; near cemetery entrance) founded the *Saturday Review of Literature* and was a literary man through and through—a novelist (his best-known work is *Kitty Foyle*), essayist, reviser of *Bartlett's Quotations*, and children's book author. In all, he authored fifty books of one kind or another. *Grounds open dawn to dusk daily.*

> **LUNCH BREAK**
>
> Nearby in Roslyn, **Mio** (1363 Old Northern Boulevard; 516–625–4223) offers osso buco, house-made, pasta and other Italian dishes at moderate prices. **Bryant & Cooper Steak House** (2 Middleneck Road, Roslyn; 516–627–7270) is a good choice for a substantial lunch or dinner.

# LAUREL HOLLOW

## MEMORIAL CEMETERY OF ST. JOHN'S CHURCH
*Route 25A; (516) 692–6748*

This old cemetery (opened 1862) is now nondenominational, though connected to St. John's Episcopal Church a few miles away in Cold Spring Harbor. The cemetery, delineated by a split-rail fence along the highway, is more of a hillside park, with half of the graves hidden in pine groves or banked by "fences" of rhododendrons. If possible, visit in the late spring, when the grounds are a fairyland of color. The Olmsted Brothers—the son (Frederick Jr.) and stepson (John Charles) of Frederick Law Olmsted, and also landscape architects—designed many of the grave sites, which explains the sense of seclusion and natural beauty that pervades the entire thirty-seven acres.

### LUNCH BREAK

**The Inn on the Harbor** (105 Harbor Road, Route 25A; 631–367–3166) is a good option for French-accented food with a view of the Sound.

When you enter the grounds, the office is on the right, facing St. Michael's Chapel, a pink building with a redbrick foundation to the left. Plot numbers are of little help, as the famous residents are so beautifully sequestered that you probably will need help from superintendent William Carew to find them.

St. John's is a sanctum sanctorum for a number of high achievers, with most of their final homes well shrouded by thickets of greenery. They include **Alfred P. Sloan** (1875–1966; section 1, plot 12), gifted auto mogul, longtime head of General Motors Corporation, and philanthropist. Also present and accounted for is **Barbara "Babe" Cushing Paley** (1915–1978; section 8, plot 14), one of the socially prominent Cushing sisters. She was a fashionista, society leader, and longtime confidante of Truman Capote—until he published chapters of *Answered Prayers*, a malicious memoir about his prominent friends. Beside her marker in a secluded hideaway is the matching slate stone of her husband, **William S. Paley** (1901–1990), the media mogul and founder and guiding light of Columbia Broadcasting System (CBS) for six decades. His gravestone is there, but he is not. Paley remarried after Babe died, and his third wife wanted him elsewhere. But the stone remains.

*Grounds open dawn to dusk daily. Office hours: 8:30 A.M.–2:30 P.M. Monday–Friday, 9:00 A.M.–noon Saturday. Restrooms.*

# OTTO HERMANN KAHN  1867–1934

orn and brought up in Mannheim, Germany, Kahn entered the banking business early. He was sent to the London office of the Berliner Deutsche Bank in 1888 and became a British citizen. Yet five years later he was in New York, where he spent the rest of his life. He joined and

became a partner in Kuhn, Loeb & Company, helped reorganize the American railroad system, supported the Allied war effort during World War I, and in 1917 took American citizenship.

Although he made his name and immense fortune as a whiz-bang financier, Kahn was also a celebrated patron of the arts, especially opera. Dubbed the "man of velvet and steel" for his arts-and-business interests, he helped finance the Metropolitan Opera and was its longtime president and board chairman. His interest in the arts went beyond music. He brought the Ballets Russes to the United States, was an art collector, and supported the Provincetown Players, the *Little Review*, poet Hart Crane, composer George Gershwin, and conductor Arturo Toscanini.

Kahn's elegant large, flat gravestone with unusual lettering is made of costly imported black slate and lies, with those of four other Kahn family members, in a secluded bower of rhododendrons, with a semicircle of fieldstone wall around one side. The Kahn address, to the right of, but totally hidden from, the similarly sheltered final quarters of Henry Stimson, is officially section 3, plot 18, on Valley Avenue.

## HOUSE CALL

After his New Jersey mansion was destroyed by fire, Kahn built **Oheka**, a 126-room estate on 500 acres in nearby Woodbury. It was the second-largest private residence in the country (after the Biltmore in North Carolina). Today Oheka's grounds have shrunk to twenty-three acres, and the estate is being converted to a spa. It is possible to have a look.

## HENRY LEWIS STIMSON   1867–1950

Stimson epitomized what used to be called, in a less stridently partisan age, The Establishment. These were public-spirited people, usually men, with Ivy League educations and business or legal experience, who believed that government service was a noble calling, regardless of whether a Democrat or Republican was at the helm.

From 1911 to 1945 Stimson served five U.S. presidents. Under William Howard Taft he was secretary of war; under Calvin Coolidge he was special envoy to Nicaragua (where he helped negotiate peace in a civil war) and then governor general of the Philippines; under Herbert Hoover he was secretary of

state (in which capacity he urged international opposition to Japan's invasion of Manchuria); and under Franklin Roosevelt and Harry Truman, he again was secretary of war.

Stimson's qualifications for such diverse jobs came from his Yale and Harvard education, his legal training, four years as U.S. attorney for the southern district of New York State, and his (unsuccessful) run for governor of New York. During World War II, as a chief advisor on atomic energy policy to Roosevelt, he argued against unconditional surrender of the Japanese, urging the president to allow them to retain their emperor. Roosevelt disagreed. Stimson later advised Truman to drop the atom bomb on Japanese cities, as a way to end the war quickly without brutal land fighting, yet he insisted on removing the city of Kyoto from the list of targets. Having visited prewar Japan, Stimson knew that Kyoto was Japan's cultural center and that destroying it would have alienated the Japanese people forever.

Stimson spent his last few years at work on controlling nuclear weapons. He can be found now in section B, plot 14, on Valley Avenue. In scenic and totally private surroundings, up a few steps from the road to a rhododendron-sheltered circle, his upright gray granite headstone is in the center. It proclaims him a "Lawyer, Soldier, Statesman." His wife, **Mabel Wellington White** (1866–1955), is with him.

# NORTH BABYLON

## NORTH BABYLON CEMETERY

*Corner of Sunrise Highway and Livingston Avenue; (631) 376–2349*

Essentially a minuscule (fourteen acres) burial ground for local residents since 1922, this nonsectarian retreat is easily walkable and home to about a hundred permanent residents. This makes it easy to find any one name among the various headstones. *Grounds open dawn to dusk daily.*

### LUNCH BREAK

The wood-paneled, wood-floored, rustic ambience of the **Argyle Grill & Tavern** (90 Deer Park Avenue, Babylon; 631–321–4900) makes for a congenial lunch stop. Steaks, chops, and seafood are all prime attractions. For tasty Italian fare, there's **Gemelli Ristorante** (175 East Main Street, Babylon; 631–321–6392).

# MARIO PUZO   1920–1999

This Italian-American son of immigrants wrote about the Mafia, yet claimed that he never met a gangster until his *Godfather* novel was published in 1969. To write the book, after he had written three others on diverse subjects (including a children's book), he had to research material and stories about la Cosa Nostra and other organized crime families for authenticity.

Up to that point, Puzo's freelance writing career consisted of articles for men's magazines, book reviews, and two novels, well-enough reviewed but with little financial reward. He made a living, supporting his wife and five children, but just barely. He wanted to write a best-selling commercial success. Little did he dream what a blockbuster it would be.

*The Godfather* and the movies based on it humanized (critics say romanticized) crime figures in a way that nothing had before. What made Puzo's *Godfather* saga so successful was his skill at dialogue and the strong, interesting characters. The themes of family ties, love, crime, and nostalgia for old-world values were so basic and strong that they translated beautifully to the screen in the three *Godfather* movies, although the books were tougher, with greater violence (hard to believe).

*The Godfather* and *The Godfather: Part II* received Oscars for best picture and best script (the work of Puzo and director Francis Ford Coppola), but they weren't appreciated by the Italian-American Civil Rights League, which held rallies to stop production until Coppola agreed to delete the words "Mafia" and "Costa Nostra" from the script. Frank Sinatra, who disliked the parallel between him and one particular character, accosted Puzo in a restaurant in 1972.

Although Puzo grew up living above railway yards, where his father was a railway trackman, he pretty much had a regular American life. During World War II he served in the U.S. Air Force in East Asia and Germany (not Italy). Postwar he enrolled at the New School for Social Research and Columbia University, studying literature and creative writing. In later years Puzo wrote other novels, including one about the mafiosos (*The Last Don*), but none had the impact of *The Godfather*. Puzo's final domicile is in the older part of the cemetery, section 1, block H, lot 14, southwest grave.

## YOUNGS MEMORIAL CEMETERY

*Cove Road; (516) 922–3200*

This tranquil hillside burial ground has been the private final quarters of the Thomas Youngs family since 1658. Scattered along the incline are white wooden crosses without names, the graves of "faithful slaves of the Youngs family." The last male in the Youngs line, **William Jones Youngs** (1851–1916), was Theodore Roosevelt's secretary during his governorship.

The area surrounding the cemetery forms the oldest National Audubon Society bird sanctuary in the country (see House Calls, page 136). At the top of the cemetery hill, enclosed by a cast-iron fence, is a graceful headstone with the presidential seal flanked by Greek pilasters, commemorating Theodore Roosevelt and his second wife, **Edith Kermit Carow Roosevelt** (1861–1948). Twenty-six steps lead up to TR's grave, symbolizing that he was the twenty-sixth president of the United States. A plaque on a boulder nearby bears these words: "Theodore Roosevelt said, Keep your eyes on the stars and keep your eyes on the ground." Graves of other Roosevelts trail back down the hill. Only two of Roosevelt's six children are buried on the premises: **Ethel Carow Roosevelt Derby** (1891–1977) and **Archibald Roosevelt** (1894–1979). *Grounds open dawn to dusk daily.*

## LUNCH BREAK

**Cafe Girasole** (1053 Oyster Bay Road; 516–624–8330), a cheerful trattoria, serves reliable Italian dishes; in warm weather you can dine outside. **Fiddleheads** (62 South Street; 516–922–2999), a self-styled American fish house and grill, is another excellent option, casual and creative.

## THEODORE ROOSEVELT   1858–1919

Few U.S. presidents have evoked the double image of toughness and good humor that Theodore Roosevelt did. Whether bear-hunting in the West (which led to a certain stuffed animal being dubbed a "teddy bear"), on safari in Africa, or exhorting his Rough Riders to *Charge!* at San Juan Hill during the Spanish-American War, Roosevelt (called TR or Teddy) expended energy and exuberance rarely seen in staid nineteenth-century public life. He

is a shining example of how a determined, aggressive, resolute person can surmount liabilities—in his case a high, squeaky voice, sickly physique, and lack of natural grace and athletic ability—and create a persona so colorful and dynamic that it is remembered by later generations.

Roosevelt rose from a member of the New York legislature (elected at age twenty-three) to mayor of New York City (at age twenty-eight), assistant secretary of the navy, a national hero (by age forty), governor, vice president, and then president at age forty-two (the youngest ever). This short, stocky man was an improbable leader, but a leader he was. His bravery in the Spanish-American War made him a lock for vice president on the Republican ticket, a job that Party leaders (who disdained him) thought would banish him to oblivion.

To their dismay, William McKinley was assassinated in the first year of his second term (1901), and Roosevelt roared into the White House. He used this "bully pulpit," as he called it, to fight the corruption of politics by big business. In record time he upheld the antitrust laws and punished violators, got the Pure Food and Drug Act passed, set aside 230 million acres for conservation— perhaps his greatest legacy—and created the U.S. Forest Service. He proved himself a populist, progressive president.

There were contradictions: Roosevelt fomented a revolt in Panama in order to assume control of the Panama Canal, built up the navy, and espoused the idea of an imperial presidency with his "speak softly but carry a big stick" philosophy. Yet in 1905 he won the Nobel Peace Prize for brokering peace

## HOUSE CALLS

Roosevelt's home, **Sagamore Hill** (20 Sagamore Hill, Oyster Bay; 516–922–4447), now a National Historic Site managed by the National Park Service, was the president's summer White House from 1901 to 1909. For anyone intrigued by the twenty-sixth president, his sprawling Queen Anne–Victorian home is a treasure house, chockablock with original furnishings and all kinds of artifacts, including a chair made of moose antlers, an elephant-foot wastebasket, and a bearskin rug given to Roosevelt by Admiral Perry. The trophy room with mounted specimens from Roosevelt's Wild West and Africa visits evokes the enthusiasms of the man as words alone cannot. Bordering Youngs Cemetery is the **Theodore Roosevelt Memorial Bird Sanctuary and Trailside Museum** (Cove Road; 516–922–3200), with nature trails amid eleven acres of woods. The museum contains bird exhibits and displays on Roosevelt and his role in the conservation movement.

between Japan and Russia. All the while he found time for family life, hunting, hiking, reading, and writing. He wrote forty books, the best known of which is *The Winning of the West*. In 1912, dissatisfied with President William Howard Taft (whom he had supported for a first term), Roosevelt ran again, this time on the Bull Moose ticket. This split the Republican vote and assured the election of Woodrow Wilson, the Democratic candidate.

Roosevelt's personal life was not without tragedy. His first wife, Alice Lee, died of Bright's disease in 1884, just after the birth of their only child, Alice, and eleven hours after Roosevelt's mother had died of typhoid fever. He was so devastated that he never mentioned his wife's name again and ignored his daughter for most of her childhood. Happiness came with his marriage to Edith Carow. Their five children romped happily in the White House during the Roosevelt presidency, but the youngest son, Quentin, the apple of TR's eye, was killed in World War I. Another son, Kermit, became an alcoholic and later committed suicide.

# REMSENBURG

## REMSENBURG CEMETERY
*Main Street at Basket Neck Lane*

On the main thoroughfare of a quiet, scenic south-shore village is the simple Remsenburg Community Church (Presbyterian), built in 1853. Behind the old-fashioned little church (more of a chapel really) is the cemetery, as small and countryish as an ancient burial ground. Only one headstone dominates—that of P. G. Wodehouse. The others are mostly small headstones in casual rows behind the church. There is no problem finding the star attraction. He rests at the end of the drive into the cemetery (to the right of the church), his grave set back but highly visible at the turn in the drive. *Grounds open dawn to dusk daily.*

## P. G. WODEHOUSE    1881–1975

Bertie Wooster would have loved the joke of it: A writer connected in the public mind with the starchiest of upper-class England ends up having his last word in a remote Long Island village. Actually, the

author of the fifteen Jeeves/Wooster novels seemed to have spent most of his adult life *outside* of England—by choice in France, New York, and Hollywood; by the Nazis in Belgium and Upper Silesia (now Poland).

Sir Pelham Grenville Wodehouse—or "Plum," as friends called him—began life in Guildford, Surrey, England, and studied at Dulwich College. Early on he discovered a talent for writing, especially light, comic works that were send-ups of the aristocracy. He knew whereof he wrote: He had his own deep noble roots, dating back to Anne Boleyn and earlier.

With enormous facility and a light touch, he wrote like an assembly line, turning out novels (around ninety), short stories, plays (collaborating on thirty or more), film scripts (twenty), and lyrics for musical comedies. What most kept him in royalties and still keeps him in the public eye were the stories about the gentleman's gentleman, the clever valet Reginald Jeeves, and his dim bulb of a master, Bertie Wooster. Wodehouse's twelve *Blandings Castle* novels are almost as engaging. Many songwriters, including Cole Porter and Ira Gershwin, thought he had enormous talent as a lyricist for Broadway musicals.

The Jeeves/Wooster books may seem interchangeable, but they are all entertaining, producing such lines as these: "It is not aunts that matter, but the courage that one brings to them" (from *The Mating Season*), and "I could see that, if not actually disgruntled, he was far from being gruntled" (from *The*

*Code of the Woosters*). Although his books were lighthearted, many writers consider Wodehouse the twentieth century's master of English prose style.

Much of his life was uneventful—until 1940 when he and his wife were living in the French seaside town of Le Touquet. The Nazis, by then in France, rounded him up and sent him to a series of internment camps. As carefree of world events as his books, Wodehouse was a naïf politically, so when the Nazis asked him to broadcast a series of radio talks, he did so without a thought about consequences. He treated internment like boarding school and wrote of it with the flippant tone of his other works. Naturally, in wartime the British were not amused. Wodehouse was denounced as a quisling in the press and Parliament, and friends like A. A. Milne deserted him.

No wonder when the war ended he did not return home, but settled in America and eventually became a U.S. citizen. He apologized for having been an "ass," and eventually his reputation was rehabilitated by writers who remained his friends. Shortly before his death Wodehouse was awarded a knighthood, though he was not well enough to return home for the ceremony. Throughout the postwar years he continued to write. He grew older, but Bertie remained the same, forever young.

Wodehouse's large gray granite headstone-monument is larger than life and a glowing memorial to the man, erected by his doting wife of sixty-one years. The stone is beautifully carved and bears the words "Sir Pelham Grenville Wodehouse, author, beloved husband of Ethel." In the four corners of the headstone are carved pictures of a quill pen, a knight in visor, an oil lamp, and a rosette, respectively. On top of the stone is an open carved book (in the same gray granite) with the titles of four of his books: *Jeeves, Blanding's Castle, Leave It to P. Smith,* and *Meet Mister Mulliner.*

# SAG HARBOR

## OAKLAND CEMETERY
*Jermain Avenue*

Organized in a city-block layout, this sleepy, cozily tatty old burial ground has graves from the early 1800s, a few even earlier. Well named for all the oak trees, the leafy, deeply shaded grounds are also home to hemlocks, cedars, rhododendrons, and shaggy forsythia. Moss has crowded out grass in many areas, and the paved road just inside the main entrance eventually gives way to a road of packed dirt and grass.

Oakland has a nautical air; it is home port to many seamen and whalers who were active during Sag Harbor's whaling days. Graves are marked by stone anchors, buoys, and ships. The most famous memorial, signposted from the entrance, is the four-sided Broken Mast Monument, which honors five whalers who "perished in actual encounter with the monsters of the deep" on Pacific and Atlantic ocean voyages, and Captain John Howell, who lost his life in the Pacific. The other sides are well carved with sea motifs. Seated atop its sturdy pedestal, on a coil of rope-shaped marble, is a marble column cut in the shape of a mast broken off at the top.

Just left of the monument is the small granite gravestone of **Captain David Hand** (1756–1840), buried in a row with his five wives. Hand, who five times was captured by the British during the Revolutionary War and escaped imprisonment in Halifax, was the model for James Fenimore Cooper's Natty Bumppo in *Leather-Stocking Tales*.

Also inhabiting these shadowy grounds is **William Gaddis** (1922–1998), a respected contemporary author whose best-known novels are *Carpenter's Gothic, JR, The Recognitions,* and *A Frolic of His Own.* Around the corner from George Balanchine's grave are those of **Alexandra Danilova** (1903–1997), a Russian-American dancer and choreographer, and ballerina **Tamara Glassberg** (?–2001). *Grounds open dawn to dusk daily.*

> **LUNCH BREAK**
>
> For ambience, good French-American food, and an extensive wine list, **American Hotel** (25 Main Street; 631–725–3535) is a village mainstay (built in 1846), with a handy central location. There are also eight guest rooms.

## NELSON ALGREN   1909–1981

This leftist, working-class writer is better known today for two films than for any of the eighteen books he wrote in a long, mercurial life. Nelson Algren was forty-one before he sold *The Man With the Golden Arm*, which won the first National Book Award for fiction in 1949 and became a Frank Sinatra film in 1955. *A Walk on the Wild Side*, published in 1956, was made into a movie in 1962 with Laurence Harvey.

Born in Detroit to parents of Swedish descent, Algren grew up in Chicago, earned a BA at the University of Illinois in 1931, and spent much of his writing life in the Windy City—when he wasn't traveling. After school, while looking for a newspaper job, he ended up in Texas, where he spent four months in jail for stealing a typewriter. Back in Chicago, he used his Texas experience in his first novel, *Somebody in Boots,* which sold all of 750 copies.

The next years produced more books, work on a WPA Illinois writers' project, a stint in World War II in the U.S. Army medical corps, awards, grants, lecture tours, and still more books. Essays, poems, short stories, and a column for the *Chicago Free Press* were interspersed with Algren teaching creative writing at universities in Iowa and Florida.

A self-destructive lifestyle of heavy drinking and gambling almost ended, at least once, in a suicide attempt that landed him in the hospital. Almost everything he wrote was about troubled people. Sometimes he laced his realistic style with humor, as in this observation: "Never eat at a place called Mom's. Never play cards with a man named Doc. And never lie down with a woman who's got more troubles than you."

Ironically, despite his talent and output, Algren may be best remembered as the sometime-lover of French feminist writer Simone de Beauvoir. He met her in Chicago when she was on a postwar lecture tour. She later wrote of their affair in her best-selling 1957 book *The Mandarins,* which she dedicated to him. They traveled in Latin America and to Istanbul, Athens, and Crete. Algren moved to Long Island in 1980 and died there a year later. Now, in such peaceful surroundings, he may have found the pastoral Eden that eluded him in life. His grave is near the entrance gate on the right.

## GEORGE BALANCHINE   1904–1983

Sometimes procrastination can have positive results. If young Balanchine had been on time with his application to the Imperial Academy, he might have become just another Russian navy officer instead of the greatest ballet choreographer of the twentieth century.

From studying ballet as a child in St. Petersburg at the Royal Imperial Ballet School, he went on to the Conservatory of Music to study piano and musical theory. In 1924, at age twenty, he and three other Russian dancers left Russia to tour Europe; in Paris they joined the Ballets Russes. A knee injury forced Balanchine to abandon dancing and become a ballet master. After Ballets Russes dissolved in 1929, he worked on several projects, choreographing, staging extravaganzas, making a dance film, and forming his own company.

The year 1934 was a turning point. Dance connoisseur and balletomane Lincoln Kirstein persuaded Balanchine to join him in founding the School of American Ballet. The next year they organized a touring company called the American Ballet. It was Kirstein's dream to establish a truly American ballet, and the timing was perfect. Their mutual efforts eventually led to the formation of the New York City Ballet. Kirstein saw his dream fulfilled; Balanchine had carte blanche to create as he desired.

With Balanchine's choreographic genius, his ability to blend classical as well as modern music with dance, and his development of a corps of superb American dancers, his company became the world's finest. It was known for its diversity and its ability to perform classics as well as imaginative contemporary ballets. Balanchine created ballets like *Firebird, Orpheus,* and *The Four Temperaments* to the music of modern composers. Igor Stravinsky was a special favorite. The son of a composer, Balanchine had a love of music as well as a great musical ear and musical knowledge. His full-length ballets—*The Nutcracker, Coppelia, A Midsummer Night's Dream*—were magical. His output was prodigious: In his long career he created 425 works.

It is less widely known that Balanchine also choreographed musical comedies (*On Your Toes, Cabin in the Sky, The Boys from Syracuse,* and *The Merry Widow* among them) and several movies (*Goldwyn Follies* and *Star Spangled Rhythm*). He had a talent for developing and bringing out the best in ballerinas, three of whom he married (Vera Zorina, Maria Tallchief, and Tanaquil LeClerq). Married a total of five times, Mr. B. (as his dancers called him) received endless awards and honors, including a knighthood from Queen Margrethe II of Denmark, the French Legion of Honor, and, shortly before his death, the Presidential Medal of Freedom. After the final curtain, Kirstein said, "Mr. B. is with Mozart, Tchaikovsky, and Stravinsky."

If you drive up the main cemetery road and turn right at the sign for the Broken Mast Monument, you will find the well-tended Balanchine rose-gray gravestone in the middle of the third block on the left. It is marked with a Russian cross and lyre and surrounded by low ewe shrubs, holly, rhododendron, hydrangea, a bank of cedar, and (in spring) tulips, hyacinths, and daffodils.

# ST. JAMES

## ST. JAMES EPISCOPAL CHURCHYARD
*490 North Country Road (Route 25A); (631) 584–5560*

Tucked behind an attractive clapboard Carpenter Gothic church, which dates back to 1853, is a small, walkable cemetery dotted with pines, weeping willows, azaleas, forsythias, and other shrubbery; small headstones; a few monuments; and funereal statuary. *Grounds open dawn to dusk daily. Office hours: 9:15 A.M.–4:00 P.M. Monday–Friday. Map; restrooms.*

### LUNCH BREAK

There is no shortage of good restaurants in this small town. For a casual lunch, try **Tic Toc Cafe** (410 Lake Avenue; 631–584–2074), which serves freshly made soups and panini, sandwiches, rolls, bagels, and brownies, all baked on the premises. If you crave something fancier, **Bella Vita City Grill** (430-16 North Country Road; 631–862–8060) has good Italian fare, with a super wine list. **Mauricio's** (645 Middle Country Road; 631–265–9228) offers well-priced northern Italian fare.

## STANFORD WHITE   1853–1906

There are so many great Beaux-Arts buildings by McKim, Mead & White throughout New York as it is, think how many more there might be if Stanford White hadn't died at age fifty-three, murdered by the jealous husband of one of the many young beauties the architect had seduced.

For most of his years, White led a charmed life. The son of a Shakespearean scholar (Richard Grant White), young Stanford was born into a privileged family and trained in the architectural firm of Henry Hobson Richardson. A superb draftsman, White founded his own firm in 1879 with two other architects, Charles Follen McKim and William Rutherford Mead. Before long,

because of talent and valuable social connections, McKim, Mead & White became the most sought-after architectural firm in the country.

White was the golden boy of the Gilded Age, when money flowed as freely as champagne. His firm designed libraries, apartments, offices, private clubs, municipal buildings, and the second Madison Square Garden (demolished 1925) and even restored Theodore Roosevelt's White House. Some of their landmarks are the Washington Square Arch, the First Bowery Savings Bank, Judson Memorial Church on Washington Square, and the Century Club, as well as summer homes for various Astors and Vanderbilts. Success came easily to the affable bon vivant White and he enjoyed it, with parties, good living, and plenty of good loving of an illicit variety.

The hidden side of White's life, unknown to his wife, was spent in a tower apartment he kept in Madison Square Garden. It was the scene of wild parties and orgies; a red velvet swing hung from the gold-leaf ceiling, and an array of young chorus girls visited. One of the girls was seventeen-year-old Evelyn Nesbit, a Pennsylvania beauty in the chorus line of the Floradora review. The story reads like a B movie (aspects of which are in *Ragtime, The Girl in the Red Velvet Swing,* and other films): After seducing Nesbit with drugged champagne, White had an affair with her. She later married Harry Thaw, a Pittsburgh railroad millionaire known as a bully with a ferocious temper. Nesbit confessed her affair with White to her new husband. In a rage, Thaw approached White at a supper club theater on the top of Madison Square Garden and shot him fatally three times in the head.

Thaw was tried twice and found not guilty by reason of temporary insanity (the first time that defense was used successfully). He divorced Nesbit, wrote a book, and lived to age seventy-six. Nesbit went on to work in vaudeville and died in a nursing home at age eighty-one.

White is still remembered for the beauty of his buildings, but there will always be an invisible asterisk by his name for the lifestyle that killed him well before his time, and in his own edifice. His grave, about halfway down the main drive (to the right side of the church; Allée, section G, plot 195/196), is easy to spot. It is marked by the tallest pine tree on the grounds, just to the left of the drive. A small angel statue near this point marks a grave labeled JEANETTE; straight back from that is a graceful gray granite stele with a shell-shaped top. It reads "Stanford White architect and his wife Bessie S. Smith." The intimate, secluded White section, consisting of his stone and several horizontal ones of relatives, is sheltered by boxwood and other plantings.

# SOUTHAMPTON

## SACRED HEARTS OF JESUS AND MARY CEMETERY
*County Road 39 (Route 27); (631) 283–0097*

Affiliated with Sacred Heart Church but located on the other side of town, this modest rural cemetery dates back to 1896. It is not even ten acres, which makes it a cinch to wander and look for graves of interest, most of which are small headstones or stones flush to the ground. The office at Sacred Heart Church does not reveal grave locations, but in a very short time you can find the final habitat of the most famous permanent resident. *Grounds open dawn to dusk daily. Office hours: 7:00 A.M.–3:00 P.M. Monday–Thursday.*

### LUNCH BREAK

**The Golden Pear** (99 Main Street; 631–283–8900) is fun for a late breakfast or casual lunch (good pasta and chili). For a top-notch dining experience, **Le Chef** (75 Job's Lane; 631–283–8581) is inventive and surprisingly *un*pricey for the quality.

## GARY COOPER  1901–1961

One of America's best-loved movie stars in the golden age of Hollywood, Cooper was most convincing when he seemed to be playing himself, with his shy, boyish smile, sly twinkle in the eye, wholesome good looks, lanky figure, and western voice. Some of this persona was real. He was born in Helena, Montana, but lived and studied for seven years in England. After a car accident at age thirteen, he returned to Montana to recuperate. While there he learned horseback-riding skills.

At twenty-three Cooper went further west, to Hollywood, where he planned to be a commercial artist or cartoonist. That didn't pan out, so he tried the movies as an extra. He soon had a role in a two-reeler and was offered a long-term contract at Paramount. Among his more than one hundred films, many were blockbusters: *The Lives of a Bengal Lancer, Beau Geste, Sergeant York* (for which he won an Oscar), and *High Noon* (another Oscar). Cooper received three other Oscar nominations, for *Mr. Deeds Goes to Town, The Pride of the Yankees,* and *For Whom the Bell Tolls.*

Off-screen Cooper wasn't quite the "aw shucks" naïf he often projected on-screen. Early in his career he had liaisons with actresses Clara Bow and Lupe Valez and socialite Dorothy Caldwell Taylor. After his marriage to another socialite, New Yorker Veronica Balfe, he had other affairs, including one with Grace Kelly and later with Patricia Neal. But he remained married and eventually converted to his wife's Catholic faith.

So why is westerner Cooper spending his postmortem retreat on Long Island? After his death and interment in California, his widow married a Southampton doctor and returned east. She had her first husband reinterred near where she lived and where she wanted eventually to be—at Sacred Heart. Things are often simpler than they initially seem.

## SOUTHAMPTON CEMETERY
*Route 27; (631) 283–3212*

This small rural cemetery was incorporated in 1885, but some graves are older. Considering its location in the fashionable Hamptons, it isn't surprising that the cemetery is the final home of at least two celebrated people. While their graves are unspecified, they are easy to find as you meander over the grounds. If the custodian is on the premises, he will help. *Grounds open dawn to dusk daily. Office hours: 8:00 A.M.–4:00 P.M. Monday–Friday. Map.*

### LUNCH BREAK

As an addition to the Southampton restaurants mentioned above (under Sacred Hearts Cemetery), consider the **Southampton Publick House** (40 Bowden Square; 631–283–2800). This rollicking microbrewery serves lunch and Sunday brunch, in addition to dinner.

# ROONE PINCKNEY ARLEDGE   1931–2002

*N*ot many network television executives are household names, but sports fans generally know the name Roone Arledge. He was the man who created the most successful sports program of all time—ABC's *Wide World of Sports*—as well as *NFL Monday Night Football* on ABC. He also introduced the techniques of slow motion and instant replay into televised games, put cameras in race cars, and added up-close-and-personal interviews of athletes. He was one of the first to use the Atlantic satellite to produce shows live from all over the world.

In short, Arledge revolutionized the way television covered sports. In 1994 *Sports Illustrated* ranked him third (behind Muhammad Ali and Michael Jordan) in a list of the forty people who had the greatest impact on sports in the previous forty years. After covering and producing ten Olympics, he was inducted into the Olympics Hall of Fame and later awarded the Medal of Olympics Order by the International Olympics Committee.

Although Arledge, as vice president and then president of ABC Sports, catapulted the network from so-so sports coverage into the leader in the field, he wasn't a Johnny-one-note. In 1977, restless and seeking more fields to conquer, he was promoted to president of ABC News while still heading ABC Sports. He used his innovative skills to revamp network news, turning it from the poorest network performer to the best.

For a man who began as a production assistant with the DuMont Television Network in 1952, Arledge rose rapidly. After a brief stint in the army, he joined NBC Television, becoming a director and producer, but left in 1960 for ABC. Then his many talents began to emerge. His successes at ABC brought him scores of medals and journalism awards. These included thirty-seven Emmy Awards (including the first-ever Emmy for lifetime achievement), four George Foster Peabody Awards, the John Jay Distinguished Achievement Award from Columbia University (his alma mater), and membership in the Academy of Television Arts and Sciences Hall of Fame. Suffering from cancer, Arledge retired in 1998.

# JACK DEMPSEY   1895–1983

*W*illiam Harrison "Jack" Dempsey was the ninth of eleven children in a family of Manassa, Colorado, sharecroppers. Jack was pulling his weight in the fields at age eight. No wonder boxing was a step up in the world. He left home at age sixteen, hopping freight cars like a hobo and boxing in the back rooms of frontier towns to pay his way, going by the moniker "Kid Blackie." Once Jack "Doc" Kearns began to manage him, he got better fights and began beating legitimate contenders. Dempsey became known as the "Manassa Mauler" for his rough, aggressive punching style.

His career hit a turning point in 1919, when he fought heavyweight champion Jess Willard, knocking him down seven times in the first round. Willard lasted less than three more rounds, and Dempsey was the new champ. Immensely popular with fans, he continued to win against other contenders until 1926, when he met his nemesis, Gene Tunney, in a classic match between a boxer (Tunney) and a puncher (Dempsey). Dempsey lost in a fifteen-round decision.

Two years later he had a return match at Chicago's Soldiers Field. In the seventh round Dempsey knocked Tunney down. Then came a defining moment in boxing history, one that fight experts talk about even today. Dempsey stood waiting to knock Tunney down again the minute he struggled to his feet. But a new rule forced Dempsey back into a corner. It took several seconds for him to get there, and only then did the referee *begin* the count. Fans believe that Tunney was down for fourteen seconds before getting up. In any case, Tunney went on to win by decision, and the "long count" became part of boxing history.

Dempsey retired then, more popular than ever, and opened a New York restaurant that was a Broadway favorite for thirty-nine years until it closed in 1974. Dempsey loved hanging out there, greeting fans, signing autographs, and posing for pictures. Another long count: It took seven years after his death for Dempsey to be inducted into the International Boxing Hall of Fame.

# WESTBURY

## HOLY ROOD CEMETERY
*111 Old County Road; (516) 334–7990*

A venerable (1851) rural Catholic cemetery on sixty-five acres, Holy Rood has its share of notable residents—bishops, congressmen, and the like. Most newsworthy are the following: **William "Bill" Casey** (1913–1987; section 7, range AA, plot 12), controversial chairman of the U.S. Securities and Exchange Commission and later head of the Central Intelligence Agency under president Ronald Reagan, in charge when the Iran-Contra scandal hit the fan; **Don Dunphy** (1908–1998; section 11, range J, plot 106), a great boxing broadcaster for forty years; **George Martin Skurla** (1921–2001; section 2, range D, plot 3), a well-known space engineer whose company, Grumman Aircraft Engineering Corporation, was involved in the first lunar landing; **John Paul "Jay" Monahan** (1956–1998; section 7, range J, plot 33), a legal analyst for NBC and husband of *Today Show* host Katie Couric; and **Dennis McCarthy** (?–1993; section 13, range CC, plot 127), one of the six people killed on the Long Island Railroad by a

> ## LUNCH BREAK
>
> Two lively Italian restaurants that serve lunch and dinner are nearby, both on the same road as the cemetery: **Café Spasso** (307 Old Country Road; 516–333–1718) and **Cafe Baci** (1636 Old Country Road; 516–832–8888).

deranged man, Colin Ferguson. McCarthy's death led his widow, Carolyn, to run for Congress (where she still serves) as an advocate for gun control. *Grounds open 8:00 A.M.–5:00 P.M. daily. Office hours: 9:00 A.M.–4:30 P.M. Monday–Friday, 9:00 A.M.–noon Saturday.*

## MARGARET "UNSINKABLE MOLLY" TOBIN BROWN
1867–1932

Surviving the RMS *Titanic* disaster was Margaret Brown's ticket to fame, though not one she would have sought. From then on, this wealthy Colorado matron became known as "Unsinkable Molly" Brown. She moved (with her husband) to New York, studied acting, and was prominent as a do-gooder and promoter of women's suffrage. Her life had much more significance than that single unsinkable episode.

Molly was born to an Irish immigrant family in Hannibal, Missouri, studied at the Carnegie Institute, and then moved with her brother to Leadville, Colorado, at the time of the late-nineteenth-century gold rush. Her brother worked in a mine, and she met and married James Brown, a mine superintendent who later struck it rich by inventing a method of reaching the gold at the bottom of mines.

Effervescent and upbeat, Molly put her husband's new wealth to useful purposes. Together, the Browns opened a soup kitchen for mining families, and Molly ran for Congress (even though women did not even have the vote), helped organize one of the first juvenile courts in the United States, and became a prominent philanthropist. In 1932 she received the French Legion of Honor for her efforts in helping others evacuate the *Titanic,* her work with miners, and other worthy causes. A 1964 movie starring Debbie Reynolds— *The Unsinkable Molly Brown*—was based on her life. The real Molly rests posthumously from all her labors in section STB (range QUE, plot 2) along with her husband, **James Joseph Brown** (1855–1922).

# CHAPTER 6

# Westchester

$M$ any of the Empire State's most prominent twentieth-century citizens lived and died in Westchester County. The county is also the final home of many famous non–New Yorkers, distinguished people in a variety of fields—Judy Garland and Sergei Rachmaninoff come quickly to mind—who for one reason or another have ended up spending eternity in the rolling hills and quiet valleys just north of Manhattan. Here are their last known addresses.

# BEDFORD

## SAINT MATTHEW'S CHURCHYARD

*382 Cantitoe Street (Route 22); (914) 234–9636*

The stately columned Saint Matthew Episcopal Church, with its imposing belfry, will be 200 years old in 2010. It wears its age well, as does the peaceful graveyard in the rear and to the left of the church. The church office is located in a building to the rear of the church on the right side of the driveway, which is to the right of the church. You can enter the graveyard on foot through the wooden gate behind the church, or you can drive around the circle where the office is located to a gate at the far end of the chain-wire-enclosed cemetery, near which you may park your car.

Some graves may predate the official 1810 opening of this burial ground, which sprawls over six acres of grassy flat land. Shaded by towering pines and other vintage trees, the many upright headstones are punctuated by a variety of shrubs.

Among the august perpetual inhabitants are twenty-three descendants of John Jay's ubiquitous family. Also here are **Walter Tower Rosen** (1875–1951; section K8), a New York lawyer and investment banker, and his

## LUNCH BREAK

**Bistro Twenty-Two** (391 Old Post Road; 914–234–7333) is a longtime favorite for its creative French food and comfortable setting. Lunch is available Thursday through Saturday; dinner, Monday through Saturday.

musician wife, **Lucie Bigelow Dodge Rosen** (1890–1968; same section). They built Caramoor, a magnificent estate nearby that now serves as the Caramoor Center for Music and the Arts, scene of the Caramoor Music Festival every summer. *Churchyard grounds open dawn to dusk daily. Office hours: 9:00 A.M.–4:00 P.M. Monday–Friday. Restrooms.*

## JOSEPH L. MANKIEWICZ    1909–1993

Still one of the most iconic movies ever made, *All About Eve* won all kinds of awards when it appeared in 1950, not least of which were the Oscars for writer and director that went to Joe Mankiewicz. In fact, he notched a record, still unmatched, for being the only person to win two Oscars two years in a row. (His previous two were for *A Letter to Three Wives*). In all, this talented Pennsylvanian, born in Wilkes-Barre, directed twenty films in twenty-six years, beginning with *Dragonwyck* in 1946. Not bad for a man who began his association with films as a translator of movie titles, working for Paramount Pictures in Berlin.

JOSEPH L. MANKIEWICZ
FEBRUARY 11, 1909
FEBRUARY 5, 1993

TIME is finite! It's your TIME now
no longer just God's TIME – your TIME
make it good to live in!        JLM

Mankiewicz loved using flashbacks in his films, and there wasn't a genre he wouldn't tackle: westerns, Shakespeare, epics, musicals, romances. His titles ranged from *The Keys of the Kingdom* to *Guys and Dolls*, *The Barefoot Contessa*, and *The Honey Pot*. Skilled as his directing was, his real forte was as a screenwriter, especially writing dialogue, often of the clever, sophisticated kind. Bette Davis's famous line in *All About Eve*—"Fasten your seatbelts, it's going to be a bumpy night!"—is still quoted today.

Mankiewicz's flecked pink granite headstone, S99, lies at the far rear of the graveyard, just in front of the stone wall and the all-encompassing chain fence. In its own little fieldstone-bordered plot, with a small andromeda bush at each end, the stone has a black plaque at its base, with bronze lettering that says, in part, "TIME is finite! Make it good to live in!" A man of his word.

# BRONXVILLE

## CHRIST CHURCH BRONXVILLE

*17 Sagamore Road; (914) 337–3544; www.christchurchbronxville.com*

This beautiful Episcopal church, built in 1926, is located approximately 14 miles north of Manhattan—less than a half hour by train on Metro North's Harlem line. The station is 1 block from the church in the village of Bronxville. The church, designed by architect Bertram Grosvenor Goodhue in the English country Gothic style, has a beautiful interior, with vaulted ceilings and stained-glass windows. The columbarium is a small space in a garden off the apex of Kensington and Sagamore Roads. *Grounds open dawn to dusk daily.*

> ### LUNCH BREAK
>
> Bronxville has a number of highly recommendable restaurants. A local lunch favorite, the trendy **Scarborough Fair** (65 Pondfield Road; 914–337–2735), offers very good food.

## FORD FRICK   1895–1978

*I*t isn't everyone who has his life's work savaged by an asterisk. But to some die-hard baseball fans, the asterisk that Frick, as Major League Baseball commissioner, attached to Roger Maris's record-breaking sixty-one home-run season will forever smudge Frick's own name. The facts are these: Babe

Ruth had set baseball's home-run record of sixty in 1927, a season that spanned 154 games. The record seemed destined to last forever—and it did stand until 1961, when Maris broke it. But the baseball season had been expanded to 162 games, thus presumably making the record easier to break. Frick decreed that Ruth's record could legitimately be broken only within the confines of 154 games, hence the asterisk. It didn't help his reputation that he had been a close friend of, golf and bridge partner of, and ghostwriter for Babe Ruth. Not exactly an impartial arbiter, critics said.

Aside from that, Frick had an exemplary career that began as a sports-writer, first in his native Indiana, then in Colorado, and finally in New York. One of his innovations was the nightly sports report on WOR radio. In 1934 he became public relations director for baseball's National League and president of the league the next year.

Early on, Frick endorsed the idea of a baseball museum and urged that it include a Hall of Fame. (This came to pass in 1939 in Cooperstown, New York.) Other accomplishments included saving three baseball franchises from bankruptcy, disciplining unruly characters like Dizzy Dean and Leo Durocher, and supporting the Brooklyn Dodgers in 1947 when they broke the color line by hiring Jackie Robinson. At the time Frick said, "The National League will go down the line with Robinson and I don't care if it wrecks the league for five years."

Frick shepherded the National League until 1951, when he was chosen commissioner of Major League Baseball, a job he held for fourteen years. During that time he helped stabilize baseball, espoused night games and team expansion, and helped popularize the sport in many other countries. In 1970 his baseball career was capped by his election to the Baseball Hall of Fame. "I'm just a lucky fan," Frick said near the end of his career. His business and managerial skills proved that he was considerably more than that. Look for him outside in niche 177 of the columbarium, in the area around the sculpture.

# HARTSDALE

## FERNCLIFF CEMETERY
*281 Secor Road; (914) 693–4700*

When Ferncliff's main mausoleum opened in 1927, people were dying to get in. A mausoleum on such a large scale was rather a new concept in the United

States and considered very fashionable by many New Yorkers. Imagine—cremated remains tucked into marble vaults stacked aisle after aisle, or placed in private rooms, inside a massive new building. The marble interior, as restful as an upscale hotel lobby (but a lot quieter), is furnished with Oriental rugs, stained-glass windows, soothing taped music, and bathrooms as clean, neat, and orderly as the entire premises.

Through the years, Ferncliff's popularity led to the addition of a second large mausoleum (called the Shrine of Memories) on the property's sixty-six acres. Now some 30,000 people are buried on the grounds, though *buried* is a matter of speech, for many are entombed indoors in the two mausoleums. Outdoors, scores of graves are arranged in orderly rows in carefully delineated sections throughout the vast property.

> ## LUNCH BREAK
>
> At **Cafe Meze** (20 North Central Avenue; 914–428–2400) sandwiches and burgers are available, but the cafe's real tour de force is its imaginative Mediterranean menu, with many excellent dishes.

Most of the grave sites in the fresh air bear small bronze markers of similar size and design, set flush to the ground (making them a challenge to find). The map of the grounds is also difficult to decipher, so we have noted particular sections where these personalities are at rest—Rosewood, Maplewood, Pinewood, and the like.

In addition to the biggest names, whose obits are cited below, you will find scores of other terrestrial tenants at Ferncliff. These include **Harold Arlen** (1905–1986; Hickory, grave 1666), composer of "Over the Rainbow," "Stormy Weather," "That Old Black Magic," and other popular songs we still hum today; **Charles** (1874–1948; St. Paul, plot 309) and **Mary Beard** (1876–1958; same plot), husband and wife historians and coauthors of the respected *The Story of Civilization* series and other books; and **Sherman Billingsley** (1900–1966; unit 8, alcove Y, crypt 74), proprietor of New York's snooty Stork Club, which began as a speakeasy during Prohibition and evolved into a jet-set hangout in the 1930s and 40s. Also here is **Peaches Browning** (1910–1956; unit 7, alcove MM, crypt 35), a tabloid headliner (who can resist the name "Peaches"?) in the late 1920s and 30s for marrying (at age fifteen) a fifty-one-year-old "sugar daddy" and later three others like him. Her real name was more mundane: Frances Heenan.

**Michel Fokine** (1880–1942; Shrine of Memories, unit 1, tier 1, crypt 12), the world-famous Russian ballet choreographer, is at Ferncliff. So are noted psychiatrist **Karen Horney** (1885–1952; St. Paul, plot 355), one of the founders of the American Institute for Psychoanalysis and author of *The Neurotic Personality of Our Time* and other books; **Sigmund Romberg** (1887–1951; main mausoleum, section B-C-1, niche 5), the Hungarian-born composer and orchestra leader best known for his shows *The Desert Song, Blossom Time,* and *New Moon*; and **Bernard "Toots" Shor** (1903–1977; Hillcrest A, grave 1204), owner of a popular Manhattan watering hole, whose shtick was to insult his guests, including pals like Frank Sinatra and various sports figures.

**Elsa Maxwell** (1883–1963; Rosewood 2, grave 1132), a columnist and songwriter, famous primarily as a professional party-giver for fifty years, is here, as is **Ed Sullivan** (1901–1974; main mausoleum, unit 8, tier G, crypt 122), a newspaperman and the host of early television's most popular variety show. Classical composer **Bela Bartok** (1881–1945; St. Peter, grave 470) was here and gone (returned to his native Hungary); what is left is a memorial tribute. *Grounds open during office hours: 9:00 A.M.–4:00 P.M. daily; on major holidays grounds and office close at 1:30 P.M. Office is in the main mausoleum inside gate #1. Map; restrooms.*


## JAMES ARTHUR BALDWIN  1924–1987

A child of Harlem, whose father was unknown and whose stepfather was an evangelical minister, James Baldwin grew up feeling ugly and unloved, intimidated by the fire-and-brimstone preacher. Shy and small for his age, with an awkward gait and large "bug" eyes, Baldwin had a difficult childhood, alleviated by his mother's unswerving love and support and the encouragement of several teachers who recognized how bright he was. One of them taught him French (which would become his second language), and another introduced him to the world of books, research, and reading at the New York Public Library.

A teenage Pentecostal preacher, young Baldwin studied at the prestigious De Witt Clinton High School, where he became lifelong friends with classmate Richard Avedon. Later painter Beauford Delaney befriended Baldwin and became his role model and mentor. In 1944 Baldwin met Richard Wright, who encouraged his writing and secured a fellowship for him from *Harpers*. Essays, criticism, and short stories followed, but Baldwin wanted to leave the United States, so in 1948 he made his first trip to Paris, courtesy of a Rosewald Foundation Fellowship. Subsequently, he lived much of his adult life abroad, in France and Switzerland, finding them safer havens from racial and sexual prejudice than his native America.

As a novelist and essayist, Baldwin wrote with sophistication and controlled anger, in exquisite prose, about the African-American experience. His output was large, and what he wrote generally drew accolades from literary critics. His most praised books are *The Fire Next Time, Go Tell It on the Mountain, Notes of a Native Son,* and *Giovanni's Room.* He also had two plays produced on Broadway—*The Amen Corner* and *Blues for Mr. Charlie.* Baldwin won a Guggenheim Fellowship, a Ford Foundation Grant-in-Aid, many honorary doctorates, the French Legion of Honor, and other awards.

In 1957 he made his first trip to the American South to research his family roots. After observing the early glimmers of the civil rights struggle, he wrote about it in a 1961 book of essays, *Nobody Knows My Name.* He continued his interest in civil rights causes and became America's best-known African-American intellectual. Fearful for his own safety in late 1970—after the assassinations of Martin Luther King Jr., Medgar Evers, and Malcolm X—Baldwin went abroad again, this time for good. He lived and worked in Provence, in an old farmhouse in Saint-Paul-de-Vence, a village in the hills above the Riviera. There he wrote two more novels, *If Beale Street Could Talk* and *Just Above My Head* (his last); essays; and a screenplay about Malcolm X, *One Day When I Was Lost,* which was never produced. He also spent about eight years living and writing in Istanbul, Turkey, where he wrote *Another Country.*

Baldwin died of cancer of the esophagus while working on a biography of Martin Luther King Jr. His funeral at the Cathedral of St. John the Divine was attended by several thousand of his many literary, theatrical, and civil rights friends, black and white, who recognized him as one of the twentieth century's important writers and thinkers. His grave marker can be found outdoors in the Hillcrest section, grave 1203 (between the Shrine of Memories and main mausoleum).

## ADOLPH CAESAR   1933–1986

*H*ardly a household name, Adolph Caesar's life is a sad tale of fame that came too late. A graduate of George Washington High School in Harlem, young Caesar enlisted in the U.S. Navy and became a chief petty officer. He remained in the navy until he was eligible for early retirement. Still young enough at age thirty-seven for a second career, he enrolled in drama studies at New York University. In 1970 he joined the Negro Ensemble Company and appeared in *The Triumph,* his first TV movie. Some plum roles followed, with Caesar working in the New York Shakespeare Festival, the Lincoln Center Repertory Company, and the Center Theater Group at the Mark Taper Forum in Los Angeles.

A stunning and dominating performance as the vicious army sergeant Vernon C. Waters in the Negro Ensemble Company's production of *A Soldier's Story* brought Caesar an Obie and a New York Drama Desk Award. A reprise of the same role in the 1984 movie resulted in an Oscar nomination for best supporting actor. (The film turned out to be a breakthrough for actor Denzel Washington as well.) More film and television work for Caesar followed, including *The Color Purple* and his final movie, *Club Paradise.* Caesar died of a heart attack before he could enjoy his newly earned fame, however. He was fifty-three years old. His grave is number 0238 in the Beechwood section, near Secor Road.

## JOAN CRAWFORD   1906–1977

*J*oan Crawford was born Lucille LeSeuer on the wrong side of the tracks in San Antonio, Texas. In a long career she migrated from modest beginnings as a Broadway dancer to starring roles in dozens of dramatic films (eighty-one in all), beginning in 1925 with *Pretty Lady* and *Sally, Irene and Mary.* In her golden decade (1931–1941), Crawford made many classics— *Rain, Grand Hotel, The Women,* and *A Woman's Face* among them—and was considered the queen of what were called "tearjerkers" or "four-handkerchief movies." In 1945 *Mildred Pierce* won her a Best Actress Oscar.

As Crawford's career wound down, she made *Whatever Happened to Baby Jane?* with Bette Davis in 1962. The hit salvaged both of their careers and fed gossip about their mutual animosity, a feud based partly on a much earlier tug-of-war over actor Franchot Tone, whom Crawford married.

Crawford lived to the hilt her public life as the epitome of Hollywood movie star glamour. Her private life was something else, with two miscarriages, four adopted children, four marriages (including one to Douglas Fairbanks Jr.), and several affairs (including a long off-and-on relationship with Clark Gable). Crawford's private role as a mother was reported by her daughter Christina in a bitter exposé titled *Mommy Dearest.* Crawford's final address is a spacious private alcove behind bronze gates in the main mausoleum (unit 8, alcove E, crypt 42). The large pink-marble wall vault gives the word STEELE top billing; below is her name and that of her last husband, former Pepsi board chairman **Alfred M. Steele** (1900–1959). Though the birth date on Crawford's vault is 1908, experts believe that 1906 is accurate. Ever the actress, fudging her age, even unto death.

## JUDY GARLAND    1922–1969

The Judy Garland fan club is alive and well, still leaving fresh flowers at her simple beige-marble wall crypt. In fact, a good way to find her crypt (upstairs from Joan Crawford's, at the other end of the same mausoleum; unit 9, alcove HH, crypt 31) is to look for the fresh bouquets.

The story of the transformation of little Frances Gumm into a Hollywood legend is a familiar one. Old-timers remember her as Mickey Rooney's girlfriend in the Andy Hardy series, but *The Wizard of Oz* brought her eternal stardom, and *A Star Is Born* proved she could really act, a fact punctuated by her role in *Judgment at Nuremberg*. Her tremulous voice, bittersweet smile, and soulful brown eyes gave her a poignancy that fans adored.

An endless series of concert tours, while successful, were a constant drain on her energy and her voice, which finally gave out by the late 1960s. Still, the sad saga of her personal life—the bouts with alcohol and drugs, the five failed marriages, and her death from a barbiturate overdose—merely added to the Garland mystique, making her larger than life, or death. Even today the name Judy evokes thoughts of only one star, proof of her eternal popularity. Her performances, via films and television concerts, go on and on, over the rainbow.

## MOSS HART    1904–1961

A chance pairing turned this minor-league playwright, librettist, sometime-actor, and theatrical wannabe into one of Broadway's biggest names for decades in the mid-twentieth century. A series of flops (the first of which cost Hart his job and his producer $45,000) didn't deter this ambitious and talented man. In 1929 he conceived a comedy, *Once in a Lifetime*, and showed it to producer Sam Harris. Harris liked it but said he would produce it only if Hart agreed to have a more seasoned playwright, George S. Kaufman, help with a rewrite.

Thus the team of Kaufman and Hart was born. It was a collaboration that was, if not made in heaven, meant to flourish on Broadway. Their styles jibed, and the two went on to such comic successes as *Merrily We Roll Along, You Can't Take It With You* (which won a Pulitzer Prize), *The Fabulous Invalid, I'd Rather Be Right,* and *The Man Who Came to Dinner.* Most of these have endured and are still performed from time to time. *New York Times* theater critic Brooks Atkinson said of the dynamic duo that they "gave Broadway not only wit and skill but also integrity . . . They presided over an era and pioneered the withering, iconoclastic play that made routine comedy obsolete."

Nothing lasts forever, and in 1940 the team split. Hart continued to write both comedy and serious works for Broadway (*Lady in the Dark* in 1941) and Hollywood (his screenplays included *Winged Victory, Gentleman's Agreement,* and *A Star Is Born*) and to direct. In 1956 he capped a fabulous career by directing *My Fair Lady*, for which he won a Tony Award. Look for his wall crypt upstairs in the main mausoleum (alcove EE-FF, column D, niche 4), just below that of Ed Sullivan.

## JEROME KERN   1885–1945

A New Yorker born, bred, and for eternity, Jerome Kern detoured briefly as a youth of nineteen to study operettas and the musical theater in London. There he met Eva Leale, who became his wife in 1910 and was with him unto his death. In a career that spanned forty years, Kern wrote almost 700 songs for 117 Broadway musicals and movies. Early on, he had as many as seven or eight Broadway shows running at the same time, a megaaccomplishment. Major lyricists for his music were Guy Bolton, P. G. Wodehouse, Ira Gershwin, Otto Harbach, and Oscar Hammerstein II.

A turning point in an already successful career came in 1925, when Kern worked with Harbach and Hammerstein on a show called *Sunny*. From then on Kern teamed up with both men, but most often with Hammerstein. In 1927 they worked together on *Show Boat*, producing what many believe to be their masterpiece, with "Can't Help Lovin' That Man," "Make Believe," and "Old Man River" among the songs that have lasted to this day.

Kern worked with Harbach on *Roberta*, creating such memorable music as "I Won't Dance," "Lovely to Look At," "Smoke Gets in Your Eyes," and "Yesterdays." In 1934 Kern went to Hollywood, and two years later he won an Oscar for "The Way You Look Tonight," sung by Fred Astaire in the movie *Swing Time*.

In 1941 Kern and Hammerstein wrote "The Last Time I Saw Paris," a heartrending tribute just after the French capital had fallen to the Nazis. Kern's dark green marble wall crypt, with a miniature fountain beneath it, is unique in a wall of white marble on the main floor of the main mausoleum (section 4, alcove 3). His wife, **Eva Leale Kern** (1891–1959), is with him.

## THELONIOUS MONK   1917–1982

The fact that full frontal fame didn't come to this pianist and jazz composer until he was in his early forties may have been a good thing. He was mature enough to handle it, unlike some musicians who peak early and fizzle fast. While he came from the jazz tradition of Willie "The Lion" Smith, Duke Ellington, and other mainstream jazz pianists, Monk was never easy to categorize. He played with Dizzy Gillespie and Charlie Parker, but he wasn't totally in their bebop mode.

Many jazz critics consider Monk a true original, for his witty style and musical clarity, all the more remarkable because he was mostly self-taught. Some of his dissonant compositions (called weird at one time) are considered masterpieces—the likes of "Round Midnight," "Blue Monk," and "Bemsha Swing."

Monk made his first recordings with Coleman Hawkins in the mid-1940s, but it took another twenty years for wider recognition. By then he was riffing in clubs—the Five Spot in New York was his steady base for years—concerts, international festivals, and finally with big orchestras at Philharmonic Hall and Carnegie Hall. A marvelous run for a syncopating artist. You will find Monk outdoors in the Hillcrest I section, grave 405, beneath a bronze marker (resembling wood) with flowers etched into it. His wife, **Barbara E. Monk** (1953–1984), is there, too.

## BASIL RATHBONE   1892–1967

For fans of old movies, Basil Rathbone is the eternal Sherlock Holmes, but the South African–born British actor began his career as a leading man, traveling through England in a repertory company. Then came World War I, during which he served in the British army and received the Military Cross. By the time talking pictures arrived, Rathbone was in Hollywood, where his beautifully resonant voice and perfect diction made him a natural for the new medium. His darkly handsome looks soon had him cast as a villain, a type he played endlessly and with gusto in all kinds of delightfully wicked roles, including those in *Captain Blood, If I Were King, David Copperfield, Anna Karenina, The Last Days of Pompeii,* and *A Tale of Two Cities.*

His first Sherlock Holmes role, in *The Hound of the Baskervilles* (1939), proved so popular that thirteen other Holmes films followed. *The Adventures of Sherlock Holmes,* a radio series, was also a hit for six years. Holmes gave Rathbone the steady meal ticket all actors crave, but he relished other roles as well. All in all, he made some 150 films (69 of which had nothing to do with Mr. Holmes), working almost to the end of his life.

He alternated movies with live theater (which he loved), Shakespeare readings on college campuses, and recordings of classic plays. Not so elementary, my dear Rathbone. You will spot his wall vault in the Shrine of Memories mausoleum (top row, unit 1, tier K, crypt 117). Michel Fokine is nearby, at a lower level.

## PAUL ROBESON   1898–1976

"The artist must elect to fight for freedom or slavery. I have made my choice. I had no alternative." So says the bronze marker of this proud man. A powerful singer, actor, and political activist, Robeson lived— and died—in controversy. Born in Princeton, New Jersey, the son of a former slave, he inherited from his Presbyterian minister father a stentorian baritone, sense of dignity, and devotion to social justice. The latter defined his entire life.

PAUL ROBESON
APRIL 9, 1898     JAN. 23, 1976
"THE ARTIST MUST ELECT TO FIGHT
FOR FREEDOM OR SLAVERY. I
HAVE MADE MY CHOICE. I HAD
NO ALTERNATIVE"

Robeson might have had it easy; he was a star football player and Phi Beta Kappa at Rutgers, earned a law degree at Columbia, and was a successful Broadway actor, concert singer, scholar, and ladies' man. He scored major Broadway successes in *Emperor Jones, Othello,* and *Show Boat.* But his left-wing politics during the 1930s, when he was an apologist for the Soviet Union, did him in professionally. He was blacklisted and persecuted by the FBI, which tapped his phone. Pride and a certain arrogance kept him from recanting earlier idealistic beliefs. He suffered in other ways: from depression and several suicide attempts. Robeson's long, sad life ended in loneliness and despair. His grave can be found in Hillcrest A, grave 1511, next to the walk between Hillcrest and Knollwood. His wife, **Essie Goode Robeson** (1896–1965), has a marker next to his.

## PRESTON STURGES   1898–1959

oll the credits: *Sullivan's Travels, The Great McGinty, The Lady Eve, Christmas in July, Hail the Conquering Hero, The Palm Beach Story, The Miracle of Morgan's Creek, The Sin of Harold Diddlebock, Unfaithfully Yours.* Fans of these and other films by this writer-director may be disappointed at the minimalist final tribute to his memory at Ferncliff. The bronze Sturges marker, with name and dates only, located in front of the Shrine of Memories mausoleum inside the second hedge in the Maplewood 4 garden section (grave 74), was half-covered by crabgrass the last time I visited. But Sturges's movies live on as testament to his originality, farcical style, satire, and madcap fun.

Born in Chicago, Sturges lived in France as a child, served with the Signal Corps of the U.S. Army in World War I, spent six years in his mother's cosmetic business (where he invented kiss-proof lipstick—how Sturgesian!), worked briefly on Broadway, and started writing plays. But his real career and life's work as a screenwriter-director began when he headed to Hollywood in 1932.

Sturges defined himself as a humorist working in movies, and most of his best work has a wry, witty slant. He was at his best when he could control everything—production, direction, and writing—giving his best films his distinctive, slightly skewed point of view. The last reel: While working on his autobiography, *The Events Leading Up to My Death,* at New York's Algonquin Hotel, he had a fatal heart attack. He would have loved the irony. In fact, it might have been his next movie.

## MALCOLM X, AKA EL-HAJJ MALIK EL-SHABAZZ  1925–1965

*M*alcolm X, born Malcolm Little, had a life fraught with discord, from its early beginnings in Omaha, Nebraska. His father, Earl, outspoken in the cause of racial justice, was savagely killed by white bigots when Malcolm was six years old. In 1946 Malcolm was jailed for burglary; while in prison he became a member of the Nation of Islam. This period led to his belief that for blacks to survive, they couldn't depend on whites.

In the *Autobiography of Malcolm X*, which he related to Alex Haley, he describes his conversion from street hood to follower of Elijah Muhammed and the Black Muslim movement. As a minister in the Nation of Islam, Malcolm took X as his last name, a common practice of the group who rejected their slave names. (X signified a lack of knowledge of their real African names.)

In the 1960s, as Martin Luther King Jr. was preaching integration, Malcolm X promoted separatism for African Americans, with red-hot rhetoric that inflamed blacks and terrified whites. Handsome, outspoken, and charismatic, he eventually aroused the envy of some of his fellow Muslims.

Then came a trip to Mecca and Africa in 1964. It was an eye-opener to discover that people of many colors and beliefs *could* live together. At thirty-nine he was still a work in progress, returning to the United States with a new perspective, a new name (El-Hajj Malik El-Shabazz), a new religion (orthodox Islam), and a desire to share the African-American experience with receptive whites. At the same time he became highly critical of the Nation of Islam leaders, questioning Elijah Muhammed's ethical and fiscal probity. The war of words between the two sides escalated, and on February 19, 1965, Malcolm was shot to death by three hit men at the Audubon Ballroom in Harlem just before his fortieth birthday. Although the killers were caught, convicted, and sentenced to life imprisonment, they denied that Elijah Muhammed had a part in the crime.

Many believe that had Malcolm lived, he would have reinvented himself one more time. With his intelligence and articulateness, there was the potential for better, more constructive things ahead. They were not to be. He can now be found outdoors near two dogwood trees in Pinewood B, grave 150, to the rear right of the Shrine of Memories, next to his wife, **Betty El-Shabazz** (1936–1997).

## WHITNEY M. YOUNG JR.   1921–1971

To participants in the civil rights movement, Whitney Young is a revered name. Although lacking the verbal eloquence of a Martin Luther King and the flamboyance of a Jesse Jackson, his leadership (as executive director) of the National Urban League was so effective that in just four years he expanded the organization from 38 employees to 1,600 and its annual budget from $325,000 to $6.1 million. In his ten-year tenure, the organization grew to more than one hundred affiliates in thirty-plus states.

Young's ability to communicate with white business leaders (to create job opportunities through education for minorities) turned a somewhat passive organization into a dynamic force for social justice—and jobs. He was one of the organizers of the 1963 March on Washington and an advisor to three U.S. presidents. Lyndon Johnson capped Young's successes by awarding him the Medal of Freedom, the country's highest civilian honor.

Though he grew up in a segregated society, Young was well prepared for his work with the NUL, where he dealt with America's corporate CEOs on a first-name basis. The son of an educator at the Lincoln Institute of Kentucky, in Simpsonville, Young graduated from Kentucky State College, earned a master's degree at the University of Minnesota, and joined the faculty of the School of Social Work at the University of Nebraska. During the 1950s he taught at Creighton University, became dean of social work at Atlanta University, and served as state president of the Georgia NAACP. A Rockefeller Foundation grant gave him a postgraduate year at Harvard and led to his appointment as executive director of the National Urban League in 1961. While there, he produced two books, *To Be Equal* and *Beyond Racism*.

Young lived for many years in New Rochelle with his wife, Margaret, and two daughters. Forceful, persuasive, personable, and knowledgeable, he seemingly had years of accomplishments ahead of him. But in 1971, while at a conference in Lagos, Nigeria, he went for a swim and drowned, possibly because of strong currents and undertow. Young's grave site (Knollwood Garden 2, plot C, grave 5) notes his convictions: "Every man is our brother and every man's burden our own. Where poverty exists, all are poorer; where hate flourishes, all are corrupted; where injustice reigns, all are unequal."

# HAWTHORNE

## CEMETERY OF GATE OF HEAVEN

*10 West Stevens Avenue; (914) 769–3672*

When this 250-acre property along the railroad tracks (and parallel to the Taconic Parkway) became a cemetery in 1918—owned and operated by the Catholic Archdiocese of New York—prominent New York architect Charles

Wellford Leavitt was hired to lay out the grounds along rural lines. And so it remains, with iron entrance gates and stone pillars, rolling hills, steep embankments, an abundance of sheltering oak and pine trees, and a Gothic bridge spanning a little lake (sporting a NO FISHING sign).

Section 45, home of the "Stations of the Cross" shrines, was designed for meditation. Fourteen stations, or rest stops along the way, commemorate Christ's tortuous journey with the cross to Calvary. The beautiful floor-to-ceiling stained-glass windows in the modern, circular St. Francis of Assisi Chapel, also in section 45, were designed by Benoit Gilsoul.

For all its acreage, Gate of Heaven is one of the most easily navigable cemeteries; the map available at the office is a cinch to use, with the graves of notables clearly identified. If you travel by rail (via Metro North's Harlem line), disembark at the Mount Pleasant stop. The cemetery is right there, but check the train schedule ahead, as times vary from weekdays to weekends.

The privileged residents here include **Bob Considine** (1906–1975; crypt in Our Lady of Peace garden mausoleum), a famous sports columnist and the author of *Thirty Seconds Over Tokyo* and twenty-four other books; **Anna Held** (1872–1918; division 2), a French musical-comedy star and the first wife of Broadway showman Florenz Ziegfeld; **Fulton Oursler** (1893–1952; division 5), a religious writer; and **Michael Quill** (1905–1966; division 47, corner of 47, 44, and 22), a labor leader and powerful head of the Transport Workers Union. *Grounds open 7:30 A.M.–4:30 P.M. daily. Office hours: 9:00 A.M.–4:30 P.M. daily; closed on major holidays. Restrooms; map; drinking fountain. Mass held at 9:30 A.M. every Saturday in St. Francis of Assisi Chapel.*

## LUNCH BREAK

Just outside the cemetery, **Spadafino** (15 Commerce Street; 914–769–3725) offers reasonably priced Italian and American specialties.

## FRED ALLEN   1894–1956

Fans of Fred Allen's nasal voice and deadpan humor in his longtime radio program, the *Fred Allen Show*, usually think first of "Allen's Alley." This popular segment of the program featured such oddball characters as Mrs. Pansy Nussbaum, a Brooklyn Jewish housewife; Titus Moody, a frugal New England farmer; Ajax Cassidy, a lazy Irishman; Falstaff Openshaw, the resident poet; and Senator Beauregard Claghorn, a pompous, bloviating southern politico. Portland Hoffa, Allen's real wife, was also a regular.

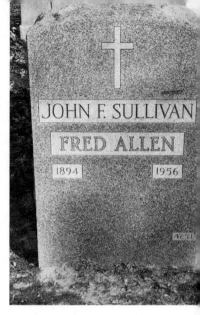

Allen—whose birth name, John F. Sullivan, is also etched on his headstone—developed his interest in comedy at the Boston Public Library, where he worked nights during his high school years and read joke books endlessly. After graduation he headed for the vaudeville circuit, billing himself "The World's Worst Juggler," with an act that juggled tenpins with jokes. An eleven-month tour of Australia and New Zealand gave him time to rethink his career and create a new act and a new name, which, on his return to New York, brought him top billing at the Palace. Then came raves—for his stand-up monologues in *Three's a Crowd* and several other musical revues.

Throughout his career Allen wrote most of his own material, lines such as "When you get through all the phony tinsel of Hollywood, you find the genuine tinsel underneath" and "Imitation is the sincerest form of television." Even on rebroadcasts today, his jokes sound remarkably fresh. He loved sarcasm, irony, and puns, though he once said, "Hanging is too good for a man who makes puns; he should be drawn and quoted."

After quitting radio Allen joked, "I was able to live on the money I saved on aspirins." He contemplated the transition to television, which so many radio performers were making, but seemed uncomfortable in his few guest appearances. His humor was dry and verbal, his voice was grating, and he looked like a dour curmudgeon. The transition became a moot question. Allen was scheduled to give TV a try in 1952, but a heart attack forced him into semiretirement. He died two years later, after collapsing on the street near Carnegie Hall. A rare example—for him—of bad timing. Allen's headstone is near the road in Division M.

## JAMES CAGNEY    1899–1986

Jimmy Cagney didn't have the face of a matinee idol, but he played just about everything else throughout almost sixty years of acting and dancing, in a career that began in vaudeville in 1919 and ended with the television movie *Terrible Joe Moran* in 1984. To break into show business, Cagney taught himself to dance (with help from actress-dancer Frances Vernon, who later married him) and then danced his way in Broadway chorus lines throughout the 1920s. His grace of movement was evident later in the movies, even when he portrayed the worst of hoodlums—as in *Public Enemy*, his breakout movie, and *Angels With Dirty Faces*. (His knowledge of gangsters was firsthand from the rough New York neighborhood in which he grew up.)

After years of playing crooks and cops in 1930s movies, he astonished audiences with his rousing, cocky *dancing* performance as showman George M. Cohan in the 1942 musical *Yankee Doodle Dandy*, for which he won a Best Actor Oscar. *Mister Roberts* (1955) revealed his comedy talents, but by then he was ready for early retirement. He retreated to his New York horse farm, raised Morgan horses, farmed, sailed, played classical guitar, painted, puttered, wrote poetry, and worked on an autobiography, *Cagney By Cagney* (with a little help from a ghostwriter). In 1981 he was lured from retirement to play Commissioner Waldo in *Ragtime*. Diabetes and circulatory problems brought down the final curtain in 1986. He and **Frances W. Cagney** (1899–1994), his wife of sixty-four years, now reside side-by-side in marble wall vaults in the St. Francis of Assisi mausoleum Garden Crypt, just beyond the entrance on the right. No doubt about it, Cagney *was* a Yankee Doodle Dandy.

## DOROTHY KILGALLEN   1913–1965

*I*t is surprising to anyone who remembers the acid tongue and sharp gossipy tones of this well-known syndicated newspaper columnist and radio-television performer to see her flat gravestone in division 23, carved with roses on the right side and a Celtic cross on the left. The stone reads "Dorothy Kilgallen Kollmar, beloved wife and mother—In God's Care." Not at all the image the public had of this influential personality in her heyday, which lasted for decades.

For years Kilgallen and her husband, Richard Kollmar, entertained radio listeners with a morning talk show. She also wrote a weekly column, "The Voice of Broadway," for the *New York Journal-American*. Her

last media hurrah was as a guest panelist on the television show *What's My Line?* Kilgallen's life ended mysteriously in her own bedroom, with alcohol and Seconal. Accident? Suicide? No one knows for sure, but if Kilgallen could have reported it, it would have been a good story. Sadly, her husband overdosed in the same place six years later.

## BILLY MARTIN  1928–1989

O n a hillside in section 25, plot 21, grave 3, around the corner from Babe Ruth's last address, is a former Yankee of a very different (pin)stripe. Alfred Manuel "Billy" Martin's horizontal, mottled brown granite memorial with a cross on top has baseballs inserted in niches at both ends. It also features a white bas-relief of St. Jude, the patron saint of lost causes, as well as a white bas-relief cross. Etched into the imposing stone are the words "I may not have been the greatest Yankee to put on the uniform but I was the proudest" and "Until we meet again."

Considering Martin's dysfunctional life, it is easy to forget that this pugnacious man was a better-than-average ball player and a canny manager. It was off the field that he had trouble: too many nightclubs, too much drinking, too quick a temper, too many fistfights, too many tabloid headlines. As a shortstop

he played on six World Champion Yankee teams, but he was traded after a brawl at the Copacabana.

When Martin's playing days ended, he worked his way up to major-league managing in the aggressive, scrappy style that sportswriters dubbed "Billyball." In sixteen years—with five different teams—he won five divisional titles, two American League pennants, and one World Series, that one with the Yankees. In several cases he brought a team up from the cellar to an impressive first- or second-place finish within one year. His Yankee years were fractured by frequent combat with owner George Steinbrenner, who fired and rehired him three times. Martin's heart was always with the Yankees, who retired his #1 uniform and hung a plaque at Yankee Stadium in his honor. He died in a car accident on Christmas Day—one call he couldn't argue.

## SAL MINEO   1939–1976

All but forgotten except by fans of old movies, Mineo had a short, meteoric life. In effect, it began when Salvatore Mineo Jr., son of Sicilian immigrants, was tossed out of parochial school at age eight. Sal became a member of a Bronx street gang, took part in a robbery at age ten, and was given the choice of juvenile detention or enrollment in a professional drama school. Guess which he chose? His first break was in *The Rose Tattoo* on Broadway. Then it was off to Hollywood, a part in *Giant* and in several forgettable films, and then a catapult to instant fame in *Rebel Without a Cause*. Mineo's portrayal of Plato, a psychotic teenager, won him an Oscar nomination. Oscar called again with another nomination for his performance as Dov Landau in *Exodus*.

Those were the peaks, followed by some minor films, television, a brief fling as a singer, and some stage work in Los Angeles. Then one day, after rehearsing a play, Mineo returned home, parked his car, and was stabbed to death in the parking lot of his apartment. He was thirty-seven years old. A random killing? Mistaken identity? A homosexual encounter that went wrong? His wallet was still in his pocket, so robbery did not seem to be the motive. Two years later the case was solved when a man named Lionel Williams, in prison in Michigan, boasted of having killed Mineo. Williams was tried and convicted and received a life sentence, but his motive is as unknown now as ever.

Mineo's gravestone in division 2 bears the words "In God's care." Above the stone are a framed photograph of Sal with James Dean (both looking heart-wrenchingly young), a plastic vase of real and artificial flowers, and a wooden statue draped with a rosary. Sal's brother, **Michael Mineo** (1937–1984), is buried in the same plot.

## CONDÉ NAST   1873–1942

*I*t may come as a surprise that Condé Nast, best known as a conglomerate publishing company, actually was a real live human being. Condé Montrose Nast was born in New York, raised in St. Louis, and educated at Georgetown University. Though possessed of a law degree, he joined a friend as advertising manager of *Collier's Weekly* in New York but soon left to cofound the Home Pattern Company, which made and sold dress patterns. In 1909 he bought *Vogue*, which he and his brilliant editor, Edna Woolman Chase, converted from a small society magazine to the arbiter of good taste and fashion for upper-class women and wannabes.

Nast's appetite for acquiring magazines continued with *Vanity Fair, House and Garden,* and a European edition of *Vogue*. After a brief setback during the Depression, he bought *Glamour,* a magazine for young career women. Nast had more success in his choice of editors than in wives: His two marriages failed. He succumbed to a fatal heart attack in 1942, but the publishing empire bearing his name lives on and on and on, ever acquisitive, ever successful—like Nast himself. His grave is in section 25, plot 25, grave 4.

## WESTBROOK PEGLER   1894–1969

*A*nyone who thinks that fame isn't fleeting might check the record of the now-forgotten Westbrook Pegler. In full throttle in the 1930s and 40s, he ruled the roost of journalism and commentary. From simple beginnings as a sportswriter (at which he excelled), he moved on to a column in the *New York World-Telegram* and then to a national beat with a syndicated column called "Fair Enough." Writing in an acerbic, hard-hitting, often witty style, he spared nothing and no one, ridiculing hero worship and lambasting politicians, sports figures, and anyone in public life. His favorite targets were Franklin Roosevelt (whom he called a "feeble-minded Führer") and Eleanor Roosevelt ("La Bouche Grande"—the big mouth), author Upton Sinclair, fellow columnist Drew Pearson, politician Huey Long, and, surprisingly, Frank Sinatra. Labor leaders, Nazis, Communists, gamblers, and the IRS all felt the sting of his words.

In his prime, Pegler's direct style earned him a Pulitzer Prize for an exposé of a corrupt union leader. But times changed, and Pegler began to sacrifice accuracy for pure vitriol. In 1954 Quentin Reynolds, a war correspondent, sued him for libel. Admitting under oath that he had made 130 false statements, Pegler was ordered to pay $175,001 in damages. He soon lost his audience and influence and became embittered and shrilly reactionary, ending up writing for the John Birch Society magazine and other right-wing publications. Thrice-married, he finally lost a long battle with stomach cancer. His gray granite upright stone in division 40 bears the nonironic words "Rest in Peace."

## BABE RUTH   1895–1948

No sport has been as defined by one man as baseball has by George Herman Ruth, aka the "Sultan of Swat." Record after record (for home runs and hits) and the visceral joy of playing the game—these are part of the Babe Ruth legacy. Yet he hardly fit the image of the athlete-as-Adonis. Among his signature excesses were drinking, overeating (a pint of ice cream as a between-meal snack), womanizing, driving fast, and sleeping and exercising too little. Even so, he played the game with a zest rarely seen before or since.

From shaky beginnings as a truant and reluctant student at a school for underprivileged boys in Baltimore, Ruth could have drifted into adulthood as a small-time loser, but baseball saved him and he never forgot. The Babe began his career as a pitcher (a good one) with the Baltimore Orioles and then with the Boston Red Sox, where he also became a hard-hitting outfielder. After being traded for beans (a mere $125,000 and a loan) to the New York Yankees, he came into superstardom as the Babe Ruth of legend, playing fifteen years in a Yankee uniform, on a team that made seven World Series and won four of them. One of the first five players elected to the Hall of Fame, Ruth held fifty-four major-league records when he died.

On his large white marble headstone in section 25, plot 1115, is a bas-relief of Jesus instructing a young boy wearing modern clothes (the Babe?), with a quote by Cardinal Spellman: "May the divine spirit that animated Babe Ruth to win the crucial game of life inspire the youth of America." The grass in front of the memorial is perpetually strewn with bats, balls, Yankee caps, pebbles, fresh flowers, American flags and handwritten notes. A relatively recent one, from a Red Sox fan, begged Ruth to "Give it up!"—a reference to the "Curse of the Bambino" (as Ruth was sometimes called). The curse, supposedly for trading him to the hated Yankees, deprived the Boston Red Sox of a World Series for eighty-six years, until their jubilant 2004 win. The curse has ended, but for Ruth fans, the Babe will *never* have a final at bat.

## DUTCH SCHULTZ   1902–1935

*I*t is surprising to find in such a serene Catholic cemetery one of the most vicious gangsters of the Prohibition era. Schultz, whose real name was Arthur Flegenheimer, was a member of New York's "Jewish Mafia." Racketeer, bootlegger, and cold-blooded killer, he made millions on the numbers racket. As he laid plans to kill U.S. prosecutor Thomas E. Dewey, he was gunned down by Murder Inc. hit men—as at that time the mob feared retribution if Dewey were killed. At his Catholic wife's request, and over his mother's fierce objections, Schultz was baptized, received the last rites, and was buried in Gate of Heaven unceremoniously. You will not find his grave marked on the cemetery map, but it is in section 42, plot 96, grave 1-3.

## JAMES "JIMMY" WALKER JR.   1881–1946

"*G*entleman Jim" was the epitome of an affable bon vivant, a witty, charming New Yorker. A much-admired fashion plate, he once packed twenty identical white piqué vests and more than one hundred neckties for a short European vacation. As the lackadaisical, leisure-loving mayor of New York (elected in 1926), he suited the free-living times, spending charm as freely as treasury dollars.

The dark side surfaced within a few years, when prosecutor Samuel Seabury charged "Beau James" with kickbacks, bribes, and payoffs in city government. The charges stuck, and in 1932 Al Smith and other Tammany leaders forced him to resign. In full retreat, Walker sailed for Europe. By the time he died fourteen years later, of a blood clot on the brain, he was back in New York's good graces. Thousands attended his wake and High Requiem Mass at St. Patrick's Cathedral. Was he a rogue, a crook, or an ineffectual bumbler? Possibly all of the above, but his personality almost carried the day. Located across from the lake, at the corner of division 41, Walker's handsome red granite headstone bears an incised ornate cross.

# RYE

## MARSHLAND CONSERVANCY

*210 Boston Post Road; (914) 835–4466*

This beautiful, wooded 165-acre natural conservancy is run by the Westchester County Department of Parks. It is free and open to the public, with trails for walking, hiking, and observing nature. The Jay family cemetery is on

the grounds, about a quarter mile from the entrance, and can be reached via a woodland trail. The cemetery is gated and private. To visit the grave of its most prominent member, you must obtain permission from the conservancy in advance.

The Jay graveyard is enclosed by padlocked chain-mail fencing. Inside the fenced-in area, the small burial ground is framed by an old-fashioned, higgledy-piggledy fieldstone wall, punctuated by white pine and oak trees, mountain laurels, and rhododendrons. John Jay's squarish gray granite headstone is of medium size, its lettering almost indecipherable from the ravages of long Westchester winters. He is surrounded by seven generations of Jays, most with small and modest headstones. The ground throughout undulates slightly and is carpeted with springy club moss. Quiet and natural, this is a final refuge to be admired and envied. *Grounds open dawn to dusk daily. Office hours: 9:00 A.M.–5:00 P.M. Wednesday, Thursday, Saturday, and Sunday.*

## LUNCH BREAK

One of Westchester's best restaurants is in Rye: **La Panetière** (530 Milton Road; 914–967–8140) is the place to go for elegant, memorable food in a country house setting. If you want something a bit less fancy, there is **Black Bass Grille** (2 Central Avenue; 914–967–6700), popular for American comfort food in a homey setting with fireplace.

## JOHN JAY   1745–1829

American history books cite John Jay as the first chief justice of the United States Supreme Court, but few say much more about this exemplary lawyer, jurist, and statesman who played an important role before, during, and after the American Revolution. Jay was the son of Peter Jay, a prominent New York merchant of Huguenot heritage. Educated at King's College (later Columbia University), John became president of the Continental Congress in 1778–79, helped draft New York's constitution, and served as the state's chief justice. In 1781 he (along with John Adams, Ben Franklin, Thomas Jefferson, and Henry Laurens) was commissioned to negotiate the peace treaty at the war's end.

In a time of savage political partisanship and corruption in elections and appointments, Jay's well-known independence and integrity won him the trust of many people of opposing parties. (We could use him today.) George Washington chose him to be the first chief justice of the U.S. Supreme Court, where he served from 1789 to 1795. While Jay was still on the court, Alexander Hamilton hand-picked him to run for governor of New York without even telling him. Jay was in Britain at the time, negotiating what became known as the Jay Treaty (1794), which helped remove British troops entrenched in the northwest territory after the war had ended. Returning home, Jay found that although he had neither accepted the nomination nor campaigned, he won the election by 1,589 votes. (They did things differently back then.) Becoming governor, he had to resign from the Supreme Court.

As governor, Jay was a dynamo of accomplishments: He reformed the prison system, limited the death penalty, abolished flogging, and worked to improve New York State's canal system and to abolish imprisonment for debt. He even pushed a bill that would eventually abolish slavery. In 1801 he retired from public life to his comfortable home in Katonah.

## HOUSE CALL

The **John Jay Homestead** (400 Jay Street, Route 22, Katonah; 914–232–5651) is about 30 miles north of the grave site, but it is worth a visit for history buffs. His home, built in 1800, was dubbed the "Mount Vernon of the North," something of an overstatement for a clapboard farmhouse. Jay spent the last twenty-eight years of his life there.

# VALHALLA

## KENSICO CEMETERY

*Lakeview Avenue; (914) 949–0347; www.kensico.org*

There are few resting places as paradisial as the arboreal Kensico, set among the Westchester hills, with circular drives and well-manicured lawns accented by flowering trees. It is at its most beautiful in springtime, but serene and contemplative in any season. Can it be a coincidence that such a heavenly place exists in a town called Valhalla (the final resting place of heroes slain in battle)? The rolling hills are graced with obelisks, cenotaphs, sculptures (including a statue of Christ with angels by Augustus Saint-Gaudens), tombs shaped like classic Greek pavilions and pyramids, and a small lake. Thirty-six native, ornamental, and rare tree species, identified with black vinyl labels, are on the grounds—magnolia, birch, juniper, sassafras, grand fir, and sugar maple among them.

Kensico began in 1889; the first interment was in 1891. At that time a private railroad car, luxuriously equipped for funeral parties, brought guests from Grand Central Station in New York directly to the Kensico gates. It is still possible to visit Kensico by rail by taking Metro North's Harlem line train to the Valhalla stop.

Since its beginnings, Kensico has been a favorite final address of high-profile New Yorkers—business tycoons, theatrical stars, authors, and musicians. With your map (available at the office), you will find memorials to the Friars Club, the Actors Fund, the Order of Elks (with a full-size elk statue), and the Kane Lodge, all marked.

Here are but a few souls who have found final peace among the trees and graceful slopes: **Henri Bendel** (1868–1936; Pocantico plot), a leading and influential clothes designer; **Vivian Blaine** (1921–1995; Actors Fund plot, grave 462), a musical comedy performer who was renown as the adenoidal Adelaide in *Guys and Dolls* on Broadway; **Paul J. Bonwit** (1862–1939; family mausoleum, section 52, Powhatan plot, lot 4673), retailer and founder of the former high-fashion Bonwit Teller department store in Manhattan (now replaced by Trump Tower); **Evangeline Booth** (1865–1950; section 2, Salvation Army plot), daughter of the founders of the Salvation Army and herself the army's head in the United States; **Marc Connelly** (1880–1980; Tower Garden, lot 799, grave 3), a playwright and winner of a Pulitzer Prize for the play *Green Pastures*; **Milton Cross** (1897–1975; section 156, lot 10397, grave 2), a radio commentator and for thirty-five years the radio voice of the Metropolitan Opera; and **Guy Kibbee** (1882–1956; Actors Fund plot), a comic character actor in movies.

**Herbert Lehman** (1878–1963; Katahbin plot), a banker, popular four-term Democratic governor, and U.S. senator is here, as are **Allan Nevins** (1890–1971; section 75, Garden of the Apostle, lot 124), a Columbia University history professor, prolific author, and two-time winner of the Pulitzer Prize for history; and **Harriet Quimby** (1884–1912; Katonah plot), the first licensed woman pilot. **Colonel Jacob Ruppert Jr.** (1867–1939; section 53, lot 2618), a beer tycoon and owner of the New York Yankees during the golden era of Ruth and Gehrig, is in Kensico. Also present is **Edward Grant Barrow** (1868–1953; family mausoleum, section 79, lot 10501, grave 6), baseball Hall of Famer and manager of the Boston Red Sox, who converted Babe Ruth from a pitcher to an outfielder and later followed Ruth to New York as general manager of the Yankees. *Grounds open 8:30 A.M.–4:30 P.M. daily. Office hours:*

9:00 A.M.–5:00 P.M. *Monday–Friday, 9:00 A.M.–4:00 P.M. Saturday and Sunday; closed Thanksgiving, Christmas, and New Year's Day. Map; tree map; restrooms.*

## LUNCH BREAK

Reasonably priced sandwiches and continental meals are available at the **Valhalla Station Restaurant** (2 Cleveland Street; 914–682–7445), less than a mile outside the cemetery grounds.

## PETER ARNO   1904–1968

The *New Yorker* has spawned dozens of notable cartoonists, but few captured the magazine's spirit of urbane sophistication as successfully as Peter Arno, whose cartoons were a regular feature for forty-three years (1925–68). Even as he was dying of emphysema, Arno continued drawing. His last cartoon was published the week he died.

If Arno—who was born Curtis Arnoux Peters Jr., son of a New York State Supreme Court judge—hadn't sold his first cartoon to the *New Yorker* (after scores of rejections from other magazines), he was ready to accept an offer to play in a band in Chicago. Our funny bones are healthier for his decision. His métier was New York's cafe society: gold-digger showgirls, tuxedoed roués, and pouter pigeon-bosomed dowagers. A bon vivant-around-town, the well-bred, well-dressed Arno knew this scene intimately.

He was multitalented—he drew; painted; played the piano, accordion, and banjo in a college band at Yale (called the Yale Collegians); composed music; and even coauthored a Broadway musical, *Here Comes the Bride*. Though unlucky in two marriages, he was at the top of his form at the drawing board. His bold, strongly drawn satiric cartoons live on in *New Yorker* book collections and his own stand-alone book collections. Arno's large upright headstone is located at the south edge of the West Pocantico plot, section 15/168.

## BILLIE BURKE   1884–1970
## FLO ZIEGFELD   1867–1932

Today, Mary William Ethelbert Appleton Burke is best remembered as Glinda, the Good Witch of the North, in the movie classic *The Wizard of Oz* (a role she loved). As a shy, young actress in New York who played ingénue roles, she met Florenz Ziegfeld in 1913, and they soon married. He

produced revues called the *Ziegfeld Follies*, which featured beautiful showgirls parading around the stage in scanty costumes in extravagant musical tableaux. He also knew talent when he saw it and is credited with introducing Fanny Brice, W. C. Fields, Will Rogers, and Billie Burke. Ziegfeld was a notorious lothario, but Billie averted her eyes and stayed married. She juggled her career, mixing stage work and silent films with a comfortable private life at their luxurious Westchester estate.

Ziegfeld lost heavily in the Wall Street bust of 1929, and after his death Billie had to cope with his heavy debts. A real trouper, she turned to Hollywood and began her longest run. Specializing in ladylike but scatterbrained roles, she made more than sixty films between 1933 and 1960, among them *Dinner at Eight, Topper, The Man Who Came to Dinner,* and *Father of the Bride*. A touching aspect of the secluded Burke-Ziegfeld residence at Kensico (in section 78, the eastern edge of the Powhatan plot) is the life-size bronze sculpture by R. Aitken of a demure lady seated under a beautiful weeping beech tree. This sculpture was commissioned by Burke and dedicated to **Blanche Beatty Burke** (1844–1921), with the words "In memory of my mother." Burke and Ziegfeld's bronze markers in the ground nearby are modest by comparison.

## TOMMY DORSEY   1905–1956

*I*n the era of Big Bands, the Dorsey brothers could really swing. Tommy and older brother Jimmy learned how in Shenandoah, Pennsylvania, from their miner father, a self-taught musician determined to keep his sons from having to work in the coal mines. Seeing music as their passport out, he gave them cornet lessons and soon had them tooting in his part-time band. By the time Tommy was sixteen, the brothers had their own Dorsey's Wild Canaries, with Tommy on trombone and Jimmy on sax.

They went on to play with Jean Goldkette's jazz band in Detroit and hung with the best of 'em: Bix Beiderbecke, Joe Venuti, Eddie Lang. Then they joined Paul Whiteman, cut records with Bing Crosby, and formed the Dorsey Brothers Orchestra. That didn't last—too many temperamental differences. In a dramatic moment before a packed house at the Glen Island Casino in New Rochelle, New York, the brothers had a bruising row. Tommy walked off the bandstand, and the two stopped speaking for eighteen years. Jimmy kept the Dorsey Brothers name; Tommy took over another outfit. By the mid-1940s he was leading one of the smoothest dance bands in the country, with vocalists Frank Sinatra, Connie Haines, and, later, Jo Stafford.

A perfectionist, Tommy attracted, then lost, a procession of star sidemen: Bunny Berigan, Buddy Rich, and Ziggy Elman among them. His theme song, "I'm Getting Sentimental Over You," earned him the public soubriquet "sentimental gentleman"—which must have seemed ironic to his two ex-wives, his estranged third wife, and certain colleagues with whom his relations were more tempestuous than tender.

By the 1950s, when the Big Band era was over, the Tommy Dorsey band was still going strong. In 1953 the brothers made up and Jimmy joined the group, taking it over three years later when Tommy died suddenly. Within seven months Jimmy was dead, too. They are separated in death as they were in much of life: Jimmy is at home in Shenandoah, and Tommy is in Kensico, in the southeast sloping edge of Kensico Gardens plot, facing Cherokee and Powhatan Avenues. His name, musical notes, and a trombone are carved into a giant oblong granite marker. Behind is the Dorsey headstone, surrounded by hedges and well-pruned evergreens.

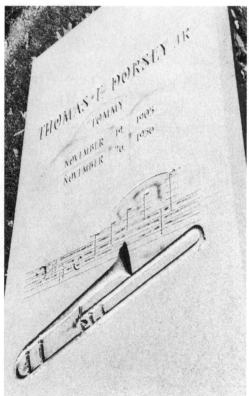

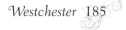

espite all the negative headlines, there *are* some nice guys in sports, and Henry Lou Gehrig was one of the nicest—not a publicity-hyped hero, but the real thing. He was born in the German Yorkville section of Manhattan to a German ironworker and Danish maid. His baseball skills in high school led him to Columbia University, where a New York Yankees scout signed him, despite his dominating mother's wishes. She wanted him to finish college, and she aimed to keep tight control over her only child. And so she did, until the very day he married (an action she strenuously opposed).

Within two years, after a brief stay in the minors, Gehrig was with the Bronx Bombers. There he played for the next fourteen years as one of the hardest-hitting members of "Murderers' Row," so called because of their slugging ability. Although he was always overshadowed by (and had a sometimes-stormy relationship with) his showier teammate, Babe Ruth, Gehrig considered Ruth a mentor, and the two had a friendly home-run competition. Gehrig never won it, but he accomplished something Ruth *never* did: four homers in a single game, a rare feat. Shy and unassuming, Gehrig played every regular-season game—2,130 games in a row. This steadiness earned him the nickname "Iron Horse."

While statistics aren't the whole Gehrig story, his record is impressive: a lifetime batting average of .340, 493 career home runs, 1,990 RBIs (runs

batted in), four Most Valuable Player awards, and one Triple Crown. He also is remembered for his fortitude and gallantry in coping with amyotrophic lateral sclerosis (ALS)—later called Lou Gehrig's disease—a progressive disease with no known cure. Even as his muscles deteriorated, he behaved with grace and courage, returning as team captain in 1939, even though he could hardly play. That year, on a special Lou Gehrig Day, he spoke these famous words: "I may have been given a bad break, but I've an awful lot to live for. With all this, I consider myself the luckiest man on the face of the earth."

At the end of that final season, the rules were waived and he was elected to the Baseball Hall of Fame, without the usual five-year waiting period. He was not quite thirty-eight when he died. That fans still honor Lou is evident at his granite headstone (with two decorative bronze doors at the top) under a big shade tree in the south side of the Cherokee plot (section 93, lot 12686). There bats, balls, rain-faded Yankee caps, and gloves are clustered between two small, round hedges. With him is **Eleanor Twitchell Gehrig** (1905–1984), his wife of eight short years. His parents' and Eleanor's parents' gravestones are in front by a granite bench, convenient for contemplating the family scene.

## DANNY KAYE    1913–1987

When Danny Kaye double-talked and scat-sang his way through *Up in Arms*, his hilarious debut film in 1944, he seemed to movie audiences a breath of fresh air. But Kaye was no newcomer to show business. As a vaudevillian and nightclub performer, he could sing, act, do comic sketches, and move with a dancer's grace. He really hit his stride and defined his talent when he married Sylvia Fine, a comedy writer, pianist, composer, and lyricist. She created so much of the material that made Kaye a star that one critic joked that Kaye "had a Fine head on his shoulders." Songs forever associated with him were her handiwork: "Anatole in Paris," "Pavlova," and his signature tune, the tongue-twisting "Tchaikovsky," rattled off at Kaye's inimitable machine-gun speed.

Because of his virtuosity, he was difficult to pigeonhole in movies, which may be why so few of his seventeen films were real successes. The exceptions include *The Secret Life of Walter Mitty, The Inspector General, Hans Christian Andersen,* and *The Mad Woman of Chaillot.* Kaye also tried his hand at radio, but his visual antics were lost.

 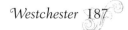

In later years Kaye spent so much time as a goodwill ambassador for the United Nations Children's Fund (UNICEF) and on other charitable work that he was recognized with the Jean Hersholt Humanitarian Award in 1982. His memorial granite bench, in section 19, Valhalla plot, depicts his hobbies and interests sculpted in bronze on the back—a music scroll (for Sylvia), a chef's hat (he loved cooking Chinese food), a baseball and mitt (he was part-owner of the Seattle Mariners), and an airplane (he had a license to fly jumbo jets). If a grave site can be called "charming," this one more than qualifies. It perfectly reflects the man.

## TOMMY MANVILLE   1894–1967

*I*n section 77, a monumental Greek temple-like mausoleum with Corinthian columns and the name MANVILLE above the imposing door suggests that a man of great importance lies within. Thomas Franklyn Manville Jr. was well known solely for being well known. He had two claims to fame: lots of money (as heir to the Johns-Manville fortune) and lots of wives. Called the "marrying Manville" by a gossip-hungry press, he made getting married his full-time occupation.

A precocious boy, Manville smoked at age eleven, drank and began shaving at twelve, ran away from school eight times by age fifteen, and married for the first time at seventeen. It was the first of thirteen marriages (to eleven different women). Most of the wives were blond, gold-digging chorus girls. His longest marriage lasted seven years; his shortest, seven hours and forty-five minutes. His reported engagements ranged from 27 to a preposterous-sounding 529, depending on which newspaper report you believed. Considering Manville's wealth—a $10 million fortune inherited from his father in 1925—his divorce settlements were surprisingly modest: $2.5 million in all.

Psychiatrists would have a field day with Manville's psyche: What motivated him? Why did he make himself the butt of so many jokes? Why did he seem to encourage and revel in notoriety? A mere footnote in the social history of the twentieth century, he provided merriment to millions of readers and full employment to scores of tabloid newspaper reporters.

## SERGEI RACHMANINOFF   1873–1943

When we think of Sergei Rachmaninoff today, it's his music that floods our minds—compositions like his Second Symphony, the tone poem *The Isle of the Dead*, his Third Piano Concerto, and his preludes for the piano (Thirteen Preludes, Six Etudes Tableaux, and Nine Etudes Tableaux). Along with seventy or more songs with piano accompaniment, he wrote a choral symphony (*The Bells*) and a Vesper Mass for male voices. Yet while Rachmaninoff was alive, it was his work as a concert pianist and conductor that sustained him, both in his native Russia—where he came from an impecunious but noble family—and later, after the 1917 Russian Revolution, on tour in the United States, England, and continental Europe.

From 1921 to 1925 the composer and his family were Manhattanites, summering near Paris. They later lived full-time on Lake Lucerne in Switzerland. The Soviet Union banned Rachmaninoff's works briefly in 1931, but the music was too popular and the decree was soon lifted.

SERGEI AND NATALIE RACHMANINOFF
APR 2 1873 - MAR 28 1943 · MAY 26 1877 - JAN 17 1951

SERGEI RACHMANINOFF
APRIL 2, 1873 - MARCH 29, 1943

A perfectionist, he seldom felt at the top of his form as a pianist—usually wearing, in Igor Stravinsky's words, his "six and a half foot tall scowl." Rachmaninoff yearned for more time to compose. During World War II he left his beloved villa on Lake Lucerne and resettled in Beverly Hills, California. Although he was a generous man and contributor to many charities, he was obsessed with fears and phobias most of his life. In his words, he feared "everything: mice, rats, cockchafers, bulls, burglars." He neglected to put lung cancer in that list, but he died of it just before his seventieth birthday.

The inner distress that Rachmaninoff felt through much of his career is nowhere evident in the composer's current home, where hedges, rhododendron, and pachysandra provide a serene privacy for his Eastern Orthodox cross, two granite benches, and the gray granite gravestone he shares with his wife, **Natalie Satin Rachmaninoff** (1877–1951), who was his cousin and life's companion. Their daughter, **Princesse Irina Wolkonsky née Rachmaninoff** (1903–1969), is nearby in the same woodsy alcove. Their final abode on a rolling northern hillside of the Pocantico plot near Pocantico Avenue is secluded, yet scores of admirers find it year after year.

## AYN RAND   1905–1982

*T*oo bad she died when she did (of lung cancer). Ayn Rand would have loved the "me" era of personal consumption—the 1980s and 90s. Her lifetime political philosophy, which she called objectivism, was one of self-centered "me first" individualism and unfettered capitalism. She promoted this not through dull economic texts, but in fiction that pulsed with heroes who *behaved* as she *thought*. The most famous example is Howard Roark in *The Fountainhead,* a controversial and successful novel (that as a movie starred Gary Cooper). The book made Rand's name and fortune while sparking an ultraconservative movement that continues to this day. (Her most fervent disciple today is probably economist Alan Greenspan, chairman of the Federal Reserve Board.)

In a sense, Rand created herself as well as her fiction. Born Alyssa Rosenbaum in St. Petersburg, Russia, she left in 1926, changing her name en route.

The Rand part was lifted from a Remington-Rand typewriter, an omen, perhaps, of the writer she was to become. Although critics give short shrift to her writing style, many of her books, including the novel *Atlas Shrugged*, continue to sell well.

Sharing her piece of real estate here is **Frank O'Connor** (1897–1979), Rand's husband of fifty years, whom she met when they both were working as extras in a Cecil B. DeMille movie—her first Hollywood job. Their twin upright headstones are side by side in the south side of Kensico Gardens plot, off Cherokee Avenue. Not in evidence is the 6-foot-high dollar sign that stood next to her coffin at her memorial service. That says it all.

## DAVID SARNOFF   1891–1971

To the left of the mausoleum of mercantile magnate Paul J. Bonwit, in the northeastern section 40, Powhatan plot, lies another massive monument of gray granite with the words DAVID SARNOFF on the facade. This is the final home of the radio pioneer, chairman, and guiding genius of RCA and later NBC, as well as his wife of fifty-four years, **Lizette Hermant Sarnoff** (?–1974), and their eldest son, **Robert Sarnoff** (1918–1997), who succeeded David as RCA president.

For a Russian-born immigrant who studied to be a rabbi, Sarnoff had a remarkable, worldly life. Sometimes it is difficult to separate the truth from the "spin" or exaggerations. Truth: Sarnoff was nine when he, his mother, and two brothers sailed to New York to join his father, who was living in a tenement in the Lower East Side of Manhattan. When David was fifteen, his father died and David became the main support of his family. This meant quitting school to work for a commercial cable company. There he taught himself Morse code and learned about the new, wireless invention—radio. Later, at the Marconi Wireless and Telegraph Company, he began as Guglielmo Marconi's messenger and soon, with Marconi's blessing, became a wireless telegraph operator.

Radio fascinated the young, ambitious Sarnoff. With hard work and study, he was hired by John Wanamaker (himself intrigued by radio) in 1912 to run the Marconi wireless station at Wanamaker's New York department store, which he had installed as an attraction for shoppers. The first momentous event of Sarnoff's life occurred that April 14, when he arrived at work to the first reports of the sinking of the *Titanic*. Spin: Legend says that Sarnoff was

the sole radio operator and worked tirelessly for three days and nights, relaying word of the missing and dead to relatives and to newspapers. In fact, he was one of a team. Sarnoff later commented that he owed his success to tragedy: "The *Titanic* disaster brought radio to the front, and also me."

In record time the importance of radio, um, telegraphed itself and the Marconi Company flourished, as did Sarnoff. When the newly formed Radio Corporation of America (RCA) bought out Marconi in 1919, Sarnoff became commercial manager. He was influential in founding the National Broadcasting Corporation (NBC), an RCA subsidiary, in 1926. Eventually Sarnoff became chairman of the RCA board of directors. Along the way, he was a tireless promoter of radio (and later of television), with the vision to see the infinite possibilities of the medium and the energy and knowledge to make them happen.

During World War II he was a communications consultant to General Dwight D. Eisenhower and was appointed brigadier general. He loved the title "General Sarnoff" and used it happily the rest of his life, even after becoming chairman of the RCA board (in 1947), a job he held until his peaceful death at age eighty.

Not everything for Sarnoff was always peaceful. He battled hard and long (and won) with competing radio titan CBS over the issue of compatible color television. Even more acrimonious was his feud with Edwin Howard Armstrong, a former friend, over patents and the development of FM radio; the dispute ended in Armstrong's suicide in 1954.

## SHARON GARDENS

*Kensico Cemetery, Lakeview Avenue; (914) 949–0347; www.kensico.org*

In 1959 Kensico began an addition called Sharon Gardens as the final residence for Jewish families. The seventy-six-acre grounds have a separate entrance with fieldstone portals, located just opposite the faux-Tudor administration building. A prominent lodger is **Joseph Baum** (1920–1998; family lot AA), a pathfinding food entrepreneur whose La Fonda del Sol, Four Seasons, and Windows on the World were landmark restaurants in their time. *Grounds open 8:30 A.M.–4:30 P.M. daily. Office hours: 9:00 A.M.–5:00 P.M. Monday–Friday, 9:00 A.M.–4:00 P.M. Saturday and Sunday; closed Thanksgiving, Christmas, and New Year's Day. Map; tree map; restrooms.*

## PADDY CHAYEFSKY   1923–1981

The most notable resident of Sharon Gardens is Paddy Chayefsky, whose headstone is located in section 6, on the edge of Sharon Drive opposite the entrance to Paradise Road. "Paddy," an unlikely moniker for a Jewish child of the Bronx, was born Sidney Aaron Chayefsky and was a New Yorker through and through. After studies at the City College of New York and Fordham University, he served in the U.S. Army in World War II and was awarded a Purple Heart.

Unlike many writers who jump from Broadway to television, Chayefsky won his playwriting stripes first on TV, later moving to films and then to Broadway, where four of his plays were produced (*Middle of the Night, The Tenth Man, Gideon,* and *The Passion of Joseph D.*). *Marty,* a bittersweet study in loneliness, was his first big hit, produced live on television in 1953 during what has been called the medium's "golden age," a period when most shows *were* live. Quickly made into a movie starring Ernest Borgnine, the film won the 1955 Academy Award for best picture, and Chayefsky won an Oscar for best screenplay. It also sent him packing for Hollywood. What followed were two decades of successful screenwriting.

After *Marty* came *The Goddess,* for which Chayefsky was nominated for another Oscar, followed by such films as *The Bachelor Party, The American-ization of Emily,* and *Paint Your Wagon.* In the 1970s he received another two Oscars and two Golden Globe Awards, for *The Hospital* and for *Network.* The latter, perhaps his best work ever, is a savage satire about television (about which Chayefsky knew more than a little and referred to as "democracy at its ugliest") and yielded a line that has become an American classic: "I'm mad as hell and I'm not going to take it anymore!"

One aspect of Chayefsky's skill as a writer was his ability to sift comic elements into dramatic themes and use satire to focus attention on serious subjects (as in *The Hospital* and *Network*). His last film—*Altered States* (1980), based on a novel he had written—was a mishmash, probably because of infighting between Chayefsky and the director. The author didn't want to be publicly connected with the film, so he hid his credit as screenwriter under his real first and middle names: Sidney Aaron. The following year he died of cancer.

# CHAPTER 7

# Along the Hudson River

The Hudson River is so beautiful that it is easy to understand why so many prominent people—including the Roosevelts, the Vanderbilts, Washington Irving, and Samuel F. B. Morse—built their homes on the eastern side of its majestic bluffs. The west side of the river has more than its share of American history, too, as home to West Point Military Academy, the Storm King Art Center, and the historic Dutch-founded, pre–Revolutionary War town of Kingston.

In this chapter the first five towns mentioned are on the Hudson's east side, while the final three are on the Hudson's west banks. It is easy meandering to crisscross the river from New York City via the George Washington, Tappan Zee, Bear Mountain, and New-burgh Bridges and the bridges at East Kingston, Catskill, and Castleton-on-Hudson.

## BARD COLLEGE CEMETERY

*Bard College, Route 9G; (845) 758–6822*

This minuscule burial ground lies in a sheltered, wooded area behind Bard College's Stevenson Library. It is best to park in the library lot, just off Annandale Road (which loops around the campus), and climb the stairs on the right side of the building. At the top of the stairs, turn left and follow a path into the woods. The cemetery is in a quiet oak-shaded setting, with only a few dozen graves, mostly of Bard faculty members and their families. There are no mausoleums, no obelisks reaching to the sky, just an intimate, old-fashioned graveyard. One can fantasize about it being spooky at midnight, but on a sunlit autumn day it is aglow with fiery and golden foliage, a calm oasis on a busy campus.

A map of the campus, with the cemetery noted, is available at the security office in the Old Gym, but the best way to find it is to ask a passing student. The entrance to the cemetery is marked by a quaint little roof-topped wooden gate. *Open dawn to dusk daily.*

There are several cafes on campus for a quick bite, but if you have time for a leisurely lunch, I heartily recommend **Calico Restaurant & Patisserie** (9 Mill Street; 845–876–2749) in the center of Rhinebeck, about 7 miles south of Bard on Route 9. The setting is cozy, the food is lovely, and the house-made desserts are out of this world. Another pleasant choice is across the street from Calico in a historic inn. The **Traphagen Restaurant** in the Beekman Arms (Routes 9 and 308; 845–871–1766) offers pizzas, salads, and sandwiches in an airy, glass-fronted dining room and a greenhouse.

## HANNAH ARENDT   1906–1975

The writing of this German-born scholar–political philosopher is most often recapped with the words "the banality of evil," a phrase that Arendt used to describe Nazism in her on-the-scene reporting of the Adolf Eichmann war crimes trial in Jerusalem (1961) and two years later in her book *Eichmann in Jerusalem: A Report on the Banality of Evil*. With the genocides and horrors engulfing the world since the Nazi period, it is no wonder the phrase still resonates today.

In her lifetime Arendt was known in intellectual circles for her studies of totalitarianism and anti-Semitism. Her 1973 book *The Origins of Totalitarianism* is still read today. She was criticized in some American Jewish circles at the time for her harsh observations about certain Jewish leaders in Nazi Germany who, she felt, betrayed their own people. "To a Jew," she wrote, "this role of the Jewish leaders in the destruction of their own people is undoubtedly the darkest chapter of the whole dark story."

Arendt knew her subject matter firsthand. She was born in Hanover, Germany, to a middle-class Jewish family of Russian descent, studied philosophy with Martin Heidegger (with whom she had a short-lived affair) at the University of Marburg, and published a dissertation on St. Augustine. As a Jew she couldn't teach at German universities, so she fled to Paris, where she helped aid Jewish refugees from eastern Europe. In 1940 she was sent to a notorious internment camp at Gurs, near the French Pyrenees, before being deported to a concentration camp in Germany. At the last moment, in 1941, she escaped with her husband and mother to New York, via Lisbon.

Eventually Arendt found work as a journalist, alerting the American public to Hitler's persecution of the Jews. Soon she became established as a political philosopher and held teaching posts at Princeton, Harvard, Berkeley, and other American universities. She became friends with the American novelist

Mary McCarthy, and a book of their friendship, *Between Friends: The Correspondence of Hannah Arendt and Mary McCarthy 1949–1975,* was published in 1995.

One can only speculate how Arendt would feel about the ways in which her birth city has honored her posthumously. Hanover now has a Hannah Arendt Way, Hannah Arendt Path, Hannah Arendt Days, and the Hannah Arendt Stipendium, which offers aid to persecuted writers.

Arendt's gravestone is flush with the soil, to the right of the same-size stone of her second husband, **Heinrich Blücher** (1899–1970), a German poet and philosopher. The markers usually have pebbles on top, following a Jewish custom of honoring the deceased. From the entrance gate, walk straight ahead on a dirt path, past a few headstones. As you round a corner in the path, the Blücher graves are just beyond, in the second row on the right. Ironically, they lie next to a large stone cross.

# HASTINGS-ON-HUDSON

## WESTCHESTER HILLS CEMETERY
*400 Saw Mill River Road; (914) 478–1767*

Cited as the Memorial Park of the Stephen Wise Free Synagogue, this compact Jewish cemetery was founded in 1921 and named in honor of a respected Reform rabbi, **Stephen S. Wise** (1874–1949; block C), who is buried here. Wise was known as a tireless promoter of world peace and a labor reformer.

The seventeen-acre burial ground climbs a steep hill around a circuitous drive and down again. It is chockablock with large, imposing mausoleums, like that of the **Barricini family** (block D), the candy manufacturers, with the name across the facade engraved in the same script that graces the candy boxes.

Here also rest **Sidney Hillman** (1887–1946; block J), an influential union leader and head of the Amalgamated Clothing Workers of America; and **Judy Holliday** (1922–1965; block B), a comic actress whose movie career was truncated by her

**LUNCH BREAK**

Just ten minutes from the cemetery in Dobbs Ferry is **Chart House** (High Street, opposite the Metro North station; 914–693–4130), with views of the Hudson, decent food, and moderate prices.

death of cancer at age forty-two. Holliday was best known for her role as the not-so-dumb, sensitive blond in *Born Yesterday*, for which she won an Oscar, and for her parts in *Bells Are Ringing* and *PHFFFT*. In block C is **Max Reinhardt** (1873–1943), an internationally renowned producer and director who fled Nazi Germany in 1933 and later produced Shakespeare and Shaw plays in New York. *Grounds open during office hours: 8:00 A.M.–4:00 P.M. daily except Saturday. Map; restroom.*

## JOHN GARFIELD    1913–1952

John Garfield began life as Julius Garfinkle and first gained attention as a Golden Gloves boxing semifinalist. He worked in New York with the Group Theatre and then moved to Hollywood, where during the 1940s his career as a tough yet sensitive hero took off in such films as *Tortilla Flat* (1942), *Destination Tokyo* (1943), *The Postman Always Rings Twice* (1946), *Humoresque* (1946), and *Gentleman's Agreement* (1947). Twice he was nominated for an Oscar for best supporting actor, for *Four Daughters* (1938) and *Body and Soul* (1947); the latter may have been the best performance of his career.

In 1951 Garfield was called to testify before the House Un-American Activities Committee for reputed Communist ties. He swore under oath that he had never been a Communist but declined to "name names" of friends who were. The experience took a personal and professional toll; Garfield was blacklisted in Hollywood, and opportunities for work evaporated. The next year, at age thirty-nine, he made tabloid headlines when he died of cardiac arrest in a girlfriend's apartment, days after leaving his wife. Fresh flowers frequently surround his gray headstone and marker in block H. Obviously, someone still remembers.

GEORGE GERSHWIN

## GEORGE GERSHWIN    1898–1937
## IRA GERSHWIN    1896–1983

orn between an affinity for popular music and admiration of the classics, George Gershwin managed the unthinkable: He bridged the gap between them. Beginning with "Swanee," one of his first pop hits, he wrote all the songs in the *George White Scandals*, annual Broadway revues of the 1920s. His ticket to ride the classics train came with a commission from Paul Whiteman to compose a big orchestral work in the jazz idiom. This was *Rhapsody in Blue*, whose success in 1924 made Gershwin famous overnight and rich forever.

But he was just hitting his stride. *An American in Paris* followed four years later, and concurrently there were his scores for *Lady Be Good, Girl Crazy, Funny Face,* and *Strike Up the Band,* Broadway shows that also have become classics. Then came *Of Thee I Sing,* for which his brother Ira wrote the lyrics and George S. Kaufman the book. Gershwin's *Porgy and Bess* folk opera, with words by Ira (his favorite lyricist) and DuBose Heyward, was not a success at the time (1935), but it has since become an important part of the Gershwin— and American music—legacy.

Always seeking to improve his already considerable piano skills, George wanted to study with Maurice Ravel, but Ravel said, "Why should you be a second-rate Ravel when you can be a first-rate Gershwin?" Prolific, talented, and inspired, George felt that the world was his. He collected art and took up painting while savoring the role of debonair man-about-Manhattan. Pianist and friend Oscar Levant said, "He had a little love for a lot of people, but not a lot for anybody." George's last romance was with actress Paulette Goddard, who was married to Charlie Chaplin at the time.

After George and Ira moved to Hollywood to work on movie musicals, George began suffering from headaches, memory lapses, and poor coordination. A brain tumor was confirmed. An emergency operation removed only part of it; his life ended abruptly at thirty-eight years. But had he lived, he might have been blind and disabled.

Ira's many songs with George included "Let's Call the Whole Thing Off," "Fascinating Rhythm," and "But Not For Me." After George's death, Ira remained in Hollywood and collaborated with Jerome Kern, Harold Arlen, and Kurt Weill. He is now reunited with George in a spacious mausoleum, the third one on the right facing the main driveway, block B. Note the panels to the right and left of the tomb doors: bas-reliefs of musical instruments, interwoven with notes from *Rhapsody in Blue*.

## BILLY ROSE   1899–1966

Broadway producer, songwriter, showman, and self-promoter, Billy Rose was a diminutive man—barely 5 foot, 3 inches (without his elevator shoes)—which may be why he compensated by doing everything on a gigantic scale. His name, shortened from William Rosenberg, was probably the only thing he cut down to size.

Rose is little remembered today, but in his time he enjoyed a long, successful career. One of his first jobs was as a stenographer for Bernard Baruch during World War I, but Broadway was the magnet that drew him. He wrote more than 400 songs, including "That Old Gang of Mine," "It's Only a Paper Moon," "K-K-K-Katy," "I Found a Million-Dollar Baby in a Five-and-Ten Cent Store," "Me and My Shadow," and "Without a Song."

The owner of several nightclubs in New York, Rose was best known as a producer of *Crazy Quilt* in 1931, *Jumbo* in 1935, and *Carmen Jones* in 1943 and as the onetime husband of comic actress Fanny Brice (from 1929 to 1938). His four other marriages were also failures. It seems ironic that such a

short man has such a grandiose mausoleum on such a large plot. Built for $60,000—a fortune in 1966—the tomb is highly visible, on the left side of the main drive through the grounds in block A, opposite that of the Gershwins.

## LEE STRASBERG    1902–1982

he common denominator that links actors Dustin Hoffman, James Dean, Robert De Niro, Anne Bancroft, Julie Harris, Paul Newman, and Marilyn Monroe is Lee Strasberg, a Polish-born actor-director who taught them all at the Actors Studio in New York in a style known as "Method." Strasberg derived it from a technique formulated by Russian director Konstantin Stanislovsky, who encouraged actors to use their subconscious to develop their roles. The most celebrated exponent of Method acting was probably Marlon Brando, but, like it or not (and some critics decidedly did *not*), Strasberg's version of the style influenced at least two generations of American actors.

Even successful movie stars like Monroe considered it modish to study with Strasberg. For many beginners, his tutelage was a great leap forward in their careers. Plays were developed under his aegis at the Actors Studio, too, notably *A Hatful of Rain, The Night of the Iguana, The Zoo Story,* and *The Death of*

*Bessie Smith.* Although Strasberg stopped performing in public in 1929, he constantly acted in class as a teaching tool. Eventually Al Pacino, one of his students, persuaded him to take a supporting role in the movie *The Godfather: Part II,* for which Strasberg received an Oscar nomination. Several other movie roles followed. That Strasberg, resting in block C, is mourned and still missed by devoted students, playwrights, and other theater-connected folks is no act.

# HYDE PARK

## FRANKLIN D. ROOSEVELT NATIONAL HISTORIC SITE
*Route 9; (845) 229–9115; www.nps.gov/hofr*

The graves of both Franklin Roosevelt and his wife, Eleanor, are in the rose garden of Springwood, the family home, which overlooks the Hudson River from a majestic height. Also on the grounds: the Franklin D. Roosevelt library and museum. The property is under the supervision of the National Park Service. *Grounds open 7:00 A.M. to sunset daily; closed Thanksgiving, Christmas and New Year's Day. Free access to the grounds and rose garden; nominal admission fee to the house. Restrooms.*

### LUNCH BREAK

For a special treat, plan to lunch at the **Culinary Institute of America** (433 Albany Post Road/Route 9; 845–471–6608). It has five restaurants on the premises, where students show off their skills. The most casual and least pricey is the Apple Pie Bakery Café. The remaining four require advance reservations but are worth it. St. Andrew's Café has contemporary American food, wood-fired pizzas, and vegetarian dishes. The Escoffier is French and fancy, and the Caterina de Medici is northern Italian and elegant. My favorite is American Bounty, with dishes from various regions of the country.

## FRANKLIN DELANO ROOSEVELT   1882–1945

ranklin Roosevelt, born to a New York family of Dutch descent, was an only child and the apple of his mother's eye. An indifferent student at Harvard and a drop-out at Columbia Law School (but admitted, nonetheless, to the New York bar), handsome young Franklin was attracted to politics. He held a string of political jobs, including state senator and assistant secretary of the navy under Woodrow Wilson, and ran unsuccessfully for vice president. Then in 1921 disaster in the form of polio struck, leaving both of his legs paralyzed. The promising politician's career seemed over. No one at the time would have foreseen that it was really just beginning.

Roosevelt had married Eleanor—a shy, plain cousin from the Theodore Roosevelt branch of the family—in 1905. With her encouragement and his own determination, Franklin learned to stand and, with leg braces, even walk a few steps. Though seriously disabled, he managed through sheer willpower (and the help of a compliant press corps) to project the image of a strong, vigorous man, which, mentally, he was. After two terms as governor of New York, Roosevelt ran for president in 1932—and won. At his inauguration he declared that "the only thing we have to fear is fear itself," which inspired the multitudes bogged down by the Great Depression.

Our thirty-second president's policies were so popular that he easily won a second, then unprecedented third and fourth terms. Early on, he repealed Prohibition and introduced his "New Deal," which carried the country out of the Depression with innovative public-works projects and relief programs. Millions listened to his fireside chats on radio. His acceptance speech for a

## HOUSE CALL

Well worth a visit is **Springwood,** the Roosevelt home on the grounds. Comfortable and affluent for its time, but not in the least opulent, the rambling neo-Georgian house (parts of which date back to 1826) is in a time warp: Its furnishings are still as they were in 1945 when FDR died. An excellent tour conducted by park rangers highlights the personal side of FDR's life, even showing the primitive elevator by whose ropes the president hauled himself upstairs.

second-term nomination included this memorable line: "This generation of Americans has a rendezvous with destiny."

FDR, as he was known, also introduced legislation that established Social Security. He later initiated a lend-lease program to Britain and, once the Japanese attacked Pearl Harbor, guided the country through its worst world war. While vacationing in Warm Springs, Georgia, at the "Little White House," he died of a cerebral hemorrhage on April 12, 1945, just after his fourth term had begun.

Like all great leaders, FDR had ardent admirers and fierce opponents (who referred to him as "that man"). Today most historians consider him the greatest of our twentieth-century presidents, high in the pantheon of all-time leaders.

## ELEANOR ROOSEVELT  1884–1962

Alongside Franklin is his independent-spirited wife of forty years. What began as a love match between two distant (fifth) cousins, resulting in six children in ten years, evolved, due to Franklin's infidelities, into a détente and then a solid political partnership. Eleanor traveled the country

## HOUSE CALL

**Val-Kill** (2 miles east of Hyde Park; 845–229–8114) is a more informal house that Eleanor Roosevelt maintained as a weekend retreat (away from the pressures of Franklin's strong-minded mother, Sara, who ruled Springwood with an iron hand). After FDR's death, Eleanor lived there full-time. It is open to visitors and offers a fascinating glimpse into Eleanor's relaxed lifestyle when she was away from official duties at the White House. A shuttle bus takes visitors from Springwood to Val-Kill and back.

and the world on behalf of various causes—minorities, working-class women, the poor, the oppressed of all nations—and articulated their frustrations and goals in speeches, a newspaper column, and other writings. Newspaper editorials and cartoons had a field day ridiculing her constant travels, but FDR called her his "eyes and ears" for gauging public opinion and reporting back to him.

Hated by those who felt that she had "betrayed her class" (a charge leveled against FDR as well), Eleanor was beloved by millions of others. In 1939 she resigned from the Daughters of the American Revolution when the organization refused to let the African-American singer Marian Anderson perform at Constitution Hall.

Eleanor was always more liberal than her husband, and after his death she devoted her time and boundless energy to a number of worthy causes. In 1945 President Harry Truman appointed her to the U.S. Delegation to the United Nations, a position she held until 1953; John F. Kennedy reappointed her to the same in 1961. A popular speaker and lecturer, Eleanor wrote nine books, including a multivolume autobiography and numerous magazine articles. She continued writing "My Day," a syndicated newspaper column that she began in 1935, until shortly before her death.

# ST. ANDREW'S CEMETERY

*Culinary Institute of America, 433 Albany Post Road (Route 9);*
*(845) 451–1267*

The redbrick, cream-trimmed colossus that is now Roth Hall, the main building of the Culinary Institute of America (CIA), was once part of St. Andrew-
on-Hudson, a Jesuit seminary. The seminary closed up shop years ago, but the
minuscule cemetery is still intact. To find it, stop for instructions and to pick
up the key at the safety office of the CIA, in a diner-like building to the right
of Roth Hall. The small burial ground is beyond the safety building at the far
end of the parking lot, to the right of a metal fence. The cemetery itself is
behind a wrought-iron padlocked gate. Once inside the gate, just beyond a
graceful split-leaf Japanese maple tree, there are rows of identical white headstones of the many Jesuit priests who died in the late nineteenth and mid-
twentieth centuries. To the left of the pathway on a tiny hillside is a sculptural
crucifixion scene. The juxtaposition of this peaceful burial ground right next
to a parking lot and hyperactive school is striking. *Open 7:00* A.M. *to dusk daily*
*(with key). Restrooms in Roth Hall.*

## PIERRE TEILHARD DE CHARDIN   1881–1955

*I*n his day, this French Jesuit was a widely known paleontologist, with a
doctorate from the Sorbonne, who was also respected as a philosopher
and visionary. He entered the Jesuit order at age eighteen and was
ordained at thirty. He taught at the Institut Catholique in Paris, visited China
several times, and was an advisor to the National Geological Survey, collaborating on research that led to the discovery of Peking man.

Teilhard's goal was to integrate natural science with a religious life. He was
an ecologist before the word became common coinage, writing in *Building the
Earth* that "The task before us now, if we would not perish, is to build the
Earth." Ever the optimist in his view of man and the world, he wrote many
books in a long productive life, most of them published posthumously. The
most famous was *The Phenomenon of Man*; others were *Science and Christ*,
*Man's Place in Nature*, *Hymn of the Universe*, *The Future of Man*, *Writings in
Time of War*, and *The Divine Milieu*. Teilhard is still read today, both in Europe
and North America, by those seeking to balance religious thought with daily
life.

His grave, framed by two small peony bushes but otherwise identical to all the others, is in the third row from the rear, nine headstones in on the right. As a touchstone, look for the large square mausoleum on the left side of the path. It is just opposite the last three rows of headstones.

# NORTH TARRYTOWN
# SLEEPY HOLLOW

## THE OLD DUTCH BURYING GROUND OF SLEEPY HOLLOW

*540 North Broadway; (914) 631–1123; www.olddutchburyingground.org and www.retode.org*

North Tarrytown can be confusing. Originally a spin-off of Tarrytown, it became its own entity in 1874 but was officially renamed Sleepy Hollow in 1996 to invoke memories of the village's more bucolic past and its Washington Irving heritage. (Signage throughout the village uses both names.) The two

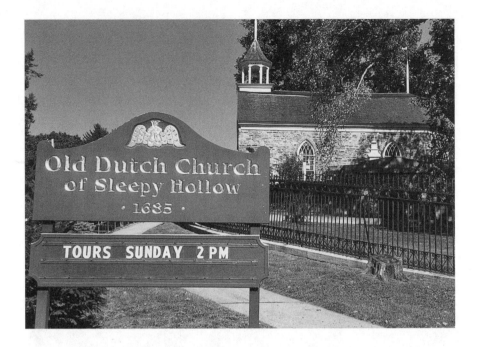

intriguing burial grounds here—Old Dutch and Sleepy Hollow Cemetery—
are contiguous, which simplifies a visit.

On the right (east) side of North Broadway, heading north, is the Old Dutch
Church of Sleepy Hollow. This wood-and-fieldstone edifice with a steeple is a
National Historic Landmark. It is owned by the Reformed Church of Tarrytown and was built in 1685, restored in 1837, and then restored again in 1897
and within the past few years. Surrounding the pristine church on three sides,
covering about three and one-half acres, is the Old Dutch Churchyard, officially called the Old Dutch Burying Ground of Sleepy Hollow. You needn't be
a cemetery connoisseur to relish this old-fashioned graveyard.

Late in the afternoon on a chilly, rain-threatening day, a walk through the
grounds might seem sepulchral and evoke a shudder and images of Ichabod
Crane and the Headless Horseman, even though the cemetery is not scary in
itself. Many of the old tombstones, some of which date back to 1650, are
engraved in an antiquated Dutch patois, long forgotten today. These weathered,
near-obliterated limestone markers—bearing names like Van Aken, Couenhoven,
and Arser—remind us of the Dutch heritage in this part of the Hudson Valley.

Many of these early settlers were colorful individuals whose stories are
recounted on a tour offered from time to time. Some of the epitaphs engraved

on the stones are alone worth a visit, such as the one for **Deleverence Acker** (1784–1804), buried to the left of the church next to the path:

> Call and see as you pass by
> As you are now, so once was I.
> As I am now you must so be
> Prepare for death and follow me.

Death is a recurring theme on many of the stones, like that for **John Enters** (1708–1779), near the left front of the church:

> Death is a debt to nature due;
> which I have paid and so must you.

The tombstone of **Evart Arser** (1743–1765) warns:

> Hark from the tombs a doleful voice
> My ears attend the cry
> You living men come view the ground
> Where you must shortly lie.

Did I say this isn't spooky?

Note the marble urn on a pedestal in front of the Van Aken family site, to the right of the church; it belongs to **Eleanor Van Tassel Brush** (1763–1861). Legend has it that she was Washington Irving's inspiration for Katrina in "The Legend of Sleepy Hollow." Eleanor's real life was a story in itself. As a young woman she was kidnapped by a renegade band of British soldiers. Her spunky Dutch housewife-mother and aunt pursued the soldiers, punched and battered them with makeshift weapons until they released Eleanor, and then ran away.

Behind the church, near the stone wall, are three more graves connected to "The Legend of Sleepy Hollow." **Susannah** (1732–1783) and **Joseph Youngs** (1722–1789) were the parents of schoolmaster Samuel Youngs, rumored to be the model for Ichabod Crane. Brom Bones, who marries Katrina in the story, was supposedly based on **Abraham "Brom" Martling**

**LUNCH BREAK**

Down the road, closer to the center of town, is **The Horseman** (276 North Broadway; 914–631–2984), a cheerful luncheonette with moderately priced sandwiches, pizza, and Greek specialties.

(1743–1830), who, with his brother Isaac (buried nearby), gave British soldiers and Loyalists a hard time. *Grounds open 8:00 A.M.–4:30 P.M. daily; grave rubbings prohibited. Church open only for guided tours (donation requested) on Sunday at 2:00 P.M., end of May through October.*

## FREDERICK PHILIPSE  1626–1702

This Dutchman, one of the earliest settlers, merchants, and landowners in the Tarrytown area, may have been the most successful carpenter in early America. He had the good fortune to combine an upwardly mobile marriage with hard work and an entrepreneurial spirit. His wife's fortune helped him thrive in grain milling, fur trading, and especially land accumulation. By 1693 his estate, certified by a royal charter, stretched from the current North Tarrytown south to the current Bronx, between the Hudson and Bronx Rivers—an area of some 90,000 acres. The main manor house that Philipse built eventually became the Yonkers city hall. His northern manor house in Upper Mills (now North Tarrytown/Sleepy Hollow) was a model of Dutch thrift and efficient farm management. After the American Revolution, the Philipse property changed hands (and fortunes) a number of times.

Philipse and his family are buried not on the grounds but in the crypt of the church, which he was responsible for erecting in 1697. Note the blue plaque in the ground by the churchyard that says the church was built by Philipse, "first lord of the manor, in use since, except in revolution." The church is open only for guided tours (see above). The tour is worth it to see the pale blue-green pews and the replica of the original pulpit.

### HOUSE CALL

The former Philipse Manor is now called **Philipsburg Manor** (Route 9; 914–631–8200). It has been extensively restored and gives visitors an authentic picture of a prosperous colonial farm, with a gristmill, a barn, animals (the breeds used at the time), slave quarters, a dam, and a millpond bridge over the Pocantico River. There are cheese-making and other farm demonstrations. The manor house is furnished in eighteenth-century Dutch style.

## ROCKEFELLER FAMILY CEMETERY

*North Broadway, on the east side of the road*

This private family burial ground, with a veritable forest screening it from the main road, abuts the north end of Sleepy Hollow Cemetery and is enclosed by an inconspicuous high metal fence. At the entrance is an unmarked wooden gate. **John D. Rockefeller Jr.** (1874–1960) and other members of the JDR Jr. branch of this prominent American family are buried here. **Nelson Rockefeller** (1908–1979)—the popular governor of New York from 1959 to 1973 and vice president of the United States from 1974 to 1976 under Gerald Ford—has a cenotaph here, but his ashes are scattered on the grounds. The gate is as near as visitors can get, and the view over it includes little else than a hillside of trees.

## HOUSE CALLS

This is Rockefeller country. Diagonally across from the Old Dutch Church is the entrance to the Kykuit Visitor Center (Route 9; 914–631–9491). From there (by prior reservation) a shuttle bus transports you to **Kykuit,** the forty-room John D. Rockefeller Jr. estate. Here Nelson Rockefeller and his family lived for nineteen years. The Beaux-Arts mansion and beautiful sculpture gardens are surpassed only by the interior's antique furnishings and art collection. Also in the vicinity is the **Union Church of Pocantico Hills** (555 Bedford Road/Route 448; 914–631–2069), with glorious stained-glass windows by Marc Chagall and Henri Matisse, commissioned by the Rockefellers.

## SLEEPY HOLLOW CEMETERY

*540 North Broadway, just south of the Rockefeller Family Cemetery;*
*(914) 631–0081; www.sleepyhollowcemetery.org*

This sloping, eighty-five-acre cemetery with two steep tiers and undulating byways opened in 1849 and continues to be an afterlife address for the rich, famous, and fashionable. The first colonial tier abuts the Old Dutch Burying Ground and is where many Revolutionary War soldiers are buried. One plot in this southernmost section is called Beekman Mound; it belongs to the Irving family. In fact, Washington Irving, a trustee of the burial ground, wrote to a friend, "I trust I shall one day lay my bones there." He christened the cemetery "Sleepy Hollow," suggesting that the name is "enough of itself to secure the patronage of all desirous of sleeping quietly in their graves." (He could not have foreseen that a bustling, traffic-clogged road, Route 9, would develop as the main north-south artery in the area.) A short distance up the hill from the Irvings is a Revolutionary War monument.

The best way to enter the elongated grounds is through the main gate, which is past the Old Dutch Church on North Broadway, pretty much at the center of the cemetery. Facing the gate, which leads into the center of the cemetery, is a 1922 faux-Gothic fieldstone building that contains both the chapel and office. The expansive grounds are lovely, shaded by cedars, Japan-

ese maples, pines, and dogwood trees, along a road that winds, dips, curves, and then levels off. The Pocantico River, more of a stream at this point, borders the cemetery grounds along the east side.

The road to the right rear of the office leads upward to the graves of many famous nineteenth- and early-twentieth-century arrivees. One of the most impressive sights is the mausoleum of **John Dustin Archbold** (1854–1916), president of Standard Oil of New Jersey and a colleague of William Rockefeller, whose own mausoleum is directly across the roadway. Note the splendid bronze doors and the boldly engraved ARCHBOLD across the facade. If you peek, you can see the beautiful mosaic work covering the inside of the dome. It resembles a Middle Eastern sheik's tomb, which is probably appropriate, considering the source of this oil tycoon's income.

Other worthies residing here include **Major Edward Bowes** (1874–1946; Gibeon section), the host of a popular radio show called *Major Bowes and His Original Amateur Hour*; **Mark Hellinger** (1903–1947; Olivet section), a New York journalist and Broadway and Hollywood producer; and **Whitelaw Reid** (1837–1912; section 27), editor of the *New York Tribune*. The multifaceted **Carl Schurz** (1829–1906; section 71) is here, having had careers as a diplomat, Civil War general, senator, secretary of the interior under Rutherford B.

Hayes, journalist, and editor. Another notable is **Henry Villard** (1835–1900; section 62), millionaire, president of the Northern Pacific Railroad, and publisher of the *New York Post*; his art nouveau memorial of a reclining languid young man with a sledgehammer is one of the cemetery's most arresting sculptures. **Oswald Villard** (1872–1949; section 62), Henry's son and editor of *The Nation* magazine, is in the same section as his father.

Other movers and shakers at Sleepy Hollow are **Walter Percy Chrysler** (1875–1940; Altona section, next to north fence, abutting Rockefeller Family Cemetery), an inventor, an engineer, and founder of the Chrysler Corporation; **Thomas J. Watson Sr.** (1874–1956; section 49), the founder of IBM; **Elizabeth Arden** (1878–1966; section 77), the cosmetics magnate; and **Henry Sloan Coffin** (1877–1954; section 9), a famous theologian in a line of theologians. *Grounds open 8:00 A.M.–4:30 P.M. Monday–Friday, 8:30 A.M.–4:30 P.M. Saturday and Sunday. Office hours: 8:30 A.M.–4:30 P.M. Monday–Friday; closed major holidays. Map; restrooms; stone rubbings prohibited. Call the office to arrange informal private and group van-plus-walking tours (donation requested).*

## ANDREW CARNEGIE   1835–1919

*A*ndrew Carnegie's name is often lumped with robber barons of the late nineteenth century—men who made millions on the backs of their workers and reveled in opulent lifestyles. But Carnegie was a different breed. He actually believed in *giving back*. His Scottish family came to the United States in 1848 and settled in Allegheny, Pennsylvania, and little Andrew was soon put to work in a cotton factory as a bobbin boy. From a salary of $1.20 a week, he was to grow—through daring, organizational skills, and intelligence—into a multimillionaire, making a fortune in railroads and steel.

His early beliefs in labor unions, collective bargaining, and the right to strike were put to the test when his business was involved. In the 1892 strike of Carnegie's Homestead Steel Company, he gave a free hand to his plant manager, Henry Clay Frick, to use Pinkerton detectives to stop the strike by any means, brutal or not. It worked and the union was broken, but Carnegie's and Frick's reputations were stained. Relations between the two men soured when Carnegie attempted to force Frick out. Many years later, when Carnegie wanted to make amends with Frick, the latter reportedly told the go-between, "Tell Mr. Carnegie I'll meet him in Hell—where we'll both be."

Carnegie retired in 1901, early enough to enjoy life—writing, reading, traveling, buying one Scottish castle and building another one, making friends with notables in the English and American cultural and political worlds. But

he never forgot his youthful poverty and his early vow to give away as much of his fortune as he could. He was as good as his word, believing that "he who dies rich, dies disgraced." Carnegie donated some $350 million—to public libraries (his special interest), colleges, the Carnegie Institute of Pittsburgh, and the Carnegie Foundation for the Advancement of Teaching, among scores of endowments. His gifts were intended to improve the life of the common man. "Let there be light" was a slogan he placed in his libraries, for he felt that enlightenment was man's key to freedom and progress. He died the recipient of many honors and awards and a moderately wealthy man, but no longer—because of all his gifts—the megamillionaire he once had been.

Money may not buy happiness, but it *can* buy privacy. The Carnegie grave site, one of my favorites because of its seclusion and serenity, is a hidden bower surrounded by a thick circle of ancient rhododendrons and ground cover of pachysandras. It is located at the corner of Summit Avenue and Dingle Road (Hebron section). You enter the sheltered area via large stepping stones that lead past a discreet pedestal with a bronze marker and

bas-relief of Carnegie. Inside the circle is a clearing and a Celtic cross—half-hidden under pine trees—with Carnegie's name and "born Dunfermline Scotland 25 November 1835 / Died Lenox Massachusetts 11 August 1919" at its base. Modest headstones for Carnegie and his wife, **Louise Whitfield Carnegie** (1857–1946), who supported his charitable giving, are in front of the cross. At the edge of the clearing are slightly larger headstones of three "beloved members of the household" and "lifelong, loyal and devoted" staff.

## SAMUEL GOMPERS   1850–1924

*B*orn in London, Samuel Gompers was thirteen when he emigrated to New York. Later, as a worker in the Cigarmakers' International Union, he edged his way up the labor ladder, representing the union at conventions. In 1882 he became president of the American Federation of Labor (which he founded); he was reelected to the post every year until he died.

Gompers fought hard to ensure for workers better wages, shorter hours, and safer working conditions. At the same time, he battled against socialistic influences among unions. Although by nature a pacifist, he did not actively oppose the U.S. entrance into World War I. At the time of his death in San Antonio, Texas, Gompers was the most powerful labor leader in the United States and has long been considered the father of the American labor movement. Carved into the bottom of his gray headstone are the words "erected by Executive Council A. F. of L."

There is a pinch of irony in the fact that this labor leader is buried (in the south edge of the Monticello section) within sight of industrialist Andrew Carnegie.

## WASHINGTON IRVING  1783–1859

*A*uthor, poet, diplomat, and historian, Washington Irving was from a prominent old New York mercantile family with Scottish-English roots and literary and religious interests. Abandoning a legal career, he enjoyed travel and a cultural life and kept notebooks wherever he went. These were grist for his essays, sto-

ries, and travel books in years ahead. On his first tour of Europe he was captured by pirates—more grist.

Irving's first major literary effort, a magazine called *Sala-magundi* that published satirical poems and sketches, proved a big hit. In 1809 he wrote *A History of New York* as a parody of more ponderous works. It, too, was a huge success. When *The Sketch Book* was published (in 1819–20), it included "Rip Van Winkle" and "The Legend of Sleepy Hollow," combining humor with a folkloric quality that charmed readers and added to the author's reputation. A trip to Spain yielded the respected *History of the Life and Voyages of Christopher Columbus*, followed by the engaging stories and sketches in *The Alhambra*, which is still read today. Stints as a diplomat in London and as American minister to Madrid followed and enhanced Irving's renown as America's "first man of letters."

He once wrote, "If ever I should wish for a retreat, whither I might steal from the world, and its distractions . . . I know of none more promising than this little valley." He was true to his words. He spent the last thirteen years of his life at Sunnyside, his home high above the Hudson River, basking in the affection of family and admiring friends. His one known love died at age seventeen of consumption. Irving never married but was a playful, devoted uncle to numerous nieces and nephews.

Now, in his final repose, he is just where he wished to be. The large Irving family grave site, in the Beekman Mound section, is secured by concrete posts, thick iron crossbars, and a padlocked gate. It has sixty or more head-stones, an oak tree, five old granite steps leading up to the graves, and a bronze plaque in front that reads "The Irving Family Graveplot." Washington's own headstone, with much of the carving eroded, "receives perpetual care from local citizens and admirers of the author of the 'Sleepy Hollow Legends,'" as a nearby notice states. It is fitting that his grave, in the south end of the ceme-

## HOUSE CALL

Washington Irving's seventeen-room house, **Sunnyside** (West Sunnyside Lane, Tarrytown; 914–631–8200), with its Spanish tower, is nearby and is a delight to visit. It started life as a simple farmhouse, but Irving enjoyed tinkering with it, adding dormers, gables, and towers. When he finished, he described the home thus: "as full of angles and corners as an old cocked hat." That's what makes it so charming. Most of the fur-nishings are of the 1850s and were Irving's, including his sleigh bed, lap desk, books, and Moorish robe. The house evokes the man so thoroughly that it seems as if he has just stepped out for a walk and will return shortly.

tery, near the boundary of the Old Dutch Burying Ground, bridges the old and newer, just as his works did in life.

## WILLIAM ROCKEFELLER   1841–1922

Y ou have only to look at this stately, Greek temple–like mausoleum, with four imposing columns on all sides and a bas-relief frieze carved from the gray granite, to realize that the occupant was someone to be reckoned with. Indeed he was. This younger brother of John D. Rockefeller Sr. began his career as a bookkeeper for a mill in Cleveland, the family hometown. When John D. got into the oil business, founding a refining company, he invited William to move to New York to manage the export part. This became the incredibly successful Standard Oil Company of New York.

Unlike John D., whose genius was for organization, William shone as a salesman, financier, promoter, and speculator in securities. With Wall Street colleagues—called the "Standard Oil gang"— he branched into various corporate fields and became a director in many disparate companies, like gas and railroads. Unlike John D., who was serious, religious, and a renowned philanthropist, William was gregarious, high-living, and not known for charitable contributions. When he died at age eighty-one, he left the bulk of his $150–$200 million fortune to his four surviving children (of six), with no charitable bequests listed.

On its own little "island," bordered by sections Gibeon, Olivet, and Lebanon, Rockefeller's large grassy plot surrounds his mausoleum. On the grass are large, full-length gravestones of fifteen Rockefeller family members and offspring. On the left side of the lawn are three flat stones commemorating family retainers, with such words as "In remembrance of the many years of friendship and devotion to William Rockefeller and family."

# NYACK

## OAK HILL CEMETERY
*140 North Highland Avenue; (914) 358–0012*

On a spacious hillside overlooking the Hudson River, Oak Hill opened in 1848. It was one of the new rural nonsectarian cemeteries, which were a departure from the religious burial grounds or small family plots of the time. Today the slopes are prolific with oak trees (as the name suggests), dogwoods, andromeda, and other flowering bushes. Wild turkeys and black squirrels scamper over the well-mown lawns, and birds communicate through the treetops. The cemetery encompasses more than sixty-five acres. Each area is defined by name (e.g., Grand View Lawn, Oak Point, and Hudson Lawn), making it relatively easy to find a specific grave within.

In addition to being the final residence of artists and writers who lived quietly in Nyack in their other lives, Oak Hill is the last abode of the town's founders, war veterans, local politicos, scientists, and other long-time resi-

---

### LUNCH BREAK

If you like the zing of Thai food, try **The King & I** (93 Main Street; 845–353–4208) in the center of town; seafood is a specialty. For a real treat drive 4 or 5 miles south of town to Piermont for a super lunch at the **Free Lance Café & Wine Bar** (506 Piermont Avenue; 845–365–3250). The cooking is delightfully creative New American style, and the cafe has a good selection of wines by the glass. Free Lance is connected to **Xaviar's at Piermont** (same address; 845–359–7007), one of the area's very best restaurants; it serves lunch on Friday only, prix fixe dinner Wednesday through Sunday, and an exceptional Sunday brunch.

dents. *Gates open 8:00 A.M.–8:00 P.M. May through August, 8:00 A.M.–5:00 P.M. September–April. Office is inside the gates, on the immediate right. Map; restroom.*

## JOSEPH CORNELL    1903–1972

While not in the highest niche in the art pantheon—his work was too small-scale for that—Joseph Cornell is known to connoisseurs for his unique box art. The surreal quality of his small open-sided boxes is no accident. He was inspired by surrealism, especially the work of Max Ernst, though Cornell's approach was generally more upbeat than the dark, erotic side of that art movement. His boxes feature ordinary three-dimensional objects like corks, marbles, keys, balls, and feathers, with collages (theater tickets, old photographs, maps)—creating a dreamlike world that can be mysterious and off-kilter. His use of ordinary objects, which he collected at flea markets, antiques shops, and souvenir shops, preceded pop art by some thirty years.

A loner in art as in life, Cornell was born in New York City; was educated at Phillips Academy in Andover, Massachusetts; and lived most of his life in Flushing, Queens. There he shared a small one-family house with his mother

and disabled brother, Robert. As an artist—and also a filmmaker—Cornell was self-taught. His career spanned almost half a century, beginning with an exhibit of collages and found objects in 1932. His reputation has grown continuously, and his boxes are in major museum collections. Not a bad finale for an artist who thought small.

Cornell's 5-foot-tall gray granite headstone sits, along with those of family members, on the north side of the Prospect Lawn section, near the curve.

## HELEN HAYES   1900–1993
## CHARLES MACARTHUR   1895–1956

*I*n the showbiz world in which they lived, the MacArthurs' twenty-eight-year-long marriage was a phenomenon. They were polar opposites. She was shy, naive, and sheltered. He was brash, witty, a jokester, and a nonstop drinker. They met in New York, but their mutual friends tried to talk each of them out of marriage, convinced it would never last. Perhaps their union survived because they rarely worked together or because they were able to celebrate each other's noncompetitive creativity. She was an actress, long called the "first lady of the American theater." He was a successful playwright, journalist, and screenwriter. He admired her acting skills; she adored his way with words, his good nature, and his quick wit.

One of their few collaborative efforts was a success for them both: He wrote the screenplay for *The Sin of Madelon Claudet* in 1931; she won an Academy Award for her role in it. It was her film debut, and although she was only thirty-one at the time, she played an old woman. Following quickly were star turns in *Arrowsmith* with Ronald Colman, *Farewell to Arms* with Gary Cooper, and *The White Sister* with Clark Gable.

Hayes acted most of her long life, from a preschool beginning in her native Washington, D.C., to cameo appearances on television in the years just before her death (of congestive heart failure). Many of her theatrical triumphs came when she portrayed women older than herself—Queen Victoria in *Victoria Regina*, Mary Stuart in *Mary of Scotland*, and Amanda Wingfield in *The Glass Menagerie*. Never introspective as an actress, Hayes admitted that she reached outside herself for inspiration. A Method actress she was not.

Arguably her best roles were as Mrs. Antrobus in *The Skin of Our Teeth* and Nora Melody in *A Touch of the Poet*. Although Hayes made a number of movies, her early work was the most successful. In her later roles, after movie acting styles had changed, she seemed unable to adapt her broader theater style to the smaller medium of film, where facial expressions are intimate and subtle. She did, however, receive a second Oscar for a supporting role in *Airport*. Hayes's life was full of awards and honorary degrees.

She also published three autobiographical books: *A Gift of Joy* (1965), *On Reflection* (1968), and *My Life in Three Acts* (1990). On the day she died, lights all over Broadway went off at 8:00 P.M. for a full minute. Her legacy lives on, not just on Broadway, where there is a theater named after her, but in the Helen Hayes MacArthur Hospital, so named for her help in establishing a therapy center for victims of polio. The March of Dimes' Mary MacArthur Fund was named for Helen and Charlie's daughter, a talented young actress herself, who was stricken with polio at age nineteen and died within a few days. Mary's death devastated her parents, but Hayes, ever the trouper, forced herself to carry on.

Charlie MacArthur, born in Scranton, Pennsylvania, grew up in Nyack. As a young man he worked as a journalist in Chicago, then enlisted in the Illinois militia and was sent to Mexico to help capture Pancho Villa, an adventure he considered something of a lark. Later, back in Chicago, he reenlisted in World War I and saw action with the Rainbow Division in the Meuse-Argonne and Chateau-Thierry.

Even war couldn't tame his high spirits. His working life as a hard-drinking, fun-loving newspaperman in Chicago in the Roaring Twenties inspired his most famous work, *The Front Page*, which he wrote with Ben Hecht, a fellow journalist, close friend, and frequent collaborator. There were four film adaptations of the play, the funniest and most flamboyant of which was *His Girl Friday*, which starred Cary Grant and Rosalind Russell. In 1935 *The Scoundrel*, a Hecht-MacArthur film adapted from their original story, won the two an Oscar for best original screenplay. They also played cameo roles in the movie. Other Hecht-MacArthur screenplays included *Gunga Din*, an unlikely assignment for two wisecracking journalists.

Always a heavy drinker (which played havoc with his innards), MacArthur declined steadily after his daughter's death, which he never got over. He died seven years later. In life MacArthur was so well-known that his cynical, compassionate, and charming personality became a prototype for other writers, among them F. Scott Fitzgerald, Moss Hart, Thornton Wilder, and S. N. Behrman, who created MacArthur types in their own works.

The three small marble MacArthur gravestones embedded in the grass of the Grand View Lawn section are sheltered by the shade of two trees and a bush. You will find them below and in front of the Hecht family headstones on a hilly slope with a sweeping view of the Hudson below. Between Charlie and Helen is their daughter, **Mary MacArthur** (1930–1949). The sad words on her marker were composed by her father and convey her parents' grief: "Underneath this stone doth lie as much beauty as could die."

## BEN HECHT   1894–1964

Just a few steps behind the MacArthur graves, in front of a row of nine large mausoleums in the Grand View Lawn section, lies another family threesome: the upright slate headstones of Ben Hecht, his wife, and their daughter. Hecht is on the left; his stone bears the words "Sleep on! While at thy feet I weep." Next is his wife, **Rose Hecht** (1898–1979), with the words "And rooks in families homeward go." Then comes daughter **Jenny Hecht** (1943–1971), who died at age twenty-eight, memorialized with a quote from one of Ben's works: "Where was she stolen from the world, and all the world left without an elfin bugle blowing, without a breath of Eden stirring except on my daughter's face newly born?" One can feel the sadness.

Hecht and Charlie MacArthur were partners in crime—well, no, to be accurate, in playwriting about crime. Their most famous work was *The Front Page*, which captured the hard-boiled, free-for-all atmosphere of Chicago newspaper life in the late 1920s and early 30s. Although a New Yorker most of his life, Hecht feasted on his time in Chicago after World War I in colorful, cynical short stories and novels. He considered himself foremost a novelist, but objective observers preferred his short stories. One of his best collections is *1001 Afternoons in Chicago.*

Hecht was no slouch as a screenwriter either, winning an Oscar for *Underworld* and for *The Scoundrel* (with MacArthur). This didn't keep him from disparaging Hollywood (like many other writers who considered screenwriting just a way to pay the rent). He once wrote, "The honors Hollywood has for the writer are as dubious as tissue paper cufflinks." Another Hecht line: "In Hollywood, a starlet is the name for any woman under thirty who is not actively employed in a brothel." Yet among a number of Hecht screenplay credits were several big hits: *Gunga Din, Wuthering Heights, Angels Over Broadway,* and *Notorious.*

Hecht told his wife that he wanted to be buried near MacArthur—and he was. Nunnally Johnson, a friend and fellow writer, said, "Now those two are together again to engage in some of their hell-raising." Even in this graveyard shift, anything is possible.

## EDWARD HOPPER  1882–1967

*I*n our mobile society it is unusual for an artist to be born and buried in the same town. But that is the sketchy outline of Edward Hopper's life. He and his wife, **Josephine Hopper** (1883–1968), share the same rough-hewn gray granite headstone—cramped quarters, perhaps, considering their stormy (though loving) relationship. Hopper's parents are behind them beneath similar stones, and to the right of them is Hopper's sister, **Marion** (1880–1965). All reside at the edge of plot C, facing Oak Avenue.

Hopper left Nyack at age seventeen to study art (for seven years) in New York under Robert Henri, one of the founders of American realism. Hopper later visited Paris, London, Amsterdam, and Spain, but his painting style—scenes of solitary people in hotel rooms, depots, restaurants, and gas sta-

tions—remained firmly American in its transient nature, evoking loneliness, solitude, and sometimes despair.

Most of his life was actually spent in Greenwich Village. At the 1913 Armory Show, a landmark event for modern American art, Hopper sold his first painting, but full success was slow to come. He was thirty-seven when it arrived, with sales to the Museum of Modern Art and the Whitney Museum. Hopper was a late bloomer in his personal life as well, marrying at age forty-two a fellow artist from his art school days, Jo Nivison. She modeled for almost all his work, and they traveled together throughout the United States and Mexico, quarreling and making up until the very end.

## CARSON MCCULLERS   1917–1967

Considering that Lula Carson Smith McCullers had rheumatic fever at age fifteen and a series of strokes that left her an invalid and blind in one eye by her thirties, it is rather amazing that she lived to be fifty, felled at last by cancer and a stroke that led to brain hemorrhaging. While her literary output was not large, it is memorable, beginning with the novel *The Heart Is a Lonely Hunter.* All her major works—*Reflections in a Golden Eye, The Ballad of the Sad Café,* and *The Member of the Wedding*—were later adapted for the movies. The latter was a highly successful Broadway play as well; it won the New York Drama Critics Circle Award and two Donaldson Awards. McCullers also wrote plays for television, short stories, and books of poems for children.

A recurring theme in her work is loneliness and alienation. Many considered her an inconsequential Southern Gothic writer—like Arthur Miller, who called her a "minor author," and critic Stanley Kaufman, who deemed her work merely "Spanish moss hanging on the tree of American literature." McCullers's subject matter (freaks, eccentrics, and misfits) put many off, but that undervalues her subtle, nuanced style and empathetic view of society's outcasts. She once said that "writing, for me, is a search for God." She also noted, "I live with the people I create and it has always made my essential loneliness less keen."

Born in Columbus, Georgia, to a prosperous jeweler and his wife, Lula Carson was a youthful piano protégé and moved to New York to study at the Juilliard School of Music. Instead, having lost her tuition money, she survived on menial jobs, earning money to study creative writing at several New York universities, and ended up as a writer. Her personal life took various turns. She married, divorced, and remarried Reeves McCullers, another writer, whose failures eventually led him to suicide. (He wanted her to join him in a double-suicide pact; she declined.) Though southern-born, she lived much of her life in New York, Paris, and Nyack, making friends with Truman Capote, Tennessee Williams, and W. H. Auden. In Nyack, McCullers shared a house with her mother and sister, Rita Smith, who was a book editor in New York. Among McCullers's awards were two Guggenheim Fellowships and a National Institute of Arts and Letters grant.

To find McCullers's grave, walk up a steep grassy incline to the far right end of High View Lawn. If you are driving, it is easier to take a right at the end of Division Avenue, then a second right along a mere grassy track. Near the end, in the third row from the rear, are two gray granite stones, fairly low, with identical silvery plantings in front of each. The stone on the right, a bit smaller than that of McCullers, belongs to her mother, **Marguerite Waters** (1890–1955), identified as the "wife of Lamar Smith."

# POUGHKEEPSIE

## POUGHKEEPSIE RURAL CEMETERY
*342 South Avenue; (845) 454–6020; www.poughkeepsieruralcemetery.org*

This esteemed cemetery opened in 1853, on land bought and developed by sixty subscribers who paid $300 each. Originally there were 54 acres; 106 were added in 1883. What makes Poughkeepsie Rural special is its Victorian character and its proximity to the Hudson River. Family plots, imposing mausoleums, statuary, a Victorian gazebo, a pond frequented by ducks and geese, a Spanish-American War memorial, and a plethora of pine and oak trees are situated on a bluff above the water, with the river as a compelling backdrop.

A signature of the cemetery grounds is the granite sundial designed by Tiffany Studios of New York. At the Police Memorial is a granite bench donated in memory of James Cagney, who lived in the area and was a friend of the Poughkeepsie police department.

There are no "big names" residing here, but the grounds are peopled with many intriguing characters. **Gaius Bolin Sr.** (1864–1946; section 10, across from the Civil War Memorial) was the first African-American graduate of Williams College and first black lawyer in Dutchess County. **Thomas Murphy** (1877–1967; mausoleum in section 40), called "wizard of the reins," was internationally famous as harness racing's greatest trainer and driver.

**LUNCH BREAK**

Down Route 9 South a short distance is **The Coyote Grill** (2629 South Road; 845–471–0600), which serves Mexican, Italian, and American specialties at reasonable prices.

**Philip Hamilton** (1802–1884; section V), the youngest son of Alexander Hamilton, is in the Hamilton plot along with Alexander's grandson, **Captain Louis McLane Hamilton** (1844–1868), a member of General George Custer's Seventh Cavalry, who was killed in the Battle of Washita.

Several permanent residents here made contributions that far outlasted their times. Lawyer and educator **Joel Springarn** (1875–1939; section M) was one. With his brother Arthur (also a lawyer), he helped found the National Association for the Advancement of Colored People (NAACP), which awards the Springarn Medal annually to an African American for outstanding achievement. Springarn's large, flat gravestone is marked by four bushes. Twin Quaker brothers **Albert** (1828–1912) and **Alfred Smiley** (1828–1903; section 11) were famous for building Mohonk Mountain House, a still-popular resort in New Paltz, and for their longtime involvement in Native American affairs.

**Samuel Neilson** (1761–1803), born in Ireland, is better known in his home country than in America. A fearless patriot, advocate of the unification of Catholics and Protestants, and outspoken journalist-publisher, he was imprisoned and later exiled to the United States, where he founded a movement to reform the British Parliament and end persecution of Catholics in Ireland. Before he could launch a newspaper in Poughkeepsie, he died of yellow fever. His dark granite stone is in section A, near the road. *Grounds open 8:00 A.M.–4:30 P.M. daily. Office hours: 9:00 A.M.–4:30 P.M. Monday–Friday, 9:00 A.M.–12:30 P.M. Saturday; closed holidays. Restroom; detailed booklet of all significant graves with self-conducted walking tour.*

## ANDREW SMITH   1836–1894
## WILLIAM SMITH   1830–1913

Reproductions of the Smith brothers' bushy-bearded faces were better known than *they* were and far outlived them. In fact, few people who bought their ubiquitous cough drops knew that the brothers were actually real, not just a marketing device.

Born in Poughkeepsie, these sons of a local candy maker invented the cough drop, having developed a secret recipe from their father's work. In packaging their licorice-flavored throat lozenges, which they dubbed "cough candy," they used a box with woodcut drawings of their own stern, hirsute images. They trademarked their product in 1877 (one of the oldest trademarks in the United States) and put the word "Trade" under the picture of one of them and "Mark" under the other. This led to William becoming known as Trade Smith and Andrew as Mark Smith. Andrew (Mark) was known for his generosity and thus nicknamed "Easy Mark." While their box images looked similar, the two men had very different personalities—Andrew more easygoing; William the better businessman, an eccentric, and a stern advocate of

Prohibition. In 1963 the Smith Brothers Cough Drop Company was bought by Warner-Lambert Pharmaceuticals.

In section F are two granite columns, each with a round jug on top. The column on the left is the Smith family site, where Andrew and William are presumably at peace.

## MATTHEW VASSAR  1792–1868

A lordly monument on a choice site in section L, with the name VASSAR writ large on its pedestal, is crowned by a massive white marble knob (resembling an acorn)—tribute to a man who put Poughkeepsie on the national map. Who would have thought that a childless, barely educated immigrant beer maker would end up founding the first women's college in America, a beacon of enlightenment and inspiration for women's education throughout the world?

Born in Norfolk, England, Vassar came to the United States as a four-year-old with his parents, who were farmers and political dissenters. James Vassar bought a farm in Dutchess County but soon sold it, moved to Poughkeepsie, and opened a brewery. At fifteen, Matthew, with his mother's connivance, ran away from home to avoid being apprenticed to a tanner. Later, in the *Autobiography and Letters of Matthew Vassar*, he recalled that he had "set off to seek my fortune with 6/ [pence] in my pocket, two corse East India muslin shirts, a pair of woolen socks, scow skin shoes, all tied up in a cotton bandana handkerchief."

Young Vassar found a job in a store near Newburgh. Three years later, with $150 saved, he returned home and took up bookkeeper duties at his father's brewery. The next year, a fire destroyed the brewery, his brother died from the fumes, and his father retired to farm life, but Matthew persevered to become a successful brewer and saloon keeper.

Within a few years, his was a classic story of achievement. Vassar became a trustee and later president of the village of Poughkeepsie, cohosted General Lafayette on his visit to town, helped incorporate the Poughkeepsie Savings Bank, became president of the Hudson River Railroad, and had a hand in many local enterprises.

A favorite niece who ran a female seminary inspired Vassar to seek a worthy goal for his vast wealth. Another educator suggested, "If you will establish a real college for girls and endow it, you will build a monument to yourself more lasting than the Pyramids; it will be the pride and joy of Po'keepsie, an honor to the state and a blessing to the world."

In 1860 Vassar bought 200 acres (a former fairgrounds) and wrote, "It is my hope to be the instrument in the hands of Providence, of founding and perpetuating an institution which shall accomplish for young women what our colleges are accomplishing for young men." With his endowment of $408,000, Vassar College was born, and Matthew Vassar's dream eventually came true.

# SPARKILL

## ROCKLAND CEMETERY

*201 King's Highway; (845) 359–0172*

Sprawled over almost 200 acres, this slumbering resting place has been welcoming permanent residents since 1847. Its founder, Eleazar Lord, was the first president of the Erie Railroad, and he hoped the cemetery would attract New Yorkers, who could be transported there via the railroad. This happened briefly, until the rail route was diverted.

In 1880 improvements were made to roads, bridges, and the grounds with the idea of turning Rockland into a National Cemetery, with scores of military heroes choosing it for their final bugle call. The arrival of John C. Fremont, the first prominent figure to take occupancy there, raised local hopes. Alas, it proved a dead end, as Arlington bypassed Rockland as a national burial site. Fremont remains Rockland's star, although there are many local achievers and Civil War veterans sheltered among these peaceful woods. *Grounds open 8:00 A.M.–4:00 P.M. daily. Office hours 8:00 A.M.–4:00 P.M. Monday–Friday. Restroom.*

## JOHN CHARLES FREMONT   1813–1890

Life is full of ironies. John C. Fremont was born in Savannah, Georgia; was educated in Charleston, South Carolina; and made his reputation mapping territory along the Mississippi River and exploring the West. But because he died in New York (of a ruptured appendix), he is destined to recline forever in territory he scarcely knew. His large gravestone is in section H.

Fremont's diverse career reads like a true-life version of Indiana Jones. A combination of luck and pluck made it possible for Fremont to explore and map much of the land between the Mississippi Valley and Pacific Ocean in a few short years. The luck was his marriage to Jessie Benton, daughter of influential Missouri senator Thomas Hart Benton, who was keenly interested in the West and played a key role in many of Fremont's appointments. The pluck was Fremont's own; his courage and drive were legendary.

In his first job, as a mathematics teacher on a sloop-of-war, he cruised the South American coast for more than two years. As a topographical engineer with the U.S. Army, he helped French explorer Jean Nicholas Nicollet survey and map the then-unknown terrain between the Mississippi and Missouri Rivers. And as a surveyor, along with Kit Carson, Fremont marked much of the West beyond the Mississippi as far as South Pass in Wyoming, making emigration easier for those who followed along the Oregon Trail. The next year he (and Carson) completed the survey to the Columbia River's mouth. In just a few years in the early 1840s, Fremont explored much of the territory between the Mississippi Valley and the Pacific Ocean. His expedition's crossing of the Sierra Nevada in midwinter enhanced his reputation as a fearless explorer.

In 1846 he crossed the mountains again, ostensibly to explore and survey, but secretly to spy on Mexican California, in the event that the United States went to war with Mexico over the annexation of Texas. War did occur, and Fremont was appointed major of a battalion in California and helped to conquer that territory. When California became a state, he was elected one of its first two senators. Ardently antislavery, he was defeated for reelection by the proslavery party. In 1856 he ran for president, the first candidate of the newly formed Republican Party, but lost by sixty votes to James Buchanan.

During the Civil War Fremont was appointed major general and put in charge of the western department, based in St. Louis. Insufficient arms and money made organizing a Union force in a proslavery state impossible. Removed from the job, he was then assigned to a force under an old Missouri nemesis, General John Pope, and resigned.

As a civilian in 1870, Fremont squandered the fortune he had made in California on a shaky, underfinanced scheme to build a railroad along a southern route to the Pacific. To his relief, he was offered the governorship of the Arizona territory, a post he held for eight years.

Fremont may not have been a pathfinder, but he was certainly a path *marker*, and his markings made the western expansion faster and more successful than anyone in his day might have dreamed. For that he deserves lasting acclaim.

# WEST POINT

## WEST POINT UNITED STATES MILITARY ACADEMY POST CEMETERY

*West Point Visitor Center, 2107 New South Post Road; (845) 938–7049*

The Academy was founded in 1802, but the graveyard, overlooking the Hudson River, is even older, with some Revolutionary War soldiers resting in an area marked "unknown." The first known grave, that of an ensign, dates back to 1782. The cemetery was officially designated in 1817.

Here you will find **Margaret "Molly" Corbin** (1751–1800; section 6, left side of Old Cadet Chapel), a heroine of the Revolutionary War who took her mortally wounded husband's place at a cannon in the Battle of Fort Washington. Her stand-alone grave is well marked. Among many other stalwarts are **George W. Goethals** (1858–1928; section 18, row G, grave 82), a major general and builder of the Panama Canal; **Herbert Norman Schwarzkopf** (1895–1958; section 10, row I, grave 160), a general and father of the commander in the Gulf War; **Sylvanus Thayer** (1785–1872; section 25, row A, grave 22), called the father of West Point; and **Edward H. White II** (1930–1967; section 18, row G, grave 80), an air force lieutenant colonel, an astronaut, and the first man to walk in space, who died in the Apollo capsule

LUNCH BREAK

The tradition-rich **Hotel Thayer** (Building 674, U.S. Military Academy, off Route 218; 845–446–4731) offers, along with lunch, a glimpse of academy life, as officers, cadets, and parents parade (not literally) through the premises.

flash fire at Cape Canaveral. It is a surprise to find a movie actress here, but **Glenda Farrell** (1904–1971; section 7, row D, grave 211), who often took tough-girl-with-heart-of-gold roles, was married to a West Pointer and thereby entitled to make Post Cemetery her last residence.

The cemetery is located behind the Old Cadet Chapel, an 1836 Greek Revival building. As of September 11, 2001, West Point grounds are off-limits to the public. The *only* way to visit the cemetery, unless you have a relative there, is with **West Point Tours, Inc.** (845–446–4724; www.westpointtours.com), which offers two-hour tours (for a fee) April through October at 11:15 A.M. and 1:15 P.M. daily. The forty-nine-seat coach tour (a combined bus and walking tour) includes a visit to the graves of prominent inhabitants in the cemetery. It is prudent to phone ahead for a reservation. Photo ID is required.

## LUCIUS CLAY   1897–1978

Few Americans today may remember this much-decorated army general, but to Germans in West Berlin he was "Pater Urbis"—City Father. In fact, his grave, between that of General George W. Goethals and Colonel Edward H. White, has a plaque from Berliners, with six simple words: *"Wir danken dem Bewahrer unserer Freiheit"* ("We thank the defender of our freedom").

Clay, the only four-star general at the time who never saw combat, was considered a take-charge guy. One contemporary said, "He looks like a Roman emperor—and acts like one." A Georgia native, Clay was descended from a long line of public servants, including his father, who was a United States senator. His most famous ancestor was U.S. senator Henry Clay, who was known as the "Great Compromiser." *This* Clay was more the Great *Un*compromiser for his strong opinions and stands. He was also an able administrator and organizer.

He proved this in a long, distinguished career. Clay began as a cadet and later a teacher of civil and military engineering at West Point. This led to a job directing the construction of the Red River Dam near Denison, Texas, and responsibility for building 197 airports and enlarging another 227. Just after

D-Day in World War II, he was ordered to clear Port Cherbourg, a French port essential to the Allied military operation, and did so in a single day.

Appointed to succeed Dwight Eisenhower as military governor of Germany in 1947, Clay was the perfect man to be in charge when the Russians began harassing supply lines to West Berlin (at the war's end the city was divided into east and west zones) in an attempt to starve the city and push Allied troops out. On his own, Clay ordered an airlift of supplies via C-47 and C-54 planes into the beleaguered city. He then convinced President Truman that it was essential to keep Berlin free. The way to do it was inspired: by air with a steady stream of flights. The Berlin Airlift of 1948–49 became a symbol of U.S. resistance to Communism and was a key element in the escalating Cold War. To honor Clay, a wide boulevard in Berlin is now named Clay Allee.

After retiring from the military in 1949, Clay had a second career as a businessman, at one time serving on eighteen different corporate boards. His two sons also became military men—and generals. His grave is in section 18, row G, grave 79, overlooking the Hudson.

## GEORGE ARMSTRONG CUSTER  1839–1876

Idolized and then vilified, General George Custer has not benefited from the passage of time and historical research. Fearless he was, without doubt, proving it in well-publicized feats of bravery at Gettysburg and elsewhere during the Civil War, and leading the final cavalry charge at Appomattox. He was also reckless, gung-ho, and headstrong. Ever a romantic about war, he wrote his beloved wife, Elizabeth, from the Virginia battle lines in 1863 about the "Glorious War!" His exploits later in the Indian Wars were sometimes brutal—destroying a Cheyenne village in 1868, for instance—but the eastern press loved his derring-do and made his every action seem heroic.

That may have been his undoing on the plains of Montana on June 25, 1876, when federal troops converged to put down a gathering of Sioux Indians. More attuned to action than to strategy (he graduated *last* in his West Point class), Custer divided his regiment into three groups, expecting to encircle what he believed to be a small Indian force. As he moved forward with 226 of his center column, they were surrounded by a blizzard of 1,500 warriors. When the fighting ceased, Custer and more than the five companies under his command were dead. Custer's Last Stand was more hubris and folly than heroism, but in the romantic Errol Flynn movie of the same name, it's the heroism that survives.

Custer's wife, **Elizabeth "Libbie" Bacon Custer** (1842–1933), rests with him in section 27, row A, graves 1 (his) and 2 (hers). In her widowhood, she became a celebrity in her own right, writing books and articles and giving lectures on her late husband. The swashbuckling Custer myth owes a lot to Libbie.

## FREDERICK DENT GRANT   1850–1912

A soldier's son, Frederick Grant was usually eclipsed by his more famous father, Ulysses S. Grant, but he also lived an adventurous life and distinguished himself as a man of courage under fire in his own military career. While still a boy, he accompanied his father unofficially on many of the general's Civil War campaigns, often getting in harm's way. In the siege of Vicksburg, Fred came under enemy fire and suffered a leg wound.

Young Grant received an appointment to West Point in 1866 and graduated in 1871. An expert horseman, he then joined the cavalry, assigned to the Fourth Regiment. A long list of appointments and assignments followed, including stints as aide-de-camp to General William Tecumseh Sherman and later to Lieutenant General Philip Sheridan. Grant took part in scouting expeditions with General George Custer to the Black Hills, to the Yellowstone area, and in various Indian incursions. In 1877 he took a leave of absence from the army to join his parents on their travels around the world, returning the following year to fight in the Bannock Indian War.

Grant left the army, seemingly for good, in 1881 to begin a life as businessman and statesman. As his father lay dying of throat cancer, Grant was with him constantly, helping him prepare his memoirs. The pull of army life prevailed again when the Spanish-American War began: Grant earned the title brigadier general; commanded forces in San Juan, Puerto Rico; and then fought in intense guerilla warfare in the Philippines. Subsequently, he helped establish order in the civil government of that country.

While Grant may never have chosen a military career if not for the example of his father, he proved himself an able fighter, leader, and administrator. His years as a businessman and diplomat demonstrated that he was capable of success in various fields. Yet even in dying he invited comparison to his celebrated parent. In one of those tricks life can play, he *also* suffered from throat cancer. It, along with heart failure, ended Grant's life in 1912. Hereafter, you will find him bivouacked in section 26, row D, grave 39.

## WINFIELD SCOTT    1786–1866

Arguably the most distinguished military man of the first half of the nineteenth century, Winfield Scott was trained as a lawyer, not a soldier, at the College of William and Mary in his native Virginia. When war with England seemed imminent in 1807, he went to Washington to offer his services and, as they say, never looked back. For the next fifty-four years he served his country on the front lines—at the Niagara frontier in 1812, against the Seminoles in 1836—and as a skillful negotiator at the peace table. He arranged treaties after the Black Hawk War; settled a boundary dispute between Maine and New Brunswick, Canada; and mediated a conflict in the Northwest between American and British officers who were jointly occupying the San Juan Islands in Puget Sound.

Known as "Old Fuss and Feathers," Scott scored his most celebrated victory in the Mexican War, in which he captured the Mexican capital. This brought him a hero's welcome, a special gold medal from Congress, the Whig Party nomination for president in 1848 and 1852, and the creation of a special rank—the brevit rank of lieutenant general. Though a southerner, his loyalties were to the Union, and when the Civil War broke out, Scott kept command of the U.S. Army until November 1861, when he retired. A visit to Europe followed, then time spent writing his memoirs, which were published in 1864. Two years later he died, fittingly while at West Point. He is here still—in section 26, row A, grave 16.

# CHAPTER 8

# Upstate New York

North of Westchester, straight north upstate, are villages, towns, and cities where many New Yorkers have sought final sanctuaries, mostly in rural graveyards of peace, solitude, and quiet beauty.

## MAPLE GROVE CEMETERY

*Main Street, south of the junction with Church Street*

The main street in the village of Hoosick Falls (population 3,500) leads south to the cemetery (circa 1854), which lies on both sides of the road. The new part is on the left (east) side, marked by stone pillars, trimly shaped evergreen bushes, and a bronze name plaque. The pastoral scene is straight out of a Grandma Moses painting: neat, grassy mounds; a scattering of oaks and other trees; a road winding upward to a hilltop; scores of well-kept headstones and a few mausoleums; and nineteenth-century statuary.

Note the somber headstone of **Ruth Sprague** (1807–1816), which bears these words: "dau. of Gibson & Elizabeth Sprague, died Jan. 11, 1816; aged 9 years 4 mo's & 3 days. She was stolen from the grave by Roderick R. Clow & dissected at Dr. P. M. Armstrong's office in Hoosick, N.Y., from which place her mutilated remains were obtained & deposited here. Her body dissected by fiendish Men, her bones anatomised, her soul we trust has risen to God where few Physicians rise." This sorry tale is a grim reminder that grave-robbing for medical purposes was not unusual in the nineteenth century.

Coming into Hoosick Falls from the south you will see **Falls Diner Restaurant** (Route 22; 518–686–5757) on the right side of the road. It is just the ticket for a hearty breakfast or lunch. On the left inside the dinerlike entrance area is a regular dining room. The menu suits the homey atmosphere of the town, with housemade muffins and pies, blueberry pancakes, numerous egg dishes, sandwiches, and other wholesome fare, all modestly priced.

Maple Grove is relatively small and open. There is only one celebrity grave, that of Grandma Moses. If you cannot find it, ask a groundskeeper for help or inquire at the Louis Miller Museum (see House Calls, pages 246 and 247). *Grounds open dawn to dusk daily.*

## ANNA MARY ROBERTSON MOSES   1860–1961

One would never think that arthritis could have a positive side effect. But when the disease made it impossible for Anna Mary Robertson Moses to do needlework, she took up painting, rendering scenes of her farm childhood in naive fashion on pieces of old boards painted white. She was seventy-five at the time. Thus "Grandma Moses" was born—so to speak.

When Anna Mary married Thomas Moses in 1887, she was twenty-seven years old; she lived most of her married life in Virginia. Despite the late (for that era) marriage, they had ten children, only five of whom lived to adulthood. After Thomas died in 1927, she moved back to Hoosick Falls and began a career that would last until her death at 101. In the twenty-six years of her painting career, Grandma Moses made about 1,600 paintings. To create her charming, sometimes droll scenes of farm and village life, Moses said that she began from the sky down, adding mountains, then land, and finally people. The technique in her scenes of bygone country life was often called "American primitive," a term she disdained, saying that primitive was amateur art that sells. Whatever you call it, Grandma Moses's paintings have sold and sold and are in museums all over the United States and the world.

In the cemetery, follow the main road to the top of the hill. There, under the swooping branch of a huge dying pine tree, is an imposing gray granite headstone with the name MOSES writ large. Under it is the name **Thomas S. Moses** (1862–1927) as well as that of Anna Mary Robertson. In front of it, by a cluster of peony bushes, Anna Mary has her own flat marker in the ground.

## HOUSE CALL

Less than a mile from the cemetery, toward town, stands the **Louis Miller Museum** (166 Main Street; 518–686–4682), the local historical society. The two men who run it—Charles Filkins, curator, and Phillip Leonard, volunteer—are fonts of knowledge about Grandma Moses and Hoosick Falls and are delighted to share their information with visitors. The pink-and-black filigree lace dress that Grandma Moses wore for her one hundredth birthday is there, as well as a video of her interview with Edward R. Murrow on her ninety-fifth birthday. There also are numerous photographs and prints, and lore galore about her and the town itself, which once was bigger, industrial, and more prosperous than it is today.

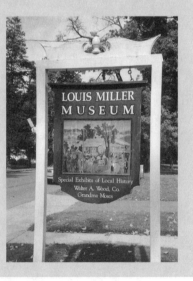

Drive north about 5 miles on Route 22 to Eagle Bridge, and turn off on Route 67 to Grandma Moses Road on the left. A short distance up the road on the left is the **Mount Nebo Gallery** (518–686–4334), a red barn-studio where Will Moses, a great-grandson, shows and sells his own naive paintings. Across from the barn is the old white frame farmhouse where Anna Mary Robertson

Moses and her family lived and where Will and his family still live. It is not open to the public, but it is visible from the road and the studio. Back on Route 67, the Moses family farm stand has delicious apples, cider, and vegetables in season, at excellent prices.

About 7 feet in front of the Moses graves a large memorial stone reads "Anna Mary Robertson Moses, 'Grandma Moses'—Her primitive paintings captured the spirit and preserved the scene of a vanishing countryside." Amen to that, though in this part of the state, these landscapes still exist.

# KINDERHOOK

## KINDERHOOK REFORMED DUTCH CEMETERY

*Albany Avenue; (518) 758–6735*

This old-fashioned nineteenth-century burial ground, at the edge of town, lies on both sides of an old country road on flat land dotted with pines and other trees and bushes. It is as plain, straightforward, and countryish as the Dutch village has always been. Visitors park along the road, step over a low metal chain, and walk in. Signposts directing visitors to the grave of the most famous resident are clearly visible at the edge of the graveyard on the east (right) side of the road (coming from town). *Grounds open dawn to dusk daily.*

## MARTIN VAN BUREN   1782–1862

Judging by Martin Van Buren's prominent obelisk (which resembles a small-scale Washington Monument), easily seen from the road, one would think that this son of Kinderhook was one of the nation's major presidents. In point of fact, he was a mostly unpopular one-termer, criticized for his lavish lifestyle and reputation as a bon vivant. He lost his bid for reelection partly because of the gold spoons used at White House functions. To his opponents, they symbolized (unfairly) his extravagance and fancy ways.

Much of Van Buren's bad luck as president was not his fault. He succeeded his popular mentor, Andrew Jackson, who called him "a true man with no guile." In office, Van Buren faced the worst economic depression since the United States was formed, which led to his defeat. Even so, he had accomplishments: He opposed the extension of slavery, blocked the annexation of Texas (in order to avoid conflict with Mexico and an increase in U.S. slaveholding areas), kept the United States out of war, overhauled the nation's

### HOUSE CALL

After leaving office, Van Buren purchased **Lindenwald** (1013 Old Post Road, Route 9H; 518–758–9689) and converted the Federal-style house into a graceful Gothic Italianate mansion. He furnished it elaborately, constantly adding tasteful *objets* and adornments. Richard Upjohn, the famous architect of that era, also added many decorative touches, as well as a porch and four-story brick tower. Visitors today thus can get a glimpse of the lifestyle of a well-to-do mid-nineteenth-century gentleman. The house is part of the Martin Van Buren National Historic Site (www.nps.gov/mava), which is managed by the National Park Service.

financial system, and established an independent treasury. Not bad for four years.

The son of a Dutch tavern-keeper and farmer, Van Buren apprenticed to a local lawyer at age fourteen, became a lawyer, and married his childhood sweetheart, **Hannah Hoes** (1783–1819), who is ensconced in the same grave site. She died young (age thirty-six) and he never remarried, bringing up their four sons alone. A series of state appointments led to top-level jobs for Van Buren: as U.S. senator, governor, secretary of state, ambassador to Britain, vice president under Jackson, and finally president.

After losing his reelection bid in 1840 and losing the nomination four years later, Van Buren made a final run at the presidency in 1848 on the Free-Soil Party ticket, which opposed the extension of slavery. With his final defeat he retired to Kinderhook and his Lindenwald estate, where he lived happily his last fourteen years.

# LAKE PLACID

## ST. AGNES CEMETERY
*Cascade Road (Route 73); (518) 523–2200*

This small, rural Catholic cemetery belongs to St. Agnes Church (169 Hillcrest Avenue) but is located about a mile away, toward the John Brown Farm Historic Site (another place of grave interest). St. Agnes Cemetery dates back to 1909 and covers almost twelve acres. The relatively flat ground, encircled by hundreds of red pine trees, with the Sentinel mountain range in the distance, gives the property a distinctive Adirondacks look.

A main road runs through the graveyard, with the priests' lot in the rear; behind it is a statue of Mary and a bench for contemplating the scenic views. Resting in this soulful place, along with many others, is **Artur Rodzinski** (1892–1958; back row, section L), a Yugoslav-born conductor of the Los Angeles Philharmonic Orchestra, Cleveland Orchestra, and Chicago Symphony Orchestra. Among his achievements: conducting the world pre-

**LUNCH BREAK**

The bistro ambience, open kitchen, decent prices, and good food at **Le Bistro LaLiberte** (51 Main Street; 518–523–3680) fit the character of this popular resort village.

miere of Sergei Prokofiev's *War and Peace* in 1953 and Aaron Copeland's ballet *Appalachian Spring*. Also located herein is Olympic athlete **Jack Shea** (1910–2002; section C-D), who won two gold medals at the 1932 winter Olympics and was the father and grandfather of two other Olympic-caliber athletes. *Grounds open dawn to dusk daily, except when snow makes the roads impassable (usually December). Queries should be addressed to the church.*

## KATE SMITH   1907–1986

Kathryn Smith's mausoleum, with two crosses engraved in its austere facade, lies at the end of a short shrub-punctuated walkway lined with fresh flowers, near the left side of the back edge of the cemetery. Once a household name, Kate Smith, as she was known professionally, was a musical icon from the 1930s well into the 1970s, famous for her magnificent contralto voice and her upbeat personality. Her forte was radio and her signature song was "God Bless America," which became an unofficial national anthem during World War II. Highly patriotic, she ordered all of her profits on the song to go to the Girl Scouts and Boy Scouts of America, an arrangement still in place.

Hers was a career that surmounted physical liabilities (Smith battled obesity from childhood and ultimately died of complications from diabetes). Early on, this Greenville, Virginia, woman jettisoned a nursing career to give singing a shot. Without professional voice training, she landed jobs singing at theaters and nightclubs throughout the 1920s, ending up on Broadway in such shows as *Honeymoon Lane, Hit the Deck,* and *Flying High.*

Long before the era of amplifiers and body mikes, Smith could belt out a song that reached the last row of the theater. In 1931 CBS signed her for a radio show; the theme song, "When the Moon Comes Over the Mountain," was forever after identified with Smith. The song was also her first major recording hit, with nineteen million copies sold.

Her voice was larger than life, and her figure approached the same. Even so, she enjoyed some success in movies, like *The Big Broadcast* (1932) and *This Is the Army* (1943), and even more on radio and later television, where she was introduced as the "Songbird of the South." TV variety shows, some 2,000 recordings, and frequent television guest appearances kept Smith busy and perennially popular until she retired in 1976. Her last public song was (can't you guess?) "God Bless America." In 1982 President Ronald Reagan (who had appeared with her in *This Is the Army*) awarded Smith the Medal of Freedom, the United States' highest civilian honor.

If you are wondering why Kate Smith is now sojourning in Lake Placid, the answer is simple. She had a summer home and recording studio on an island in the lake. While there, she became friends with a priest at St. Agnes (the Reverend Albert Salmon) and converted to Catholicism. She often sang "God Bless America" to end Sunday Mass; this custom has continued in her honor at St. Agnes Church. Smith's last years were spent at the Uihlein Mercy Center, a local nursing home.

# MENANDS

## ALBANY RURAL CEMETERY
*Cemetery Avenue; (518) 463–7017*

This beautiful pastoral cemetery, just 5 miles from the center of Albany, has rolling hills, wide roadways, a fountain, attractive plantings, a chapel, and numerous grand and grandiose Victorian monuments and gravestones. At its entrance, the cemetery abuts St. Agnes Catholic Cemetery, and in the rear is the Jewish Beth Emeth Cemetery—making the street name, Cemetery Avenue, triply appropriate and ecumenical.

Since its inception in 1841, Albany Rural's 467 country acres have been the final home to hosts of local achievers: five governors, three members of the Continental Congress and three of the Philadelphia Constitutional Convention, thirteen members of the Colonial Assembly, five U.S. senators, twenty-nine U.S. congressmen, five ambassadors, and eight presidential cabinet members. Fifty-five former mayors of Albany reside in this Elysium, as do numerous judges and local dignitaries. **Erastus Corning** (1909–1983; section 31), mayor of Albany from 1942 to 1983; **Peter Gansevoort** (1748–1812; section 55, lot 1), a Revolutionary War hero; **John Van Buren** (1810–1866; section 62), son of Martin Van Buren; and **Marcus T. Reynolds** (1869–1937; section 17), the architect who changed Albany's skyline, are all here. Maps are

### LUNCH BREAK

Just outside the cemetery on Route 32 is **Menands Diner** (563 Broadway; 518–465–1869), a convenient stop for modestly priced sandwiches, burgers, and the like.

available outside the big brick office on the left, just inside the main gate, even if the office is closed. *Gates open 7:30 A.M.–7:00 P.M. daily. Office hours: 8:30 A.M.–4:30 P.M. Monday–Friday, 8:30 A.M.–noon Saturday. Map; restroom.*

## CHESTER ARTHUR   1830–1886

Chester Arthur's grave is not just near the top of the cemetery's rolling hills (in section 24), but also clearly stands at the pinnacle in importance—the only grave marked (with a red X) on the cemetery map. To reach it take South Ridge Road, the first on the left beyond the office, toward Linden Avenue. You can't miss the corner site, with its huge flagpole and American flag and an awesome 7-foot-high green-oxidized bronze Angel of Sorrow. One angel arm holding a palm frond rests on the large polished gray granite sarcophagus, with the single name ARTHUR engraved in the stone. Five granite steps, each 15 feet wide, faced by bronze torchères, lead up to the tomb. On the base of the sarcophagus is a bronze plaque with Arthur's name, the words "twenty-first president of the United States," and his dates engraved in art nouveau script. The large Arthur plot includes the headstones of Chester's wife, **Ellen Herndon Arthur** (1837–1880), and their son, their grandchildren (with spouses), and Ellen's Herndon relatives.

This is a grand tribute to the man who, during his four-year tenure, was known as "His Accidency," a comment on the way he achieved the office. Republican kingmakers chose Arthur to be James Garfield's running mate in 1880 in order to appease warring factions in the Party. No one anticipated that Garfield would be assassinated shortly after taking office, leaving "elegant Arthur" in charge.

Nothing in Arthur's career prepared him for the presidency. Vermont-born and the oldest of seven children of a Scots-Irish Baptist minister, Arthur attended Union College Law School in Schenectady and moved to New York to practice law. A journeyman in Republican politics, considered a party hack by some, he was an able administrator in a series of mundane patronage jobs. As customs collector for the Port of New York, which was notorious for kick-backs and graft, he was an honest man in a corrupt system. In private life he was quite the dandy—fashionable in dress, a wine expert, and a gourmet.

As an unexpected president, Arthur exceeded expectations (which weren't high) by serving with dignity. He signed into law a major civil-service reform bill, which ended the patronage system for federal employees (thus, in effect, biting the hand that had fed him). Suffering from Bright's disease, Arthur died of a stroke a little more than a year after leaving office.

## PHILIP SCHUYLER   1733–1804

Schuyler is a name one encounters frequently in the Albany area. The most famous of the family was probably Philip, a Continental major general in the Revolutionary War, a member of the New York State Senate, and one of New York's first members of the United States Senate, serving 1789–91 and again 1797–98. His main recognition, though, is probably as the father-in-law of Alexander Hamilton. As such, he was often embroiled in Hamilton's rivalry with Aaron Burr for control of New York politics. Burr defeated Schuyler once in the senate race, but was defeated by him on the second go-around.

Although Schuyler was subject to bouts of gout and pleurisy from childhood, he lived a long, active life. By the time he became a delegate to the Continental Congress in Philadelphia in 1775, he was one of the wealthiest property owners in the region and had considerable influence (the legacy of inherited land and family credit). He assisted George Washington in developing the rules and regulations for the army. Then Schuyler helped fortify Fort Ticonderoga. Later, when blamed for the fall of the fort, he requested a military trial to clear his name of any failure of duty. He was acquitted "with the highest honor." He died a few months after Burr killed Hamilton in a duel.

## HOUSE CALL

The 1761 redbrick Georgian **Schuyler Mansion State Historic Site** (32 Catherine Street, Albany; 518–434–0834) contains a few Schuyler family furnishings and considerable history. Alexander Hamilton married Schuyler's daughter there, and other prominent colonists met there as well. The house typifies the period and has some fine furniture and detailing.

Schuyler's towering stone obelisk, with his name and dates in the base, is clearly visible from a distance. It rises from section 29 (between Cypress Fountain and section 31).

# NEW LEBANON

## CEMETERY OF THE EVERGREENS

*Cemetery Road, Lebanon Springs; (518) 794-7398*

On a twenty-eight-acre site, the graveyard is an old one, hilly and full of fir trees and other evergreens (as the name suggests), but no hardwoods. Though technically located in Lebanon Springs, locals still call this tiny area (population 5,000) New Lebanon. The abode of its most famous resident is clearly visible; it is the largest headstone on the grounds, the first left from the entrance. If he happens to be on the grounds, genial caretaker John Koepp points to the Samuel Tilden grave and tells visitors, "There's the first Al Gore." *Grounds open dawn to dusk daily; closed during snow months.*

**LUNCH BREAK**

For delicious wood-fired pizza, salads, and pasta dishes, try the handy **Fresco's** (569 Route 20; 518-794-9339).

## SAMUEL JONES TILDEN   1814–1886

Samuel Tilden was a footnote to history until the aftermath of the 2000 presidential election hurled his unfortunate presidential experience back into the news. To many historians, that 1876 fiasco was a textbook case of the most corrupt presidential election in American history.

Tilden, history buffs will recall, was the Democratic candidate for president who initially beat the Republican, Rutherford B. Hayes, by 51 percent to 48 percent of the popular vote. The Republicans challenged the votes in Florida, Louisiana, South Carolina, and Oregon, and those states sent two different sets of returns to Washington. The U.S. Constitution had no provision for settling such a dispute, so Congress appointed a special fifteen-member Electoral Commission to decide the outcome. The commission had an equal number of Democrats and Republicans, plus one independent. At the last minute, the independent dropped out and was replaced by a Republican sympathizer. Despite charges of ballot destruction (hanging chads?), threats of intimidation, and other fraud, all four contested states were decided in favor of the Republicans and Hayes won by a strict party-line vote (U.S. Supreme Court take note), an electoral college tally of 185 to 184.

It was, in effect, the end of Tilden's career, which had been a distinguished one. After a bucolic boyhood in New Lebanon, he studied law at Yale, was admitted to the bar in 1841, became corporate counsel for New York City, and was elected in 1846 to the New York Assembly. A member of the antislavery faction of northern Democrats, he urged fellow party members to support President Abraham Lincoln during the Civil War.

In 1866, as state Democratic Party chairman, Tilden clashed with the notorious Tweed ring, which had a crooked finger in every New York City pie. Tilden won, proving his independence from the corrupt influences in his own party. With his reputation as a reformer, he became governor of New York in 1874 and two years later a candidate for president. The rest is, if not history, at least a historical footnote.

Tilden bequeathed his $5 million estate to help found and maintain "a free public library and reading-room in the city of New York." Relatives contested his will, so only $2 million of the bequest was honored, but it, with two other large gifts, helped form the New York Public Library, a splendid legacy.

It isn't often that a person who has played on a larger stage returns to spend eternity in the same tiny town where he was born. Tilden did. His final home, all by itself, is beneath a huge headstone (25 feet long and 12 feet high) with the words "I still trust the people" engraved along one side.

# NORTH ELBA (LAKE PLACID)

## JOHN BROWN FARM STATE HISTORIC SITE
*John Brown Road, 1 mile off Route 73; (518) 523–3900*

Considered part of Lake Placid, North Elba was home to the famous, or infamous (depending on your point of view), John Brown. His grave, along with those of his two sons and ten followers who fought and died beside him, is on the same property as his spartan, well-restored cottage. Brown's sim-

> **LUNCH BREAK**
>
> For a casual, inexpensive lunch, try **Jack Frost** (Main Street; 518–523–9200) in the center of town.

ple headstone reads "John Brown, born May 9, 1800, was executed at Charleston, VA, Dec. 2, 1859." His statue, in rough-cut Adirondacks attire, his arm around a small black boy, stands outside his home. The stone also has the name of Brown's grandfather, for whom it was intended but not used. The grave may be visited year-round, even when the house is not open.

## JOHN BROWN   1800–1859

B rown, whose family lineage supposedly stretched back to the *Mayflower,* wasn't born a revolutionary, but slavery turned him into one. Connecticut-born and Ohio-bred, he tried the tanning business, sheep-raising, and the wool trade—wandering from Ohio to Pennsylvania and Massachusetts—and finally took up farming in North Elba.

Ardently abolitionist, Brown joined five of his sons in 1854 in Kansas, which was then a battleground territory between pro- and antislavery settlers. Not a pacifist like so many northern abolitionists but not a bloodthirsty killer, either, Brown was more in the Old Testament mold, seeking vengeance against wrongdoers. He organized the so-called Pottawatomie massacre, in which five proslavery men were killed in cold blood as retaliation for the murder of five "free-state" settlers.

From there, Brown became active in the Underground Railroad and established in the Virginia mountains a way station for escaping slaves. By 1858 he was almost delusional in his antislavery diatribes, feeling he had a mission

### HOUSE CALL

John Brown's grave is on the same property as the **John Brown Farm** (2 miles south of town, 1 mile off Route 73; 518–523–3900). His simple cottage is open to visitors Wednesday through Sunday, May to late October. The farm was his final home.

from God to free the slaves. This led to his raid on the federal arsenal at Harper's Ferry, Virginia (now West Virginia), on October 16, 1859. With only twenty-two men, he easily captured the arsenal, holding sixty people prisoner. The next day brought a quick response from a small force of U.S. troops, led by Colonel Robert E. Lee. When the gun smoke cleared, a wounded Brown and a handful of followers were captured. Twelve days later Brown was tried by the state of Virginia and convicted of "treason, and conspiring and advising with slaves and other rebels and murder in the first degree." He was hung December 2 in Charlestown (now in West Virginia).

When Brown's body reached New York City, the coffin was exchanged for another one so that he would not have to be buried in southern property. The entourage continued north; at every stop bells tolled and huge crowds greeted the procession. Abolitionists viewed Brown as a martyr, and his death became a rallying cry. As Union soldiers sang on their way to Civil War battlefronts, "John Brown's body lies a-mouldering in the grave, but his soul goes marching on."

# PAWLING

## PAWLING CEMETERY
*Route 22; (845) 855–5325*

Along the west side of Route 22, this small state-owned cemetery, which opened in 1852, encompasses about eight acres contiguous with St. John's Catholic Cemetery next door. The phone number listed above is that of George Coulter, a retired dentist who is the local historian/authority on Pawling Cemetery and its permanent residents. *Grounds open dawn to dusk daily.*

### LUNCH BREAK

For a first-rate lunch, **McKinney & Doyle Fine Foods Cafe** (10 Charles Coleman Boulevard; 845–855–3875) is a good choice. If the cafe is closed (Monday), you can still get a delicious sandwich, snack, or out-of-this-world dessert at the adjacent **Corner Bakery** (same ownership).

# THOMAS DEWEY  1902–1971

lice Roosevelt Longworth, Teddy Roosevelt's witty daughter, once said that Tom Dewey resembled "the little man on the top of a wedding cake." This observation struck home with many people, though it was markedly unfair to a decent man with credentials as a first-rate gangbuster. Her tart comment was more about his bland personality and ordinary, mustached looks than about his career.

As the U.S. attorney for the Southern District of New York, Dewey was a dynamo—in an unshowy, resolute way. In four years he obtained seventy-two convictions out of seventy-three prosecutions of leading mobsters. He had a reputation for careful preparation, efficiency, honesty, courage, and self-control under pressure. He needed all the control he could muster, having survived Dutch Schultz's assassination plot against him in 1935.

Childhood in Owosso, Michigan, college at the University of Michigan, and professional training at Columbia University Law School eventually led Dewey to practice law in New York. A lifelong Republican, he was tapped by mayor Fiorello La Guardia for the crime-busting job. He was elected governor

of New York in 1942, and two years after that he ran against Franklin Roosevelt for president—and lost by more than a two-to-one margin. Competing again in 1948 against a less-popular Harry Truman, Dewey ran a cool, calculated campaign, made only a few speeches, avoided controversial issues, and was expected to coast into the White House. In fact, the *Chicago Tribune* was so sure of his anticipated victory that its headline the day after the election read "DEWEY DEFEATS TRUMAN." Surprise! He didn't, though he came close. Instead Dewey went on to a third term as New York governor, received sixteen honorary degrees, wrote books, and toured a number of foreign countries. None of these honors, so local neighbors say, compensated for his cliffhanging loss of the presidency.

To reach the Dewey grave site from the cemetery entrance gate, take the road on the left, winding over a little bridge. As the ground rises you will see on the left, facing the road, a square gray granite mausoleum with the name DEWEY across the top of the facade. To the right and left of the name are incised circles with a lyre in each—more artistry than one might expect for the final lair of this seemingly humorless lawman and his wife. Two handsome bronze doors, each with four circles, distinguish the mausoleum, which stands alone, as stolid and steadfast as Dewey's image when he was alive.

# ROXBURY

## JOHN BURROUGHS MEMORIAL FIELD

*Burroughs Memorial Road (Hardscrabble Road), off Route 30, about 2 miles north of town; (607) 326–3722*

Burroughs requested that he be buried in the wooded and grassy field adjacent to his family's farmhouse (which still stands but is a private residence), just north of the scenic hamlet of Roxbury in the northern Catskills. His grave is, as he wished, next to his favorite childhood perch—Boyhood Rock, which overlooks the mountains. On the grounds of this New York State Historic Site is Woodchuck Lodge (currently closed), the rustic cabin where Burroughs spent summers writing. Note the plaques along the road that describe Burroughs's life and works. *Grounds open dawn to dusk daily.*

# JOHN BURROUGHS   1837–1921

*P*oet, essayist, and naturalist, John Burroughs today is just a vague name to many people. "Didn't he write 'Trees'?" one person guessed (incorrectly). In his heyday in the late nineteenth and early twentieth centuries, this nature writer was so popular that schools and parks throughout the country were named after him. At a time when the Industrial Revolution was drawing hordes to work in cities, Burroughs's zest for nature appealed to those who feared that the United States was becoming too urbanized. At his death, thousands around the country mourned.

Burroughs was the seventh of ten children born on his family's dairy farm in Roxbury. He left school at age seventeen to become a teacher. He married young and did a series of odd jobs as a journalist, farmer, fruit grower, and clerk in the U.S. treasury department in Washington during the Civil War. He stayed in the capital for nine years.

His first published work was a volume on Walt Whitman, in 1867. Burroughs especially admired Whitman, William Wordsworth, and Ralph Waldo Emerson. In fact, when Burroughs's first essay, "Expression," was published by James Russell Lowell in the *Atlantic Monthly*, Lowell feared that it was plagiarized because it sounded so much like Emerson.

*Wake-Robin*, Burroughs's 1871 work on flowers, birds, and nature, made him a popular essayist in the Thoreau mode. His major prose works include *Birds and Poets* (1877), *Locusts and Wild Honey* (1879), *Signs and Seasons* (1886), and *Ways of Nature* (1905). He also wrote poetry (*Birds and Bough*, 1906) and travel sketches (*Winter Sunshine*, 1875, and *Fresh Fields*, 1884) based on trips to England and France.

While Burroughs's works are not widely read today, you may, when visiting his grave site, want to muse over his words:

What matter if I stand alone?
I wait with joy the coming years;
My heart shall reap where it has sown,
And garner up its fruit of tears.

The grave still attracts visitors, who are invited to sign their names in a book kept in a metal box nearby.

# TROY

## OAKWOOD CEMETERY
*Oakwood Avenue (Route 40); (518) 272–7520*

There are several entrances to this venerable cemetery, whose main entrance gate and main office are on Oakwood Avenue. The chapel is just beyond the office. While Uncle Sam is the reason most tourists visit, the hills and curves of this 1848 burial ground shelter many noteworthy locals. U.S. congressmen, Civil War generals, and others whose graves, mausoleums, and memorials grace the grounds add to the pleasure of a visit.

In repose here is **Emma Hart Willard** (1787–1870; section M-1), a pioneer in women's rights, social reformer, and educator who championed higher education for women. She founded the Troy Female Seminary in 1819; it later morphed into the prestigious Emma Willard School. In her "spare time" she wrote textbooks on history and a volume of poems (*Rocked in the Cradle of the Deep*). Financier **Russell Sage** (1815–1906; section I-1), a two-term U.S. congressman who owned shares in railroads and Western Union, is also in residence. *Grounds open 8:30 A.M.–4:30 P.M. daily. Office hours: 8:30 A.M.–4:30 P.M. Monday–Friday, 8:00 A.M.–noon Saturday. Map; restroom.*

> ### LUNCH BREAK
>
> Downtown is **Daisy Baker** (33 Second Street; 518–266–9200), a handy spot for a casual, satisfying, well-priced lunch.

## SAMUEL "UNCLE SAM" WILSON   1766–1854

You may think Uncle Sam is an apocryphal figure, but those would be fighting words in Troy, which calls itself the "home of Uncle Sam." Local residents are absolutely convinced that Uncle Sam was really Sam Wilson, a local meatpacker. During the War of 1812, he supplied American troops with barrels of meat stamped U.S. (for United States). The meatpackers joked that the initials were shorthand for their employer, Uncle Sam, and eventually this name became the symbol of the country. In time, the U.S. Congress passed a resolution honoring Wilson as the nation's "Uncle Sam."

It wasn't a bad choice. Wilson, whose Scottish family migrated from New Hampshire to Troy, was, by all accounts, a fair and honest man, devoted to the country. Today Wilson's simple gravestone is flat in the ground, next to an upright, rough-hewn granite memorial stone with an eagle above a bronze plaque. The grave site is further graced by an American flag, raised daily. Troy Boy Scouts maintain the grave, which is at the edge of section F, facing section D-1. Uncle Sam is commemorated elsewhere in town, too, with a statue at River and Third Streets.

# CHAPTER 9

# Western New York

While New York City is often the tail wagging the dog of the Empire State, that doesn't mean that the western part of New York is bereft of its own celebrated permanent residents. Many influential American notables were born, resided, and ended up in various towns and cities in this part of the state. Here is a selection of those who were prime movers in their livelier days.

## FORT HILL CEMETERY

*19 Fort Street; (315) 253–8132*

A fortified Cayuga Indian village was on this land for centuries (as early as A.D. 1100), during a period of intensive warfare among the many tribes in the area. After the founding of the Iroquois Confederacy (which led to peace among the various warring tribes), the Cayugas abandoned the land for other homes.

Fort Hill Cemetery became a reality in 1851, when eight civic-minded Auburn residents purchased the twenty-two-acre tract of land for a new burial ground. It was the perfect site for a cemetery, especially one in the "rural" mode, with height, natural hillsides, and ancient, majestic trees. Since its 1852 dedication, Fort Hill has continued to add land, and its current eighty acres accommodate some 20,000 permanent inhabitants, with plenty of room for more to come. Bradley Chapel, on the right inside the imposing Bradley main gate, was modeled after an English Carpenter Gothic–style church in Cornwall, England. The office, like the chapel, is also part of the Gothic main gate.

A focal point of Fort Hill is the impressive 56-foot-high Logan Monument, made of local stone and built on the supposed site of an ancient Indian altar. It honors Logan, a proud Indian chief who was known as a peacemaker during the bloody French and Indian War (1755–63). But when a white man massacred his entire family, Logan felt forced to seek revenge. His eloquent words, reprinted by Thomas Jefferson in *Notes on the State of Virginia* and later in *McGuffey's Reader,* ended thus: "I have fully glutted my vengeance. For my country, I rejoice at the beams of peace. But do not harbour a thought that mine is the joy of fear. Logan never felt fear. He will not turn on his heel to save his life. Who is there to mourn for Logan?—Not one."

The cemetery's first full-time tenant was **Elijah Miller** (1772–1851; section 74, on top of mound), a local judge and partner in the New York law firm Cravath Swain & Moore, as well as William

### LUNCH BREAK

**Ricky's Restaurant** (266 West Genesee Street; 315-252-8887) is a convenient and inexpensive spot for burgers, steaks, and sandwiches. Older and a mite fancier is **Lasca's** (252 Grant Street; 315-253-3895), with an extensive Italian and American menu.

Seward's father-in-law. Civil War generals and local industrialists are also present, as is **Myles Keogh** (1840–1876; Mount Hope section), a U.S. Cavalry captain killed at Little Big Horn.

The talented Osbornes are in a row in the Morningside section: **David M. Osborne** (1822–1886), industrialist and founder of D. M. Osborne & Co., which became International Harvester; his wife, **Eliza Wright Osborne** (1822–1911), a philanthropist and leader in the women's rights movement; their son, **Thomas Mott Osborne** (1859–1926), a prison reformer, warden of Sing Sing, and mayor of Auburn; and Eliza's mother, **Martha Coffin Wright** (1806–1875), also active in women's rights (and the sister of feminist Lucretia Mott).

Also present on these Elysian fields are **Theodore W. Case** (1888–1944; Woodlawn Bower), scientist and inventor of the first successful soundtrack for movies; and **Allen Macy Dulles** (1854–1930; Glen Haven section, next to Seward's grave), professor at Auburn Theological Seminary and the father of Allen and John Foster Dulles. **Jerome "Brud" Holland** (1916–1985; Fairmount section) is in Fort Hill, honored in life, if forgotten now. He was a Cornell University football star, an ambassador to Sweden, and the first African-American director of the New York Stock Exchange. *Grounds open sunrise to sunset daily. Office hours: 9:00 A.M.–4:00 P.M. Monday–Friday. Map and walking tour brochure available; restroom. Tours (fee) conducted by the Cayuga Museum (315–253–8051) and Willard Memorial Chapel (315–252–0339).*

## WILLIAM SEWARD  1801–1872

Seward is best remembered as Abraham Lincoln's secretary of state, but his contributions to our history go well beyond this single appointment. A lawyer with strong political ambitions, Seward was an ardent abolitionist and a man of high principles and humanitarian impulses, willing to challenge those he considered wrong. While governor of New York, he refused to extradite to Virginia three seamen who had helped a fugitive slave. Virginia responded by ordering a ban on New York shipping, but Seward held firm. As a U.S. senator he championed the admission of California as a free state and tried to abolish slavery in Washington, D.C. When he lost the Republican nomination for president in 1860, he gamely campaigned for Lincoln. Seward's reward was to be appointed secretary of state, a job he handled with

The Federal-style **Seward House** (33 South Street; 315–252–1283; www.sewardhouse.org), the first brick house in Auburn, was built in 1816. (One of the workmen was a fifteen-year-old local boy named Brigham Young, who did carpentry in the interior.) No other family ever lived in the house. William Seward died on the green sofa in the library. For visitors, the house provides a wonderful glimpse into nineteenth-century upper-class life. It is a treasure trove of Seward artifacts, costumes, and furniture, as well as some fascinating history about both William and Frances and the period in which they lived.

lawyerly shrewdness, parrying British and French anti-Union agitation with great political and diplomatic skill.

The night John Wilkes Booth shot Lincoln, other conspirators attacked and almost killed Seward, who was left partially crippled. Even so, he continued as secretary of state under Andrew Johnson and was just as helpful to him. Though opposed to slavery, Seward advocated conciliation with the South, and he helped negotiate the purchase of Alaska. Occupying the same quarters as Seward is his wife, **Frances Miller Seward** (1805–1865), a Quaker with great influence on his liberal views. While he was in Washington, she hid fugitive slaves in the rear of their Auburn home. The Sewards share their afterlives in the Glen Haven section.

## HARRIET TUBMAN    1821–1913

Born Araminta Ross, a slave, on the eastern shore of Maryland, Harriet Tubman early on took her mother's first name. The surname Tubman came from a man her master forced Harriet to marry in 1844. Five years later, as a spunky woman of twenty-eight, she escaped from slavery, following the North Star to freedom. Her husband declined to join her. Though unable to read or write, Tubman had great strength and endurance—skills acquired during her years as a field hand.

She soon joined the Underground Railroad, working as a cook and housemaid to get money to bring members of her family and others out of the South. On an estimated nineteen trips, she guided more than 300 slaves to northern states and Canada. Nicknamed "Moses" for leading her people to the "promised land," Tubman—possessed of great daring, resourcefulness, and strategic skills—was a fearless guide, using disguises and carrying a gun. Large bounties were on her head, but it is believed she never lost a fugitive. She even rescued her own aging parents and brought them to Auburn. During the Civil War she assisted the Union forces as a cook, nurse, laundress, scout, raider, and even as a spy behind Confederate lines.

From the end of the Civil War until her death, Tubman continued to work for her people. She bought a little house in Auburn (with the profits from *Scenes in the Life of Harriet Tubman,* written and published for her by Auburn neighbors), where she lived, but soon converted it into a home for elderly African Americans and poor African-American children. Look for her grave under a giant spruce tree in the West Lawn C section on the Parker Street side of the cemetery. The stone is a simple upright with the name Harriet Tubman Davis near the top.

# BUFFALO

## FOREST LAWN CEMETERY

*1411 Delaware Avenue; (716) 885–1600; www.forest-lawn.com*

The city of Buffalo is a lot more than just the Buffalo Bills football team and the Albright-Knox Art Gallery. It is home to one of the largest and most beautiful Victorian cemeteries in the country (the first burial was in 1850). Forest Lawn, which abuts Delaware Park on the south, is also the largest arboretum and bird sanctuary in western New York State, sheltering some 240 species of birds. Among the residents are more than 200 mallards, whose favorite nesting grounds are unoccupied flower urns on various family grave sites.

Throughout the 270 arboreal acres are parklike woods, three reflecting lakes, two bridges, a glacial drift with a creek running through it, thousands of flowering trees and shrubs, and rolling hills. Fourteen miles of roadway twist and curve through the hallowed property. In springtime the grounds are a fiesta of tulips and daffodils.

Among a wealth of statuary and Victorian monuments, a standout is the spectacular dome-shaped Blocher memorial, carved from a single block of stone. Its glass-sided panels reveal a life-size scene in marble of a reclining man on a sarcophagus—the tomb of **Nelson W. Blocher** (1847–1884; section 11, lot 49, beyond the office on the left)—surrounded by his parents and, above his head, an angel. According to legend, young Blocher, son of a wealthy shoe manufacturer, was sent to Europe to get over a love affair with the family maid. It didn't work. He pined away and is now settled for eternity at Forest Lawn.

Forest Lawn's most recent architectural triumph is Frank Lloyd Wright's Blue Sky Mausoleum, built seventy-six years after its original commission by Darwin Martin, a Buffalo millionaire at the turn of the twentieth century. Martin had commissioned several homes by Wright. Unfortunately, Martin's fortune crashed with the stock market in 1929, he died penniless, and the mausoleum was not built—until 2004. Designed specifically for Forest Lawn, the mausoleum (the only one Wright ever designed) now serves as a tribute to the architect. It is a pier-and-cantilever complex of white Vermont granite, overlooking a pond, with benches for seated contemplation.

Epitaphs abound at Forest Lawn. Inspiration is the theme for **Sarah E. Steele** (1812–1875; section 1, lot 13), whose stone reads "Shed not a bitter tear / Nor give the heart to vain regret / 'Tis but the casket that lies here / The gem that filled it sparkles yet." Then there is the oft-quoted epitaph on the marker for **Amaryllis M. Jones** (1919–1983; section 8, lot 935): "I told you I was sick."

Many now sheltered at Forest Lawn were once accomplished citizens in a variety of fields. Among a cast of thousands are Buffalo mayors (forty-seven of them), congressmen, other politicians, veterans of eight wars, seven Congressional Medal of Honor recipients from the Civil War, and local VIPs.

There are such folks as **Edward Austin Kent** (1854–1912; section 7), a prominent local architect and Buffalo's only passenger on the ill-fated RMS *Titanic*; **Dorothy Goetz Berlin** (1892–1912; section 9, lot 282), the beloved first wife of songwriter Irving Berlin who died of typhoid fever within six months of their marriage; **John E. Brent** (1892–1961; section 37, lot 94), Buffalo's first professional African-American architect; **Willis Haviland Carrier** (1876–1950;  section 15, lot 76), called the father of the air-conditioning industry; and **Frederick Albert Cook** (1865–1940; chapel columbarium, section 21), explorer and discoverer of the North Pole in 1908.

**William Pryor Letchworth** (1823–1910; mausoleum, section X, lot 13) was known less for what he was than for what he did. A Quaker saddle- and harness-maker turned industrialist, he was also a social reformer and philanthropist. In 1906 he deeded his home and magnificent property (now Letchworth State Park), to the state; it is known as the Grand Canyon of the East.

Also in lodgings is **Leslie Fiedler** (1917–2003; section 33, Rosewood Atrium, north garden, row 70, tier D), an author of essays, poetry, and short stories. He was most esteemed as a professor of English at Princeton, Harvard, and elsewhere, and for his many books of literary criticism, including

*Love and Death in the American Novel* and *Being Busted*. Humorist **Edward Streeter** (1892–1976; section 9, lot 11), another resident, authored *Dere Mable*, a popular World War I–era book, and *Father of the Bride*, written after World War II. At the opposite extreme from humor is **Alfred Southwick** (1826–1898; section 31), a local dentist whose experiments with electroshock led to his invention of the electric chair.

Several of Forest Lawn's most notable inhabitants are Native Americans. Their small headstones may be found in a straight line on the right in section 12, just beyond the main entrance. Dominating the group is a commanding statue of Seneca chief **Red Jacket** (1750–1830; section 12, lot 1), a warrior and great orator, in tribal regalia on top of a large pedestal. His tribal name, Sa-Co-Ye-Wat-Ha (translated as "he who keeps them awake"), is on the base. On the left at the end of the row of stones lies **Ely S. Parker** (1828–1895), a U.S. Army brigadier general, aide to Ulysses S. Grant, U.S. commissioner of Indian Affairs, and chief of the six Iroquois Nations. Parker passed the New York State bar exam but, as a Native American, was not allowed to practice law. Undaunted, he attended Rochester Polytechnic Institute and became a civil engineer. *Grounds open 8:00 A.M.–5:00 P.M. daily. Office hours: 8:30 A.M.–4:30 P.M. Monday–Saturday. Maps and pamphlets; restroom. Guided tours with special themes (e.g., architecture, Civil War, and African-American history) are available May through September for groups of twelve or more.*

## SHIRLEY CHISHOLM   1924–2005

*I*t is something of a surprise to find former U.S. congresswoman Shirley Chisholm so far from her natural habitat of New York City, but she rests here beside her husband, **Arthur Hardwick Jr.** (1926–1986), in a crypt in Birchwood Mausoleum, center lounge, row 158, tier F.

Although born in New York, to a Guyanese factory worker and his Barbadian wife, Chisholm spent eight childhood years in Barbados with her maternal grandmother. There Chisholm studied at a British grammar school, acquiring the clipped accent that would characterize her precise speech throughout her life. She returned to New York at age eleven; later she graduated *cum laude* from Brooklyn College and earned a master's degree from Columbia University. A career in social work, first as director of a day-care center and later as consultant to the NYC Bureau of Child Welfare, led to Chisholm's interest in Democratic politics. Bright, assertive, and articulate, she went quickly from four years in the state assembly to being the first black woman ever elected to the U.S. Congress. She served for fourteen years, a total of seven terms.

Right from the beginning, Chisholm showed her mettle in Congress. As a newcomer, she was appointed to the House Agriculture Committee. Chisholm knew that this was a wasteland for her urban constituency, so she did the unheard-of for a freshman at the time: demanded a reassignment. She was given a seat on the Veteran Affairs Committee instead. Throughout her government service, Chisholm spoke her mind and followed her conscience, always seeing past race to the larger picture of what she believed was better for the country.

Some considered it chutzpah for a black third-term congresswoman to run for president of the United States. But in 1972 that's just what Chisholm did—not because she expected to win, but because she wanted to use the Democratic primary as a national platform to express her views as a woman and a member of a minority group. During that primary (which George McGovern eventually won), fellow candidate George Wallace was shot. Chisholm visited this racist governor of Georgia in the hospital, an unlikely thing for a black woman from New York to do. Two years later Wallace came through for *her*: She needed votes for a bill to extend the minimum wage, and Wallace "leaned on" several Southerners to support her.

Though she was a can-do, pragmatic person, Chisholm eventually became frustrated with the slowness of the political process and the movement in Congress toward conservatism. In 1982 she retired. Later she taught at Mount Holyoke College in South Hadley, Massachusetts; lectured throughout the United States; and wrote a book, *Unbought and Unbossed*. While the book was mostly about Chisholm's years in Congress, the title could be her epitaph.

## MILLARD FILLMORE   1800–1874

Today Fillmore is little more than a name that comics toss into a sentence for a cheap laugh, partly because of the formal sound of the name, and partly because Millard Fillmore was one of a string of nineteenth-

century U.S. presidents whom only historians remember. But Fillmore's story is worth recalling.

Even in America, it isn't often that an indentured servant who steals books to teach himself to read becomes president. Born in a log cabin, Fillmore was one of eight children of an impoverished farm family. His father apprenticed Millard at age fifteen to a textile maker. Ambition drove the young man to study, pay off his master, pass the bar exam, and open his own law practice. A keen interest in politics led Fillmore up the career ladder of congressman, state comptroller, and finally vice president under Zachary Taylor. Luck then stepped in: After a year in office, Taylor died and Fillmore became the thirteenth president.

On his watch the Compromise of 1850 bill was passed (admitting California as a free state), and Commodore Perry was sent to open Japan to western trade. What undid Fillmore was the Fugitive Slave Law, which guaranteed the return of runaway slaves to their masters. While a slavery opponent himself, Fillmore gave in to compromise in order to preserve the Union. This so displeased northern Republicans that Fillmore was denied his party's nomination for a second term.

Adding to his woes was the untimely death of his wife, Abigail. They were packed to leave Washington but stayed for the inauguration of his successor, Franklin Pierce. At the ceremonies Abigail took a chill that led to pneumonia; she died three weeks later. This was not just an ironic twist of fate, but a terrible personal loss for Fillmore. Abigail was the bright, spirited daughter of a Baptist minister. She met Fillmore in school, encouraged him to become a lawyer, and helped to raise funds for the first circulating library in the state. As First Lady, she established the first library in the White House and began the custom of hosting cultural evenings there. More tragedy for Fillmore followed when his talented daughter, **Mary** (1832–1854), died of cholera at age twenty-two.

Afterward Fillmore traveled to Europe. When Oxford University offered him an honorary degree in Latin, he declined, saying, "I had not the advantage of a classical education and no man should, in my judgment, accept a degree he cannot read." He sought the presidency again on the American (or Know-Nothing) ticket in 1856, carrying only Maryland. Though defeated, he expressed some ideas that resonate even today, saying, "In my opinion, Church and State should be separate, not only in form, but in fact—religion and politics should not be mingled."

Four years after Abigail died, Fillmore married a wealthy forty-five-year-old, childless widow and lived happily until his death of a stroke sixteen years later. Theirs might have been one of the earliest prenuptial agreements. Caroline kept her money and property in her own name but paid Fillmore $10,000 a year to manage her financial affairs. They lived sumptuously in Buffalo in a huge Gothic Revival mansion (since demolished).

Caroline's wealth gave Fillmore the leisure to devote time to more public service. He helped organize three local museums and a chapter of the Society for the Prevention of Cruelty to Animals. A monumental statue of him next to City Hall on Niagara Square sums up the city's gratitude to its benefactor. No more Fillmore jokes please, at least not in Buffalo.

A commanding pink granite obelisk, surrounded by a neatly trimmed hedge inside a cast-iron fence with gate, signals Fillmore's well-signed grave site in section F. With him in this enclave are the graves of both his wives, **Abigail Powers Fillmore** (1798–1853) and **Caroline Carmichael McIntosh Fillmore** (1813–1881), his two children (by Abigail), and Abigail's mother—quite the family gathering place.

About 10 miles southeast of Buffalo is the **Millard and Abigail Fillmore House Museum** (24 Shearer Avenue, East Aurora; 716–652–0167), a clapboard cottage

in which Fillmore lived with Abigail from 1826 to 1830. The cottage, built by Fillmore himself in 1825, was moved from its original site and later restored by the local historical society with careful attention to the characteristics of the Federal period. Many of Fillmore's possessions are here, including his furniture, his sleigh, his swords, and a rare American flag with twelve stars.

## FRANCIS WALSINGHAM TRACY    1839–1886
## AGNES ETHEL TRACY    1845–1903

The Tracys are better known today for their current habitat than for themselves, but it wasn't always so. The habitat *is* splendid, a pink granite sarcophagus designed by Stanford White, with a large bronze insert by Augustus Saint-Gaudens along the side, highlighting a bas-relief profile of Francis Tracy surrounded by a wreath. It is located in section 3, lot 17, next to Jubilee Spring. Flanking the portrait are these lines: "Tears to thee far below the earth / Tears do I bring to thee among the dead."

The epitaph has a special poignancy when we consider Tracy's life and death. He was the son of a wealthy industrialist who left him a $1 million inheritance. Young Tracy, always frail, spent much of his life in the spas of Europe. At thirty-four he married Agnes Ethel, who was six years his junior and had a thriving career as an actress with the Augustin Daly theatrical company. She played Camille and other emotional roles, but after her marriage she retired to travel with Tracy in Europe. When he died of complications from diabetes, at age forty-seven, it was Agnes who commissioned White and Saint-Gaudens to do the memorial. She commuted between Buffalo and New York City for another seventeen years, enjoying the social scene in both cities.

# CASTILE

## LETCHWORTH STATE PARK AND LETCHWORTH GORGE

*1 Letchworth State Park; (585) 493–3600*

This magnificent 14,350-acre park and recreation area along the Genesee River is the legacy of philanthropist William Pryor Letchworth, who bought the property in 1859, partly to save it from becoming Rochester's hydroelectric plant. In 1907 he donated it to the state. Within the park the river flows over three major waterfalls, one of which is 107 feet high. The Seneca Indians called this one "the place where the sun lingers." The gorge is 17 miles long and some of its cliffs, gouged out by the river, are 600 feet high. The nickname "Grand Canyon of the East," seems more than appropriate.

### LUNCH BREAK

William Letchworth's former colonnaded home is now the **Glen Iris Inn** (7 Letchworth State Park; 585–493–2622), a well-restored landmark that is agreeable for breakfast, lunch, dinner (with prime rib and venison as specialties), and an overnight stay. Closed from early November until Easter.

There are steep, winding roads, twenty hiking trails, feasts of wildflowers and flowering trees, a hundred small streams, a 270-site campground, picnic tables, two swimming pools, a trailside lodge, and views from various overlooks (especially great from Inspiration Point) that leave you gasping for breath. This woodland isn't a cemetery per se, but it has one grave that is a story in itself. The park is open year-round, but in bad weather only the south Castile entrance is open. Otherwise, you can enter from Mt. Morris or Portageville as well. *Open 8:00 A.M.–10:00 P.M. daily.*

## MARY JEMISON 1742–1833

*I*f she hadn't been captured by Indians, Mary Jemison would not be known today. She was born on shipboard when her Irish family was emigrating to the colonies. They settled in Pennsylvania but were pawns in the French and Indian War, and in 1758 they were captured by Shawnees. Only Mary, age fifteen, survived.

Given the Indian name Deh-gewanus (meaning "pretty one" or "two falling voices"), she married a Delaware brave, Sheninjee; had two children; and grew accustomed to Indian life. After Sheninjee died, she walked along the Gene-see River all the way to this parkland. Her mixed-breed children were rejected by the white settlers, so Jemison remained with the Senecas, marrying Chief Hiokatoo, with whom she had six children. Later the Senecas were placed on a reservation by the Big Tree Treaty of 1797, but Deh-gewanus, who by this time was widowed again, received her own land in the area. In 1823 she described her years among the Indians to James E. Seaver, whose book, *A Narrative of the Life of Mrs. Mary Jemison*, was reprinted many times (and is still available at Letchworth State Park).

When Jemison, known as the "white woman of Genesee," died, she was buried on the Buffalo Creek Reservation. William Letchworth later returned her remains to the area that she loved. Her grave, enclosed by a cast-iron fence, is marked by a bronze statue of her in Indian dress. It is located near two log cabins (the Seneca Council House) on a hill behind the Glen Iris Inn.

# COOPERSTOWN

## CHRIST CHURCHYARD
*River and Church Streets; (607) 547–9555*

The serene, tree-dotted graveyard of Christ Episcopal Church actually pre-dates the church, with some gravestones dating back to the 1700s. The church was built in 1813, but in 1839 James Fenimore Cooper was asked to oversee its expansion and remodeling. He considered this a job made in heaven, as he was both a serious, religious Episcopalian and had strong ideas about church architecture. His passion was the Gothic style of Europe, and accordingly he chose decorative buttresses; narrow, pointed Gothic windows; and a medieval roodscreen.

Other alterations came later, and now the church has a graceful spire and

## LUNCH BREAK

For soup, sandwiches, and assorted lunch goodies, **Tunnicliff Inn** (Main and Pioneer Streets; 607–547–9611) is handily located in the center of town. Just 2 miles outside town is **Pepper Mill** (Highway 28; 607–547–8550), which is closed at lunchtime but is a tasty spot for dinner.

stained-glass windows in keeping with the modest village church it is. The yard slumbers on, final home to many august former residents of Cooperstown and to generations of the town's founding Cooper family.

## JAMES FENIMORE COOPER   1789–1851

You can't turn around in Cooperstown without bumping into the name Cooper. Shortly after his birth in Burlington, New Jersey, James Fenimore Cooper moved with his affluent family to New York's lake region. Cooperstown village was founded by his father, Judge William Cooper. James's early life didn't foretell his later fame. He was expelled from Yale for insubordination, sailed on a merchant ship, and became a midshipman in the U.S. Navy at age nineteen. Three years later he retired to the family estate (once called the most beautiful house in America), married, and settled into the comfortable life of a gentleman.

Cooper might never have become a writer, but after reading a bad English novel, he told his wife, "I believe I could write a better story myself." She threw down the gauntlet and dared him to try. Never one to pass up a challenge, he wrote *Precaution*, which has been called one of the worst novels in history.

If it had been better, he might have let the matter rest. But Cooper was as much inspired by failure as by success, and within a year he produced *The Spy*, based on a tale told him by jurist John Jay. The book was a huge hit and soon led to six other novels, including *The Last of the Mohicans* and *The Pilot*, a novel about the sea that was the beginning of a genre of sea yarns still popular today.

In 1826 Cooper and his family sailed for Europe, where they spent the next seven years being wined, dined, and feted everywhere they went. While few of his novels are read anymore, they were pathfinders in their day, American works by a native-born American author about American subjects and places. They inspired a sense of romantic adventure in all his sit-at-home readers.

In all, Cooper wrote more than thirty novels, as well as many travel books and other works. Best known and loved are his *Leather-Stocking Tales*. It is ironic that a gentleman who knew nothing firsthand of Indians, woodsmen, and the wild life could evoke them so well, at least for the time (probably because his readers knew even less), but failed every time he tackled a story about high society, which he knew intimately.

Returning from Europe in 1833, Cooper spent the rest of his life in Cooperstown, enjoying every minute of it. His flat gravestone joins those of other family members at the edge of, but not technically in, the graveyard, their large plot cordoned off by an iron fence.

# ELMIRA

## WOODLAWN CEMETERY
*North and Walnut Streets; (607) 732–0151*

Well shaded by oak trees, Woodlawn has been open since 1858. The dark, hilly slopes might seem ghostly to anyone with a vivid imagination, but the property is merely sepulchrally peaceful. Like many burial grounds, this one has its surprise residents. One is **Thomas Kinnicut Beecher** (1824–1900; section H), a Congregational minister who officiated at the wedding of Samuel Clemens. Beecher was also a leader of the Underground Railroad in Elmira and, as a product of Lyman Beecher's second marriage, half-brother to Harriet Beecher Stowe and Henry Ward Beecher. **Ernie Davis** (1939–1963; Evergreen East) was a Syracuse University football hero and the first African American to win the Heisman Trophy. The pride of Elmira, he died of leukemia at age twenty-three. Adjacent to Woodlawn, with a separate office, is Woodlawn National Cemetery, where 2,963 Confederate soldiers lie at ease—prisoners of war in Elmira during the Civil War. *Grounds open 8:00 A.M.–9:00 P.M. daily. Office hours: 8:00 A.M.–4:00 P.M. (closed noon–1:00 P.M.) Monday–Friday. Map; restroom.*

## SAMUEL LANGHORNE CLEMENS 1835–1910

Why Elmira? Considering that Clemens was born in Hannibal, Missouri; traveled throughout the west; lived briefly in San Francisco; built his dream house (in a unique steamboat Gothic style, with interior touches by Tiffany) in Hartford, Connecticut; and later moved to Redding in the same state, this is a logical question. It wouldn't be surprising to find Clemens everlastingly in his hometown of Hannibal, which he put on the literary map with *The Adventures of Tom Sawyer* (1876), *Life on the Mississippi* (1883), and *The Adventures of Huckleberry Finn* (1884), perennial favorites among his voluminous works. Why Elmira? Because it was the home-town of his wife, **Olivia Langdon Clemens** (1846–1904), who rests there with him. The Clemenses—or Mark Twains—spent twenty summers at Quarry Farm, the Langdon home.

Though he drew on his early days in Missouri and on the Mississippi River, Clemens was a wanderer at heart. As a boy he wanted to be a river pilot, and later he took his pen name from a call that river pilots used to take soundings—"mark twain" means two fathoms deep. But river trade dried up after

the Civil War, so Clemens meandered west, briefly mining for gold and writing for newspapers in Nevada. While in San Francisco, he wrote the humorous story "The Celebrated Jumping Frog of Calaveras County," which brought him instant celebrity and money enough to write what he wanted and to wander at will. Clemens leaped at the chance and hopped all over. After marriage, he settled down in Hartford and spent thirty years there, traveling intermittently to Europe and, eventually, around the world.

Every trip, every experience, was fodder for his humor and pen. While *Huckleberry Finn* is considered the author's masterpiece, his steady out-

put produced books as diverse as *Roughing It* and *A Tramp Abroad* to *The Prince and the Pauper, A Connecticut Yankee in King Arthur's Court,* and *The Tragedy of Pudd'nhead Wilson.* He once said, "I came in with Halley's Comet . . . and I expect to go out with it." Surprisingly, he did. More than 3,000 mourners attended his funeral. This time the reports of his death were *not* greatly exaggerated.

The route to his grave in section G is well marked, following a short sloping pathway shielded by a canopy of giant oaks and lined with Langdon and Clemens gravestones. At the end of the path is a 12-foot-high granite column erected by Clemens's daughter, Clara. It features a bronze medallion of her father and another of her husband, **Ossip Solomonovich Garilowitsch** (1878–1936), a concert pianist and conductor of the Detroit Symphony Orchestra.

## HAL ROACH   1892–1992

est known as the producer of the Laurel and Hardy shorts, *The Little Rascals,* and Harold Lloyd comedies, Hal Roach had a long, rewarding Hollywood career. An Elmira homeboy, he left town as a teenager, hoping to win fame and fortune mining gold in Alaska. It didn't pan out. Doing odd jobs in the West, he chanced to notice a newspaper ad offering a dollar a day for genuine cowboys to be technical advisors to Universal Pictures in Hollywood. That beat mule skinning, his job at the time.

Making the rounds as a Hollywood extra, he met Lloyd, who later starred in many of Roach's shorts. A small inheritance enabled Roach to open shop in

1914, and his career as a producer was launched. Scores of short comedies with Lloyd, and others featuring Charlie Chase and then Laurel and Hardy, followed.

Undaunted by the arrival of the talkies, Roach went on to make the popular *Our Gang* series, three *Topper* films, and disparate movies like *There Goes My Heart, Captain Fury, One Million B.C.,* and *Of Mice and Men.* When his film career faltered, he turned to television, with *My Little Margie, Amos 'n' Andy, Topper, Racket Squad,* and *The Abbott and Costello Show,* all produced at Roach's studio. (Historical aside: During World War II, Roach permitted the U.S. government to use his studio for training films; some of them featured Ronald Reagan, who spent most of his military service in or near Hollywood.) At age ninety-two, Roach received an honorary Oscar for a lifetime spent mostly making people laugh—not a bad achievement.

Roach's gray granite headstone in section DD lies quite near the Clemens grave site. It reads, below his name and dates, "After leaving Elmira he found success in Hollywood and motion pictures, but always loved his hometown and has returned." Forever and ever, amen.

# INTERLAKEN

## LAKEVIEW CEMETERY
*County Road 150, north of town*

Just north of the old-fashioned village of Interlaken, west of Lake Cayuga in the Finger Lakes area, is this pastoral little burial ground, occupied mostly by local residents. *Grounds open dawn to dusk daily, except when forcibly closed by snow in winter.*

## ROD SERLING    1924–1975

A generation of television viewers was hooked on *The Twilight Zone* and its charismatic host. What made Rod Serling happiest about writing this series of TV plays that explored eerie otherworldly experiences was that they gave him license to write about serious social issues—race relations, bigotry, sexism, and capital punishment, for example—that otherwise were considered too daring or controversial for television at that time.

But Serling had more strings to his bow than just one TV series, popular as it was. Earlier, during the medium's so-called golden age, he won three of his six Emmy Awards for the television plays *Patterns* (1955), *Requiem for a Heavyweight* (1956), and *The Comedian* (1957). In all, Serling had more than

**LUNCH BREAK**

**Glass Magnolia** (8339 North Main Street; 607–532–8356), a gift shop in town, has a small restaurant attached, with ample choices for a satisfying lunch.

seventy television scripts produced during the early 1950s. After *The Twilight Zone* ended in 1964, he turned to movies and Hollywood (though he once wrote that "Hollywood's a great place to live . . . if you're a grapefruit"). His most praised script was a coauthored adaptation of *Planet of the Apes*.

Serling died prematurely at age fifty in Rochester, after a heart bypass led to complications. A lifetime smoking habit didn't help matters. His gravestone, flush with the ground, is just 100 feet beyond twin cedars, on the left. You may wonder why such an urban fellow would find himself in such rural quarters in Interlaken. He was, in a way, returning to his western New York roots. Born Edwin Rodman Serling in Syracuse, he grew up in Binghamton, joined the U.S. Army during World War II, and fought and was wounded in the Philippines. When Serling returned home, he attended Antioch College in Yellow Springs, Ohio, and began writing scripts. From there he went to New York, Hollywood, and ultimately—it took a while—full circle back to western New York.

# ITHACA

## LAKEVIEW CEMETERY
*605 East Shore Drive; (607) 277–2802*

Lakeview began life in 1895 on thirty acres north of Ithaca, near Lake Cayuga. It is as peaceful today as it was then. *Gates open 8:00 A.M. to dusk daily. Office hours: 1:00–3:00 P.M. April 1–October 31 and by appointment in winter months. Map, restroom.*

## CARL SAGAN   1934–1996

Y ou might call what Carl Sagan did as narrator and coproducer of *Cosmos,* a PBS television series, science for dummies. The charisma, knowledge, and easy conversational style of this articulate University of Chicago–trained astronomer attracted thousands of laymen to his show. As one fan said, "He made understanding the universe seem almost easy."

Sagan, who wrote about science even more than he talked about it, authored eight books, including *Planetary Exploration, Nuclear Winter, The Demon-Haunted World: Science as a Candle in the Dark,* and the Pulitzer Prize–winning *Dragons of Eden.* He also wrote hundreds of scientific papers and taught at the University of California at Berkeley, at Harvard, and finally at Cornell as professor of astronomy and director of planetary studies.

Sagan died of bone marrow cancer at age sixty-two. His simple gravestone, flush to the ground in section F, lot 322, states his full name, Carl Edward Sagan, and dates of birth and death. To visit the grave, it is best to park in the first paved area on the right, just beyond the Temple Bethel section, and then walk down a little hill to a chain fence (on the left). The Sagan grave is just beyond the fence.

# ROCHESTER

## KODAK PARK

*Corner of Lake Avenue and West Ridge Road;* (585) 724–4000

It may seem odd that the founder of Eastman Kodak rests on the grounds of this vast industrial park, which houses Kodak factories. Actually, it is appropriate that he is still in the center of his domain. George Eastman's grave and memorial are set within a circle of trees. His ashes are in a bronze urn inside a steel box beneath a large, sunken circular plaza of pinkish gray Georgia marble. Several steps lead down to the plaza, where a cylindrical column, made of the same variegated mar-

**LUNCH BREAK**

The best lunch stop is 2 miles away on Lake Ontario. **Mr. Dominic's** (4699 Lake Drive; 585–865–4630) serves delicious Italian specialties.

ble, stands. On one edge of its base are Eastman's name and dates. The column is a simple one, adorned with two bas-relief figures, one of a woman raising the flame of aspiration, the other of a crouching man who represents science. The banks surrounding the plaza are thick with myrtles, a fringe of low evergreens, and weeping beech trees.

The memorial is located just inside the main entrance to the park, next to the driveway, in an open area ringed by the research laboratories, the administration building, and two manufacturing buildings. The memorial is easily visible from Lake Avenue.

## GEORGE EASTMAN   1854–1932

Maybe photographers should urge their subjects to say "East" instead of "cheese," for all shutterbugs, amateur and professional, owe a huge debt to George Eastman. A self-educated man from Waterville, New York, he played a major role in turning a rich man's toy into a popular pastime. He had many photographic "firsts." Exasperated by the difficulty of developing negatives, Eastman spent three years in his mother's kitchen experimenting with gelatin emulsions. Then voilà! He came up with a dry plate coating machine, which became the rock upon which Eastman Kodak Company was eventually built. He patented the first film in roll form (1884); perfected the first camera to use roll film (1888); devised flexible transparent film (1889), which later proved vital to the development of motion pictures; started the Eastman Kodak Company (1892) to mass-produce standardized photographic equipment; and contributed to the development of the company's research facilities.

As the company grew, Eastman used much of his well-gotten gains in philanthropy. He donated more than $75 million to various projects, such as establishing the Eastman School of Music at the University of Rochester in

1918 and schools of medicine and dentistry in 1921. He was also a major contributor to the Massachusetts Institute of Technology, among many other worthy organizations. At age seventy-eight, suffering from a severe spinal disease, he committed suicide in the bedroom of his mansion, leaving a note that read "To my friends: My work is done—why wait?"

## MOUNT HOPE CEMETERY

*1133 Mount Hope Avenue; (585) 428–7999*

One of New York State's most beautiful final resting places, Mount Hope's 196 acres were dedicated in 1838 as the first *municipal* Victorian burial ground in the United States. Some Rochesterians vigorously opposed the site. One critic, General Jacob Gould, said, "It is all up hill and down dale, and with the gully at the entrance," adding, "Why that ground isn't fit for pasturing rabbits!" A supporter retorted, "But we are not going to pasture rabbits." Ironically, once the plans developed, Gould was one of the first to buy a plot; he built an ornate Egyptian-style family tomb near the entrance "gully" he had so disparaged.

Thick woods, flowering trees, steep hillsides, and twisting roadways (14.5 miles of them) offer visual treats of tombs, Greek Revival mausoleums, obelisks, and ornate headstones. Many of these are replete with the symbols of death, eternity, everlasting life, and sorrow that the Victorians loved to have carved into stone: angels, lambs, urns, anchors, roses, sheaves of wheat, wreaths, daisies, crowns, crosses, morning glories, lilies of the valley, and faux tree trunks.

There are splendid edifices as well: a Gothic Revival chapel (by local architect Henry Searle) and crematorium to the left of the main gate; an 1875 two-tiered, cast-iron Florentine fountain; and an 1872 Moorish gazebo with delicate Arabic designs on its arches and roof, all clustered near the old high-Victorian Gothic North Gate entrance. A towering firemen's monument with Egyptian symbols and a uniformed fireman on top stands on Fireman's Avenue near Grove Avenue, and a bronze Civil War monument designed by Sally James Farnham is across the road. A large stone art deco monument for shoe manufacturer **Wilbur Coon** (1870–1926; 249 MM), with a beautifully carved angel created by Tiffany Studios in 1927, required a special railway car to transport it.

Iron-and-wood benches installed at various locales on the grounds make it convenient for strollers and hikers to sit a few minutes and contemplate Mount Hope's many edifying memorials, a reminder that the cemetery is on the National Register of Historic Places.

Some 350,000 people and counting now rest in this hallowed ground. Occupants include **Dr. Hartwell Carver** (1789–1875; range 2, lot 104), father of the Transcontinental Railroad, who is immortalized by a towering Corinthian-style column topped with a toga-clad figure; **Elizabeth Hollister Frost** (1887–1958; section G, lot 119), a poet and novelist; **Frank E. Gannett** (1876–1957; section MM, lot 247), a newspaper publisher and founder of the Gannett newspaper chain; and **Myron Holley** (1779–1841; section G, lot 159), promoter and builder of the Erie Canal. **Hiram Sibley** (1807–1888; section D, lot 143), cofounder of Western Union, was the man who persuaded Czar Alexander to sell Alaska to the United States.

Called the spookiest mausoleum in Mount Hope, that of ethnologist **Lewis Henry Morgan** (1818–1881; section F, lot 65) is dug into the hillside—perhaps a reflection of his life's work as founder of the science of anthropology. Morgan studied and wrote books on American Indian culture, especially that of the Senecas. Also on the grounds are three of Buffalo Bill Cody's children—son **Kit Carson Cody** (1870–1876), who died of scarlet fever two years after the family moved to Rochester; daughter **Arta Cody**

**LUNCH BREAK**

Rochester has an abundance of agreeable restaurants. A favorite for its New American food is **2 Vine** (24 Winthrop Street; 585-454-6020), a trendy stop for a fabulous lunch or dinner.

**Thorpe** (1866–1904); and daughter **Orra Cody** (1872–1883; all in range 2, middle section, southwest corner)—as well as his foster son, **Johnny Baker** (1869–1931; section I, lot 149), a sharpshooter in the Wild West Show.

In section BB, lot 123, you will find a memorial to a military scouting party that fell victim to an Indian attack. Note as well the grave of **Josephus Requa** (1833–1910; section C, lot 128), inventor (in 1861) of the first practical machine gun. *Grounds open from dawn to dusk daily. Office hours: 8:30 A.M.–3:30 P.M. Monday–Saturday. Brochure with map; restrooms. Friends of Mount Hope (585–461–3494; www.fomh.org) offers guided tours May through October at 2:00 and 3:00 P.M. every Sunday; special tours monthly; costumed actor tour in summer.*

## SUSAN B. ANTHONY   1820–1906

*D*escended from a high-minded, prosperous Quaker family, Susan Brownell Anthony grew up in a strict, serious household in Adams, Massachusetts, and later resettled in Rochester. A precocious child— she read at age three—with a remarkable memory and hunger for knowledge, she seemed destined to become a teacher, a natural occupation for women in those days. But the classroom was too small a stage for her wide interests and restless intelligence.

Before long Anthony was active in the temperance and abolitionist movements, lecturing and participating in campaigns. After the Civil War she was drawn to the issue of equality—and the vote—for women. Writing, lecturing, and lobbying formed the steady diet of her life. With enormous fortitude, she withstood all kinds of opposition and abuse, physical (eggs and tomatoes thrown at her on lecture platforms) and verbal (hisses, shouts, and epithets). But Anthony and her colleagues—Lucy Stone, Amelia Bloomer, Lucretia Mott,

and especially Elizabeth Cady Stanton—persevered through court battles, arrests, trials, opprobrium, and vicious editorial attacks.

Anthony never married, and she didn't live to see the ratification of the Nineteenth Amendment, which in 1920 gave women the right to vote. But somewhere she must be smiling at last. Her graceful, rounded headstone is located in the north edge (lot 98) of section C in a well-tended, flower-laden plot with her parents and seven other relatives.

## FREDERICK DOUGLASS    1817–1895

*M*any self-made men boast of pulling themselves up by their own bootstraps, but few moved as far up as fast as Douglass. He spent his first twenty years as Frederick Bailey, a slave on a Maryland plantation. By age twelve he had secretly learned to read and write. In 1838 he escaped to freedom, changing his name to Douglass (from a poem by Walter Scott) to avoid the bounty hunters who were after him. He settled in New Bedford, Massachusetts; married; worked as a laborer; and became an activist in the abolition movement.

A powerful orator, Douglass traveled in New England and later in Europe as an agent of the Massachusetts Anti-Slavery Society. In 1845 he published his first autobiography, *Narrative of the Life of Frederick Douglass, an American Slave, Written by Himself.* Settling in Rochester, he founded a weekly journal, the *North Star.*

By the time of the Civil War, his was the most eloquent African-American voice speaking on behalf of freedom. He urged President Lincoln to utilize black troops, and in 1863 Douglass became active in enlisting African Americans for the 54th and 55th regiments. In 1870 he became editor of the *New National Era* newspaper in Washington, D.C., and in 1889 President Harrison designated him minister to Haiti.

A friend of Susan B. Anthony, Douglass was an enrolled member of the National Women's Suffrage Association and attended its conventions. He continued to agitate for African-American equality and voting rights until his death at age seventy-eight. "There is no Negro problem," he once said. "The problem is whether the American people have loyalty enough, honor enough, patriotism enough to live up to their own Constitution." Douglass's granite upright memorial and large, flat gravestone with raised metal letters are in section T, lot 26, near Fifth Avenue. With him are his first wife, **Anna Murray** (1813–1882); his second wife, **Helen Pitts** (1838–1903); and his youngest daughter, **Annie Douglass** (1849–1860).

## MARGARET WOODBURY STRONG    1897–1969

*M*argaret Strong's major claim to fame is the remarkable museum she left to her hometown of Rochester. She was the only child of a wealthy family that invested early in the Eastman Kodak Company. By the time Margaret died, her father's $1,000 investment in Kodak had grown to $80 million. The family had money even pre-Kodak. Strong's maternal grandfather owned a prosperous flour-milling business, and her paternal grandfather amassed a fortune making buggy whips.

Strong's childhood was marked by much travel. By age eleven, she had visited more countries in the world than most adults do in a lifetime. One six-month trip took Strong and her parents to Hawaii, Ceylon, Hong Kong, and Shanghai. Following the lead of her father, a coin collector, she began collecting and became an avid, if eccentric, accumulator of dolls, toys, and small objects. After her marriage (at age twenty-three to forty-five-year-old Homer Strong), she enjoyed the life of a wealthy matron, spending her time on golfing, gardening, flower arranging, and child rearing (the Strongs had one child, a daughter who died in her twenties). She once bought forty-six Victorian

## HOUSE CALL

The **Strong Museum** (One Manhattan Square; 716–263–2700) is one of the top children's museums in the country, displaying some 300,000 objects relating to play on two expansive floors. There are 5,000 toys, dollhouses, and miniatures and numerous hands-on activities. The doll collection is the world's largest—cases and cases of dolls.

bathtubs, planted them with flowers, and used them as a "fence" around her summer house in Maine. When neighbors protested the sight, she commissioned artists to decorate the tubs.

As part of her collecting mania, Strong concentrated on amassing the largest group of dolls and dollhouses in the world. Her thirty-two-room house in Rochester needed two gallery wings to contain her vast collection. At her death, she was the largest individual shareholder in the Eastman Kodak Company, and the bulk of her estate was used to found the Strong Museum. Her current and last address is the Woodbury mausoleum, section C, lot 109, near Linden Avenue.

# APPENDIX

## ASHES TO ASHES

Not all departed New Yorkers are resting snugly in permanent, paradisial surroundings. Some were cremated, with their ashes scattered. Others were buried privately on family grounds that are not publicly accessible. In case you are wondering, here are a few whose graves you cannot find.

**Marlon Brando** (1924–2004), legendary actor who lit up the Broadway stage in *A Streetcar Named Desire* and the big screen in the film version of *Streetcar* as well as *On the Waterfront, Viva Zapata!, The Wild One,* and other movies. Ashes scattered in Tahiti, Death Valley, and elsewhere.

**John Cage** (1912–1992), avant-garde composer of modern music, died of a stroke. Ashes scattered at sea.

**Bennett Cerf** (1898–1971), humorist and publisher. Ashes scattered at his home in Mount Kisco, New York.

**Charles Coburn** (1877–1961), genial character actor in many Hollywood movies of the 1930s and 40s. Ashes scattered in Georgia, Massachusetts, and New York.

**Peter Duchin** (1909–1951), pianist and New York society bandleader who appeared in movies in the 1930s and 40s. Ashes scattered in the Atlantic Ocean.

**Albert Einstein** (1879–1955), noted physicist; considered the most important scientist of the twentieth century. Ashes scattered in an unknown river in New Jersey.

**Spalding Gray** (1941–2004), writer, actor, and monologist (*Swimming to Cambodia*); suffered from depression and committed suicide, probably by jumping overboard from the Staten Island ferry. Location of ashes unknown.

**Woody Guthrie** (1912–1967), legendary folk singer and songwriter, known for left-leaning social causes and such songs as "This Land Is Your Land," "Union Maid," and "So Long, It's Been Good to Know You," among others. Ashes scattered in the water off Coney Island.

**Buddy Hackett** (1924–2003), rubbery-faced stand-up comedian, often on television talk shows and "What's My Line?". Ashes given to family or friends.

**Philip Johnson** (1906–2005), premier American architect and cultural tastemaker whose own glass house in New Canaan, Connecticut, was a prototype of post–World War II modern domestic architecture. Location of ashes unknown.

**John Lennon** (1940–1980), rock star, songwriter, author, peace activist, and member of the famous rock band the Beatles. Ashes given to family, although his memorial in Strawberry Fields, Central Park, Manhattan, is a much-visited pilgrimage site for many fans (see Chapter 1).

**Kay Medford** (1920–1980), stage, television, and movie actress; nominated for a Tony and an Oscar for her stage and film roles as Fanny Brice's mother in *Funny Girl*; received Tony and Critics Circle awards for mother's role in Broadway production of *Bye Bye Birdie*. Ashes scattered from the top of a building in Manhattan.

**Ethel Merman** (1908–1984), Broadway musical comedy icon for her clear diction and big belting voice; star of *Annie Get Your Gun, Call Me Madame,* and numerous other musicals. Ashes scattered on Broadway (where else?).

**Edna St. Vincent Millay** (1892–1950), poet known for her lyrical, poignant poems and sonnets in such collections as *A Few Figs from Thistles* and *The Harp Weaver*. Buried upstate in Steepletop Cemetery on the Millay family estate, at Austerlitz.

**Zero Mostel** (1915–1977), comic-turned-actor on Broadway and in movies; Tony winner for his roles in *A Funny Thing Happened on the Way to the Forum, Rhinoceros,* and *Fiddler on the Roof*. Location of ashes unknown.

**Edward R. Murrow** (1908–1965), widely respected CBS radio and television newscaster who set high reporting standards for those who followed him. Ashes scattered in the glen at his private Glen Arden Farm, Pawling, New York.

**Tony Randall** (1920–2004), Broadway, film, and television actor; best known as Felix Unger in TV sitcom *The Odd Couple,* also for roles in *Pillow Talk* and other film comedies. Ashes given to family or friends.

**Richard Rodgers** (1902–1979), acclaimed Broadway composer. Ashes scattered.

**Damon Runyon** (1884–1956), called the "sage of Broadway," author of humorous short stories. Broadway musical *Guys and Dolls* was based on characters in his stories. Ashes scattered from an airplane over Times Square, New York City.

**Bayard Rustin** (1910–1987), African-American civil rights activist, author, and organizer of protest demonstrations; engaged in first "freedom ride" to end segregation in the South and was chief organizer of the March on Washington in 1963. Ashes buried in an unmarked grave on an upstate New York estate.

**Billy Straymore** (1915–1967), brilliant jazz composer, pianist, and arranger for Duke Ellington; wrote or cowrote many Ellington classics like "Take the 'A' Train" and "Satin Doll." Ashes scattered at the 79th Street boat basin near the foot of Riverside Park in New York City.

**Norman Thomas** (1884–1968), pacifist, socialist, and six-time candidate for the U.S. presidency. Ashes scattered off Long Island Sound.

**Carl Van Vechten** (1880–1964), novelist, essayist, first American critic of modern dance, and photographer of the activists in the Harlem Renaissance. Ashes scattered in Shakespeare Gardens, Central Park, New York City.

**Fats Waller** (1904–1943), popular jazz pianist and singer. Ashes scattered in Harlem, New York.

## VANISHING ACT—WHEREABOUTS UNKNOWN

Not all ashes or remains of long-gone New York residents or visitors are accounted for. The whereabouts of the following are in *terra incognita*, simply unknown.

**Henry Hudson** (1575–1611), English explorer and discoverer of the Hudson River and Hudson Bay. Set adrift after a mutiny by his crew, he was never seen again.

**Anne Hutchinson** (1591–1643), exiled by the Massachusetts Bay Colony and killed by Indians. She is believed to be buried somewhere in the Bronx.

**Thomas Paine** (1737–1809), author of *Common Sense*, an American patriot and revolutionary, fervently admired and fiercely reviled. His body was stolen from his New Rochelle farm and shipped to England; his bones have vanished.

# INDEX

# TO'MB IT MAY CONCERN

Author Patricia Brooks admits to an endless fascination with cemeteries, dating back, she says, to too much early exposure to *Tales from the Crypt* and Edgar Allen Poe. Her long experience as a restaurant critic (for the *New York Times*' Connecticut section since 1977) and a freelance food writer (for *Bon Appetit, Food and Wine,* and *Travel and Leisure,* among many other national publications) whetted her appetite for more than just desserts.

Years of travel have taken Brooks across the United States, Europe, North Africa, the Middle East, India, Asia, and Down Under. While researching and writing guidebooks and magazine articles—and yes, even doing a little ghost-writing—she has found herself soul-searching in the sepulchral solitude of many a benign burial ground, observing statuary, graven images, and other grave matters. Her nineteen books (including guides to Spain, Britain, New York State, and New England, as well as *Food Lovers' Guide to Connecticut,* also published by The Globe Pequot Press) have not deadened her enthusiasm for spirited subjects—even those who are out of sight, but not out of mind. As Brooks averred in *Where the Bodies Are* (Globe Pequot Press, 2002), one thing special in writing about graveyards is that "you never run out of subjects. It doesn't take much digging—so to speak—to find them."